INSTRUMENT FLYING

INSTRUMENT FLYING

Richard L. Taylor

Introduction by ROBERT N. BUCK
author of *Weather Flying*

MACMILLAN PUBLISHING CO., INC.
NEW YORK

COLLIER MACMILLAN PUBLISHERS
LONDON

Macmillan Publishing Co., Inc.
866 Third Avenue, New York, N.Y. 10022
Collier Macmillan Canada, Ltd.

Library of Congress Catalog Card Number: 72-77655

Seventh Printing 1977

Printed in the United States of America

This book is dedicated to a number of people:

to Ray Petty, the pipe-smoking back-seat driver who originated the term "right on" while insisting on prescribed altitudes and airspeeds even in Cubs and T-6s;

to Bill Reynolds, military B-25 instructor, who really got me fired up about instrument flying;

to my colleagues in the Ohio State University Department of Aviation and in Traveling Aviation Seminars, whose advice has made the book more practical;

to the countless VHF voices whose owners have unknowingly suggested more efficient techniques or demonstrated how *not* to do it;

to Mary Curtiss and Donna Douglass, typists extraordinaire;

to Captain Bob Buck, whose *Weather Flying* provided a great deal of the inspiration for this book;

and, especially, to my family, who labor well under the unusual circumstances of having their bread won by an aviator.

CONTENTS

Introduction

This book is a valuable link between theory and what instrument flying is really like. It's a book to read all the way through and also one to have handy for those free moments to pick up, open anywhere, and gain a useful piece of information.

Instrument Flying is not restricted to any level of pilot experience. It will interest the person who is just beginning to think about getting an instrument rating, and it will be valuable to the experienced pilot as well.

It is difficult to dig out all the information about instrument flying. I've tried by reading stuffy technical books, the stiff FAA publications and formal study courses designed to get one through the FAA exams. And even after all this digging, there is still a long way to go to discover what it's really like—to know what's behind the scenes. Mostly this comes with experience.

Instrument Flying cuts this process short because it tells, as it teaches, all about the inside and what's behind the formal stuff. In doing this the book gives experience as it tells. It is a welcome arrival on the instrument flying scene. I wish it had been around years ago—it would have made things a lot easier.

Richard Taylor has an excellent background in flying and in education. He has had more than 17 years experience as a military and then a commercial pilot. Along with his practical background, he is an assistant professor in the Department of Aviation at Ohio State University. The book reflects this fortunate combination as he takes us from attitude flying, which is the solid basis for flying on instruments, to the sophisticated techniques of the high-altitude airways.

The complex problems of absorbing a clearance, using the radio, and staying within the law are talked about in an easy way that will help lift the pilot from a timid, unsure position to one where he can operate like a pro. The chapters on holding patterns and instrument approaches, plus all the aspects of a flight from *A* to *B* on instruments, are extremely valuable for learning and attaining proficiency through practice.

This book is an important addition to every pilot's library. But it is not a book to leave on the shelf gathering dust; rather it will be read many times and, I'm certain, consulted time and time again to refresh your memory and settle many a friendly argument.

Robert N. Buck
Pipersville, Pennsylvania
June 1972

INSTRUMENT FLYING

1. The Complete Instrument Pilot

PUT A FOOT-WIDE STEEL BEAM flat on the ground, and walk across it; a "no sweat" situation for anyone with normal balance and eyesight. Now put that steel beam between two buildings ten stories above the street, and anyone less than an experienced steel worker or a professional highwire performer would panic at the prospect of negotiating the same narrow path which presented no problem at ground level. The difference?—knowledge, experience, and practice.

Much the same reasoning applies to instrument flying; you know that you can handle your airplane when you can see the ground, but getting from here to there in IFR (Instrument Flight Rules) conditions is something else. And no matter how well you fly the machine, there's always ATC, that government monster, giving you confusing instructions, asking you to maintain cruise airspeed on an approach, clearing you to an altitude you don't want, and on and on and on. But basic principles always apply, and if you are well grounded in the "nuts and bolts" of instrument flying, there's no reason why you can't ad-

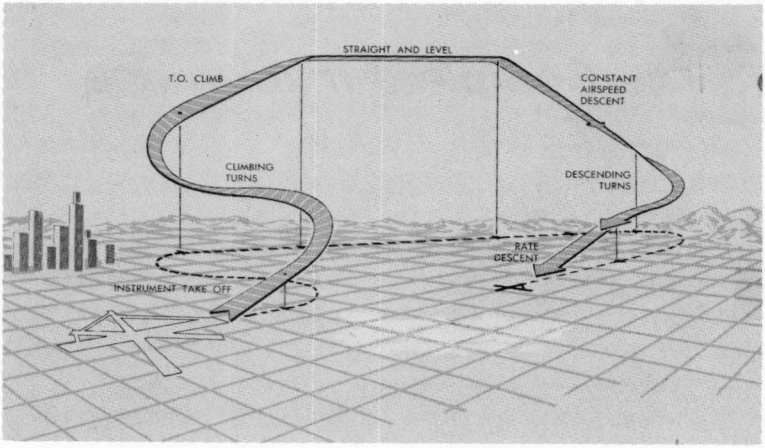

Any instrument flight, regardless of how long or how complex, is simply a series of connected basic instrument flight maneuvers.

just to changes and involved procedures IF YOU KNOW WHAT TO EXPECT, AND HOW TO HANDLE YOURSELF IN THE IFR SYSTEM. There's nothing heartstopping about flying an airplane on instruments, nor does it take a superman to do the job well. Good instrument training plus a thorough understanding of the *total* system can make it just as easy as walking that steel beam when it's flat on the ground. When you know what you're doing, you can walk it confidently and safely ten stories high.

More than seventeen years of military and civilian flying in many parts of the world, in all kinds of weather, have convinced me that once past the fundamentals, safe and efficient instrument flight is a happy combination of knowing yourself, your airplane, and the system. When you accept a clearance from Air Traffic Control to fly in the nation's airspace, you are considered just as qualified, just as capable as the airline captain who flies every day. This is not to imply that Controllers are so unrealistic that they expect your approaches to be as exquisitely precise as the "pros," but every IFR pilot *is* expected to conform to the same rules and procedures, because he becomes part of a *system* —a combination of parts into a whole, an orderly arrangement. The principal parts of this system, Controllers and pilots, must work together if the scheme is to accomplish its goal of safe separation and efficient management of the thousands of instrument flights conducted every day.

The key to the whole process is knowledge; it has been proven that the average pilot can be taught to fly an airplane by referring only to the attitude instruments (indeed, it's now a required part of the practical examination for the private pilot certificate). But throw in the confusing complications of electronic navigation and rapid-fire communication, and the average pilot can come unglued . . . unless he knows what the system is all about. "You learn something every day" is a bromide perhaps more meaningful in instrument flying than in any other endeavor; for regulations, procedures, and techniques change almost daily. In my contacts with instrument pilots as an instructor, aviation educator, and professional pilot, I come across too frequent examples of "understanding gaps" which derogate pilot performance, efficiency, and sometimes compromise safety.

For the past several years, I have been involved in a program designed to refresh the knowledge of instrument-rated pilots and to prepare candidates for written examinations relative to IFR operations. This experience has convinced me that the surface of pilot education has barely been scratched—there is a profound need to continue the training *after* a pilot obtains his instrument rating. *Instrument Flying* is intended to help put a real gouge in that surface; it has been developed with the philosophy that knowledge, added to practice and experience, will pave the way to safer and more efficient instrument flight.

This book can be used to greatest advantage as a source of information for understanding the *total* system in which we fly IFR. In addition to some basic techniques of aircraft control, you will find detailed explanations of every phase of instrument flight, from Airways to Zulu time. To help you increase the efficiency and utility of your airplane, *Instrument Flying* contains techniques and procedures for practical, legal methods of cutting down the elapsed time between point A and point B; isn't that the real reason for using an airplane in the first place?

The chapters are strung on a common thread of increased usefulness, of maximizing the dollars you spend to transport people and things through the air; chapters dealing with attitude instrument flying are not there to teach you how to fly instruments, for that is your flight instructor's job. However, you can and should use this material as a guide for practicing and polishing your flying skills. The "good" instrument pilot is the one who flies his airplane without conscious effort, conserving the major portion of his thought processes for navigation, communication, and staying at least one step ahead of the airplane all the time.

AN INSTRUMENT BOOK WITH NO CHAPTER ON WEATHER?

When you can't beat 'em, join 'em! Robert N. Buck, a *very* senior captain with Trans World Airlines, has put together the ultimate interpretation of aviation meteorology for the instrument pilot, so I defer to his work in this vital area, which has more to do with IFR operations than anything else. If you do not own a copy of *Weather Flying*, I strongly recommend that you add it to your aviation library. Seldom do we have the opportunity to share in, and profit from, the vast experience of one so eminent in his field.

BE A *LEGAL* EAGLE

When the sands at Kitty Hawk were brushed by the skids of the bicycle-builders' airplane, when theirs was the only powered flying machine in the entire country, there was no need for rules of the air—the laws of gravity kept the brothers busy enough! But soon there were two airplanes, and then more and more and more; just like the increased traffic on rivers and roads, a burgeoning aircraft population eventually had to come under regulation and control. Safety of flight has been uppermost in the minds of rule-writers from the very beginning (check your regs —almost all of them are intended to keep us pilots from running into each other), with a secondary purpose to establish who's at fault when a no-no *does* occur.

The regulations with which we must live are therefore either restrictive or mandatory in nature, letting us know those things we may *not* do, or the things we *must* do. Although the intent remains steadfast, the language and scope of aviation regulations change constantly, as the nature of flying itself changes. It would be a fool's task to list all the rules which apply to instrument flying, because they will change before the ink on these pages is dry. The regulations (and revisions thereto) are available to all, and so the smart instrument flyer (or the smart *any*-kind-of-flyer for that matter) will subscribe to those which apply to his operations, and moreover will keep his books right up to date. For noncommercial pilots (VFR *and* IFR types) Part 91 of the Federal Aviation Regulations is a bare minimum, and the quarterly Part 1 of the Airman's Information Manual will help you stay current in regard to changes in procedure and technique.

"But," you say, "I haven't time to spend going through regs and manuals—I fly good instruments, do what ATC says, keep my medical current and my nose clean." That's fine as far as it goes, but do you have the time or the resources to contend with a legal judgment against you as the result of a violation? As in any court action, ignorance of the law is never an excuse, especially when one of the very first parts of our aviation rules says that the pilot in command will, in effect, be aware of *everything* that may affect the operation of his aircraft before he even starts the engine. It takes only one small slip on your part to render yourself defenseless—there is just no way to be involved in an accident or incident with an airplane and not be in violation of some part of the aviation regulations. Unfortunately, everyone else in the world figures that a person who can afford to own or operate an airplane can also afford a huge settlement. And after you lose all your money in a court action, the government may step in and relieve you of your flying privileges—sometimes permanently.

There's a practical side to knowing the regulations, too. With the ever-increasing variety of instrument approaches and other system options that we can put to use, the less-than-current IFR pilot will sooner or later come up against a situation that could have been avoided by knowing just what he may or may not do. Current knowledge and complete understanding make the difference between the pilot who stumbles through the airspace confused and bewildered, and the one who makes things happen for his benefit, efficiency, and safety.

The point of all this is that you *must* know the rules of the flying business, you *must* stay abreast of changes as they are effected, and it's *more* important when you are IFR. The VFR-only flyer can get by with less regulation-reading because he can always rely on the see-and-avoid rule. But when you are accepted into the IFR system, you must play in the same key as everyone else; from Ercoupes to airliners, instrument pilots must operate on a common base of regulation and control. Now that you sometimes can't see where you're going, it's comforting to know that all the other pilots up there in the clouds with you are flying by the same set of guidelines.

YOUR CHOICE OF CHARTS

There are two (and only two) sources of charts for use in the IFR system. One is the federal government, the other is the Jeppesen Company, a commercial supplier. Both services include a wide range of publications, from SIDs to STARs and everything in between. You can purchase charts for the whole world, or only for the area in which you fly—it's entirely up to you and your pocketbook. Which service is best? That's an impossible question, because pilot preferences vary so widely. Get a sample of each, and try them—that's the only way you'll be able to decide which is best for you.

No matter what your choice, there is one point of commonality: IFR charts cannot fulfill their ultimate purpose unless you know precisely what every mark thereon means. New symbols are added, airway courses are adjusted, radio frequencies are changed, so it becomes nothing short of mandatory that you keep yourself up to date with current charts, and *full* knowledge of those charts. One small, seemingly inconsequential bit of information might just save your neck some day!

Realizing the same out-of-date-before-the-ink-is-dry problem that exists with regulations, *Instrument Flying* does not include a chapter on IFR charts. On occasion, it is necessary to illustrate a particular point with symbols or numbers that are expected to remain in use indefinitely—but you must realize that you are expected to know the sometimes restrictive, sometimes permissive, sometimes directive nature of *all* the chart symbols and markings. Get *very* familiar with the legend pages supplied with your charts. Jeppesen treats this problem very thoroughly in the respective sections of their IFR chart publications. If you use the government charts, you would do well to get a copy of Advisory Circular No. 90-1A, "Civil Use of U.S. Government Instrument Approach Procedure Charts," and learn it inside out.

Whenever you receive revisions to your charts, INSERT THEM RIGHT NOW, and do it yourself—don't trust anyone else, not even your wife. Allowing three or four weeks' revision notices and new charts to pile up on your desk has two bad features: First, it's very frustrating to replace the same chart several times at one sitting, and second, anytime you're flying IFR with old charts, you're an accident looking for a place to happen. When you are inserting those revisions, pay attention to the changes that caused the revision—you'll learn a great deal about the system by noticing new procedures.

THAT STILL, SMALL VOICE

There's really not much that can get you into serious trouble on an instrument flight except weather, and the consequences that develop around it. If your airplane is properly maintained, checked, and operated, chances are excellent that it will get you where you want to go. But sometimes, when "get-home-itis" is coming on strong, and your IFR capability is bolstering a "nothing-can-stop-me" frame of mind, listen to that still, small voice of reason that reminds you to back off and take another look at the situation. The temptation to press on in the face of bad weather has led many a pilot down the garden path; if you've worked out a Plan B to take care of non-flyable weather, you can make the decision well ahead of time, still get your business accomplished, and come back to fight another day.

There will be times when you cancel a flight only to have the weather gods make a fool of you with a beautiful day—those are the breaks of the game; but when you've left yourself no way out, and make a forced decision to take off into marginal weather that turns out *worse* than expected, you're in the wringer. If you're lucky, you may get by with a harrowing experience, and a monumental resolve never to do it again. It's a lot more comfortable to be on the ground wishing you were in the air, than to be up there, wishing you were on the ground! A professional pilot earns his pay, and the amateur earns the respect of his passengers, on those occasions when he overcomes pride with good sense and says "the weather looks worse than I want to tackle today; we're not going by air."

HAVE AT IT!

There is no recommended order for reading *Instrument Flying*; dig right in wherever you feel your knowledge is a bit rusty, or when you come across a situation you don't understand thoroughly. Each section is functionally complete in itself, and does not depend on previous study of some other part of the book; other chapters may be consulted for more detail, and the Glossary in Chapter 2 is available for definition of terms.

Now I have your clearance; are you ready to copy? You are cleared from here to the end of the book, via eighteen chapters packed with instrument flying information. Climb to and maintain a higher level of efficiency and safety; expect further clearance as you work through these pages and become a *complete* instrument pilot. Have a good flight!

2. The Language of Instrument Flying

PASSENGERS WHO LISTEN to the radio chatter during an instrument flight probably feel as if they have been exposed to a replay of the Tower of Babel scene. The working language, the jargon, of instrument flying does get a bit sticky at times; but then, the "at work" conversation of *any* specialized occupational group will sound like glossolalia to the uneducated.

Terms, definitions, contracted phrases can pile up into a meaningless mess of initialese and confusion when you're about the business of conducting a flight under instrument conditions. When a time-saving communications short-cut comes your way and you're not sure just what you are expected to do, or a term crops up which is completely foreign, by all means *ask*; the worst thing to do is *assume* that you know what something means—you can get in trouble doing that!

There are two ways of becoming fluent in the language of instrument flying; one is to fly IFR at every opportunity and gradually pick up the jargon, and the other is to fly IFR at every opportunity and gradually pick up the jargon. But *first* know what you and they (ATC) are talking about by studying the following glossary. It's a collection of frequently used phrases, definitions, and abbreviations to help you understand what ATC is saying to you, and to improve the propriety of your electronic conversations. There are some terms which you will probably never use, but which are included to accommodate the increasing sophistication of instrument flying. Hold on to your spoon—the alphabet soup promises to get thicker and thicker.

GLOSSARY

Abeam: a position directly off either wingtip—a relative bearing of 90 degrees or 270 degrees.

ADF: Automatic Direction Finder—refers to the low/medium frequency radio receiver in the airplane. The ADF indicator gives the pilot a readout of the bearing from airplane to station. (Cf. Relative bearing.)

Affirmative: better than "yes" because it is more easily understood.

Airport Traffic Area: a cylinder of airspace 5 miles in radius and 3,000 feet deep around and above an airport with an *operating* control tower. Exists for the protection of aircraft taking off and landing. Speed limit within this airspace is 156 knots indicated for prop-driven aircraft, 200 knots for jets, and radio contact with the tower is required.

Airspeed: velocity of an aerial machine; may be stated in a number of ways (always in knots):

Indicated—the number to which the needle points. When Approach Control says "What is your airspeed?" respond with the number of *knots* at the end of the pointer.

Calibrated—pointer indication corrected for installation and instrument error. All limiting and performance speeds are quoted in terms of calibrated airspeed.

True—calibrated airspeed corrected for pressure and temperature; the actual speed of the airplane relative to undisturbed air. This is the speed used for IFR filing purposes.

Approach Speed—a computed number used to determine the category (A, B, C, D) to be used for instrument approaches. It is the calibrated power-off stall speed of the aircraft at maximum landing weight in the landing configuration, multiplied by 1.3.

Basic rule when in flight: "Maintain thy airspeed, lest the earth arise and smite thee."

Airway: designated air route between points on the earth's surface.

ALS: Approach Lighting System—an arrangement of lights designed to provide visual guidance to a pilot breaking out of the clouds on an instrument approach. There are a number of acceptable displays; the most striking feature of a typical installation is the "ball of fire" effect from the long line of high-powered sequenced flashers cascading toward the runway.

Alternate Airport: a place to go if weather at the airport of intended landing goes sour. Must be part of an IFR flight plan under certain conditions.

Altitude: available in several models, including:

Pressure Altitude—read on the altimeter when the altimeter setting is 29.92 inches; everyone operating above 18,000 feet uses pressure altitudes. (Cf. Flight Level.)

Density Altitude—pressure altitude corrected for temperature; this is the altitude at which the airplane thinks it's flying, and the altitude upon which all performance figures are based.

Indicated Altitude—what you see on the altimeter when the current setting is shown in the window; all assigned altitudes below 18,000 feet are indicated altitudes.

Absolute Altitude—your actual height above the terrain. Used to determine decision height for Category II and III approaches, and sometimes used for over-water navigation.

Radar Altitude—same as absolute altitude; a small radar set is used to measure height above the surface.

True Altitude—your actual height above sea level.

Approach Category: grouping of aircraft according to a computed speed and maximum landing weight to determine adequate airspace for maneuvering during a circling instrument approach procedure.

Arc: a circle of constant radius around a VORTAC station. When a DME arc approach is specified, you will fly around the station at a fixed distance until intercepting an approach radial which will lead you to the airport.

ASR: Airport Surveillance Radar—relatively short-range radar equipment used primarily for approach control in the terminal area. May also be used as an approach aid, to vector aircraft to within one mile of a runway; however, no altitude information is available.

ATC: Air Traffic Control—any federal facility engaged in the direction and control of aircraft in controlled airspace; this includes Clearance Delivery, Ground Control, Tower, Approach Control, Departure Control, Air Route Traffic Control ("Center"), and Flight Service Stations.

ATIS: Automatic Terminal Information Service—a continuous broadcast of data pertinent to a specific terminal; includes weather, altimeter setting, approaches and departures in use, and other instructions.

Back Course: the "other side" of an ILS Localizer course—the electronic extension of the runway centerline, proceeding in the opposite direction from the front course. Most back courses provide an additional non-precision approach for the airport.

Back Course Marker: a range indicator similar to the outer marker, but located on the back course. Provides distance-from-the-runway information.

Bearing: the relative position of one object to another, stated in degrees. For instrument navigation, a bearing means the direction *toward* a non-directional beacon. All ADF approach charts show bearings TO the station; VOR instructions are always in terms of *radials*—bearings AWAY from the station.

Blip: the spot of light on a radar scope which indicates the position of something (hopefully airplanes)reflecting radar energy. When transponders are used, the blip shows up as two short, parallel lines separated by varying distances for different codes.

Blue: the left half of the BLUE-YELLOW color arc on the bottom of the VOR display in the airplane.

CAVOK: skies clear, or no clouds below 5,000 feet; visibility at least six miles, and no precipitation.

CAVU: an acronym for *C*eiling *a*nd *V*isibility *U*nlimited. Sky may be clear or scattered; visibility more than ten miles. Not an official Weather Service term.

CDI: Course Deviation Indicator—in the vernacular of the everyday pilot, it's known as the left-right needle on the VOR display.

Ceiling: the first broken cloud layer not reported or forecast as "thin," or an obscuration not reported or forecast as "partial."

Cell: in conjunction with a radar advisory or report, implies a strong echo, and *usually* indicates a thunderstorm. To stay on the safe side, always consider a reported cell as a thunderstorm, and request vectors around it.

Center: the ATC facility responsible for the enroute phase of IFR operations; the full name is Air Route Traffic Control Center.

Circling Approach: any instrument approach in which the runway to be used for landing is aligned more than 30 degrees from the final approach course, or when a normal rate of descent from the minimum IFR altitude to the runway cannot be accomplished. Clearance for such an approach will always be specific, i.e., "cleared for the runway 10R ILS approach, *circle to land* runway 15." A circling approach is *always* a non-precision approach.

Clearance: an authorization from ATC to proceed into or through controlled airspace. A clearance supplies, changes, or amends your limits in any one, or all three, dimensions of flight: altitude, route, point to which you are cleared.

Clearance Limit: an electronic fix (intersection, NDB, VOR, DME fix) beyond which you may not proceed in IFR conditions without further clearance. Never accept a clearance limit unless you also receive an expect-further-clearance or expect-approach-clearance time.

Cleared as Filed: a communications simplifier—means you are cleared to the destination and via the route you requested in your flight plan. Does *not* include an altitude, which must be assigned separately.

Cleared Direct: an ATC instruction which means proceed from your present position *in a straight line* to the appropriate fix.

Cleared for the Approach: proceed from your present position direct to the appropriate radio facility, and execute the approach as published.

Cleared for Straight-in Approach: proceed direct to the final approach fix and complete the approach without executing a procedure turn.

Compass Locator: a non-directional low-frequency radio beacon co-located with the outer marker, providing a signal which you can use to navigate (ADF) to the OM. Also called an "outer locator," "outer compass locator," or just plain "locator." Same as LOM.

Contact Approach: a short-cut to a published instrument approach procedure, treated in detail in Chapter 13, "Instrument Approaches."

Control Zone: airspace around and above an air terminal for the protection of IFR departures and arrivals. Control zones extend from the surface to 14,500 feet MSL and are of concern only *when the airport is reporting IFR conditions.*

Course: a line drawn on a chart between two points, and when given a direction, is referenced to either true or magnetic north. All courses on IFR charts are *magnetic.*

Cruise Clearance: always implies a clearance for an approach at the destination airport, as well as important altitude and airspace limitations. See Chapter 6, "IFR Clearances," for details.

DF: Direction Finding—a disoriented IFR pilot's last resort. Most Flight Service Stations have the capability of electronically determining your bearing and supplying headings to fly to the airport. An approach aid under emergency conditions, it is one way of becoming "unlost."

DH: Decision Height—a point on the glide slope determined by the altimeter reading. Upon reaching the DH (a published height in feet above sea level), a decision must be made to either continue to a landing, or execute the missed approach procedure. Decision heights are associated *only* with precision approaches.

DME: Distance-Measuring Equipment—an airborne navigational aid which interrogates a VORTAC or VOR/DME station, and depending on the sophistication of the black box in the airplane, can provide distance, groundspeed, and time-to-station. Frequently used to identify intersections and confirm locations.

EAC: Expect Approach Clearance time—issued to an aircraft holding in a terminal area, awaiting clearance for an instrument approach.

EFC: Expect Further Clearance time—always issued to holding or clearance-limited IFR flights, to provide time for Controllers to clear airspace ahead in the event of communications failure. EFC is associated with an *enroute* delay. (Its counterpart, EAC—Expect Approach Clearance time—is issued when holding in the *terminal* area.)

ETA: Estimated Time of Arrival.

ETD: Estimated Time of Departure.

ETE: Estimated Time Enroute.

Fan Marker: a highly directional radio transmitter used to indicate distance from the runway on an approach. The radiation pattern seen from above would look like a football with pointed ends. Outer markers, middle markers, and inner markers are fan markers. Usually shortened to "marker."

Final Approach: that segment of an instrument approach procedure which leads from the final approach fix to the missed approach point.

FAF: Final Approach Fix—the last radio-determined position before you begin descent to the minimum altitude for an instrument approach. A report is always required when passing over the FAF inbound during an approach.

Fix: a definite geographical position, determined either by crossing two bearings from radio navigation stations, or by radar observations, or by use of VOR and DME.

FL: Flight Level—term used to indicate pressure altitudes to be flown in the high-altitude route system (above 18,000 feet).

FSS: Flight Service Station.

Glide Slope: an electronic signal which provides vertical guidance during a precision approach, and which activates the horizontal needle on the ILS indicator.

GMT: Greenwich Mean Time—the standard time used throughout the IFR system; based on the time at Her Majesty's Royal Observatory in Greenwich, England. Also called "Zulu" time, but has nothing whatever to do with the position of clock hands in South Africa.

"Hard" Altitude: an altitude *assigned* by ATC; the actual altitude is always preceded by "climb to and maintain" or "descend to and maintain."

Heading: the direction in which an aircraft is pointed, related either to true north or magnetic north. In domestic IFR operations, true headings are never used—everything is magnetic.

Heavy: a term used on the air in conjunction with turbojet aircraft capable of takeoff gross weights in excess of 300,000 pounds. (Trans-Global HEAVY, 685 for example.) Controllers may not vector any other flight closer than 5 miles behind or 1,000 feet below such an aircraft, because of wake turbulence.

HAA: Height Above Airport—the number of feet you will be above the airport's published elevation when you reach MDA on a circling approach.

HAT: Height Above Touchdown—your elevation above the touchdown zone of the runway when you reach the minimum altitude on a straight-in approach.

High Altitude: refers to routes and charts for IFR operations above 18,000 feet.

HIRL: High Intensity Runway Lighting—spaced evenly down either side of the runway, these lights identify the edges of the paved surface, and differ from ordinary runway lights in that the intensity can be increased or decreased to suit visibility conditions.

Holding: an orderly means of "retaining" an aircraft at some specified point by circling in a racetrack pattern.

Holding Fix: the electronic point to which a holding aircraft returns on each circuit of the holding pattern.

Hypoxia: a physiological condition arising from the lack of sufficient oxygen to perform normal functions. Suffered in varying degrees by almost everyone when flying at altitudes above 10,000 feet. (Know well thine own symptoms if thou takest thy body higher!)

Ident; Squawk Ident: terms used by radar Controllers when requesting pilots to activate the positive identification feature of a radar transponder. Causes the blip on a radar scope to intensify, or "bloom."

IFR: stands for Instrument Flight Rules, but is used universally as a label for all instrument operations.

ILS: Instrument Landing System—a combination of electronic components which furnish information in all three dimensions (lateral, longitudinal, and vertical), designed to lead an aircraft to a missed approach point very close to the runway.

ILS Category II: a more precise system which has even lower minimums than the normal, or Category I, Instrument Landing System. Requires special certification for ground equipment, airborne receivers, and higher pilot qualifications. (ILS Category III and IIIA are even *more* sophisticated.)

IM: Inner Marker—a radio transmitter identical to outer and middle markers, except for distance from the runway and signal pattern. IMs are situated between the MM and the runway, and usually transmit continuous dots (·········).

In Radar Contact: a Controller's statement that he has positively identified your flight on radar; a polite request to "shut up"—make no reports unless requested.

Jet Routes: airways in the high altitude (above 18,000 feet) route structure, such as J50, J437, etc. Should be referred to on the air as "Jay fifty," "Jay four three seven," etc.

Jet Stream: a meandering river of high-speed air (sometimes 200 knots or more), generally found at high altitudes. Like smart people up north, it usually moves south in the winter.

Jump: what you may want to do when all your radios and navigational equipment and instruments fail at night in a thunderstorm.

Kill the Rabbit: a coded request for the Tower to reduce the intensity of the RAILs (Runway Alignment Indicator Lights). Usually heard on nights when visibility is very low and pilots are being blinded by the bright lights.

Kilometers: used to quote visibility in Europe and the Far East; designed to completely confuse all pilots accustomed to distances measured in feet and miles.

Knot: the expression of speed corresponding to 1 nautical mile per hour. Used universally by ATC and all foreign nations. Pilots are expected to accomplish all IFR operations in terms of knots.

LBCM: Locator at the Back Course Marker—A non-directional radio beacon co-located with the fan marker on a back course localizer approach.

LDA: Localizer-type Directional Aid—same as a localizer, but offset from the runway heading. Provides course guidance down to a point from which you can proceed to the airport by visual references.

LDIN: Lead-in Lighting System—a flashing (or distinctive) lighting system with light units in groups of at least three, positioned in a curved path to a runway threshold. They furnish directional guidance only, and should not be confused with ALS.

LOC: Localizer—the left-right information portion of an ILS; an electronic extension of the centerline of the runway.

Locator: same as Compass Locator.

LOM: Locator at the Outer Marker—Same as Compass Locator.

Low Altitude: when referring to airway routes and charts for instrument operations, means "below 18,000 feet."

Maintain: what you are expected to do when assigned an altitude by ATC.

MAP: Missed Approach Point—expressed in either time or distance from the final approach fix, or as an altitude on the Glide Slope; it is the point at which a missed approach must be executed if the runway environment is not in sight.

Map: usually referred to by pilots as a "chart."

Marker Beacon: same as fan marker.

Marker Beacon Lights: two, or sometimes three, panel-mounted lights which illuminate appropriately to indicate passage over radio range markers on an instrument approach. (Cf. OM, MM, IM.)

MDA: Minimum Descent Altitude—the lowest altitude (expressed in feet above sea level) to which you may descend on a non-precision approach (one without a glide slope) if the runway environment is not in sight.

MEA: Minimum Enroute Altitude—the lowest altitude at which you can receive a satisfactory navigational signal for the appropriate segment of a federal airway.

MOCA: Minimum Obstruction Clearance Altitude—guarantees terrain and obstacle clearance on the appropriate segment of a federal airway. If you should have to fly MOCA, remember that a usable VOR signal is guaranteed only within twenty-two miles of the station.

Missed Approach: a procedure specified for a "go-around" if the runway environment is not in sight at the missed approach point.

MM: Middle Marker—a highly-directional radio beacon located about one-half mile from the end of the runway on an ILS approach. A distance indicator, it transmits a signal of high-pitched alternate dots and dashes (· — · — · — · — ·). If marker beacon lights are installed in the airplane, the amber light will flash in a similar pattern. The middle marker does *not* indicate the missed approach point.

MSA: Minimum Sector Altitude—the lowest altitude within 25 nautical miles of an approach fix which guarantees 1,000 feet obstacle clearance. Found on the approach and landing chart, it may be one altitude for all directions, or may be referenced to several sectors around the fix.

Nautical Mile: one minute of latitude (measured vertically on charts); all distances in IFR charts are indicated in nautical miles; all DME indicators read nautical miles.

NDB: Non-Directional Beacon—a low-frequency radio transmitter which emanates a signal in all directions from the antenna. Its signal is not concentrated in any one direction, hence the term "non-directional."

Negative: an emphatic, easily understood "no."

No Joy: a term borrowed from our military flying brothers; means "I do not see the traffic you told me about," and saves a lot of communications time.

Non-precision Approach: a published procedure (or surveillance radar approach) which does not provide an electronic glide slope. *All* approaches except ILS and PAR are non-precision.

NOTAM: NOtices To AirMen—information pertinent to operations in the National Airspace System. May be received via teletype or radio broadcasts.

OM: Outer Marker—Usually the final approach fix on an ILS or localizer approach, this 75 mHz, non-tunable radio beacon is typically located 4 to 7 miles from the runway. Highly directional, its signal is transmitted in a narrow beam straight up, and is received only when directly overhead. The audible signal is a continuous series of low-pitched dashes (— — — — —) and if marker beacon lights are installed in the airplane, the blue light will flash in conjunction with the sound.

Omni: short for "Very-High-Frequency-Omnidirectional-Radio-Range," also known as VOR. Omni has only two syllables—don't say "om-an-ni."

Outer Locator: same as LOM.

Over: used at the end of a radio transmission to indicate that a reply is expected. Quite unnecessary; if what you have said requires a reply, you'll get it anyway.

Over and Out: used mostly by the Walter Mitty types who also wear helmet and goggles in a Learjet.

PAR: Precision Approach Radar—provides a precision approach based on vocal instructions given to the pilot, as the Controller observes azimuth, distance, and elevation on radar. Known as GCA (Ground Controlled Approach) at military airfields.

Parallel ILS Approach: in existence at only a handful of airports, and operable only within very restrictive conditions of runway separation and radar monitoring, these approaches provide guidance to side-by-side runways simultaneously.

Partial Panel: term used to describe the situation that exists when the attitude indicator and heading indicator are inoperative, or covered up with some fiendish device your flight instructor pulls from his shirt pocket. Sometimes referred to as "needle, ball, and airspeed," especially during meetings of older pilots.

Precipitous Terrain: where steep and abrupt slopes exist under the final approach course, the approach chart will display a note to that effect. In addition to causing violent up and down drafts, the sudden changes in pressure can result in wild fluctuations of altimeter and airspeed indicators. Approach planners take this into account, and boost the minimum altitudes accordingly.

Precision Approach: an approach procedure which incorporates an electronic glide slope. In today's IFR world, there is only one in regular use, the Instrument Landing System (ILS).

Prevailing Visibility: the horizontal distance at which known objects can be seen through at least half the observer's horizon. It does not necessarily mean a *continuous* half of his horizon, and so can vary considerably from the actual visibility at the approach end of the runway. Other types of visibility measurement (e.g., RVR) are considered more appropriate for instrument approaches; of course the pilot's observation is the ultimate.

Procedure Turn: a means of reversing course to line up inbound on the approach course. Generally used in non-radar situations, or when you arrive over the approach fix headed away from the airport.

Procedure Turn Altitude: found on the profile view of the approach chart, this is your vertical limit while reversing course. You are considered in the procedure turn and must observe this altitude limit until once again on the approach course inbound.

Queen, Hangar: what you call your airplane when it's in the shop more than it's in the air.

Radar: RAdio Detection And Ranging—pulses of electronic energy are emitted from a ground transmitter—objects which echo the energy show up on the radar scope as "blips" of bright light; the azimuth and distance, and in some cases the altitude can be measured. Airborne transponders cause a coded blip to appear on the scope.

Radar Altimeter: an electronic device which measures the time for a radio signal to go from the aircraft antenna to the ground and return, then displays the time interval as a precise distance. Used generally for precision approaches, and is required for Category II and III ILS operations.

Radar Beacon: the official name for a transponder.

Radar Monitored Approach: one in which a radar operator follows the progress of an aircraft in order to provide corrections in course, and sometimes elevation. Used mostly at very congested terminals. You can request a radar-monitored approach in an emergency, or when you suspect navigational equipment malfunction.

Radar Service Terminated: a phrase used by Approach Controllers when an aircraft is observed on course, headed for the Final Approach Fix. You are then expected to navigate the rest of the way by yourself. It can also be used on occasion in an enroute situation.

Radial: a magnetic course radiating, or proceeding outward from, a VOR. Controllers *always* use the term "radial" when referencing navigation instructions to a VOR.

Radio Compass: same as ADF.

RAIL: Runway Alignment Indicator Lights—the "ball of fire" you see running toward the runway in a fully-equipped approach lighting system. Sometimes called the "rabbit."

Read Back: what the Controller says at the end of an IFR clearance.

REIL: Runway End Identifier Lights—a pair of condenser discharge lights (strobes) identical to those in the RAIL system, but located on either side of the runway threshold. REILs flash simultaneously, about once a second.

Relative bearing: on an ADF indicator, the number of degrees the pointer is displaced *clockwise* from the nose (top index) of the aircraft. Add relative bearing to magnetic heading, and the resulting number is *always* magnetic course to the station.

Report Landing Assured or Missed Approach: when cleared for an approach to an airport with no ATC facility, you remain under protection from other IFR traffic. Should you be required to execute a missed approach, you go right back into the system for another try, or perhaps clearance to your alternate. The Controller would therefore like to hear from you when "landing is assured" (runway in sight), or when you start a missed approach. He will also advise whom to contact and on what frequency.

Report Procedure Turn: a request for a report as soon as you turn away from the outbound course—call the Controller at the very beginning of the procedure turn.

Report Procedure Turn Inbound: when so instructed on an instrument approach, the Controller wants to hear from you as soon as you turn toward the airport—in other words, when you are halfway around the procedure turn.

Resume Normal Navigation: usually follows "radar service terminated" and is your cue to intercept, stay on, or get back to the appropriate radial, airway, or course and get where you're supposed to go all by yourself.

RMI: Radio Magnetic Indicator—displays aircraft heading at the top of a rotating card, with pointers tied electronically to the VOR and/or ADF receivers. When properly tuned, the pointers indicate magnetic course to the appropriate station. The RMI is also convenient to use as a heading indicator.

Roger: worldwide term to indicate complete understanding of a radio transmission. Can also be used (with appropriate volume) when answering a bartender to let everyone in earshot know that you are a pilot.

Roger Wilco: means "yes, I understand and *will co*mply," and is completely out of place in today's aeronautical communications. A simple "Roger" or your aircraft number does the job.

Roger Wilco, Over and Out: be careful with the use of this phrase on the air—some enterprising musician will hear it and write a hit song.

Runway Environment: the runway threshold, approved lighting aids, or other markings identifiable with the runway. Having the runway environment in sight is one of the requirements for descending below DH or MDA on any approach.

RVR: Runway Visual Range—a photoelectric device called a "transmissometer" measures the visibility immediately adjacent to the runway, then computes what a pilot would see, and converts this observation to hundreds of feet. Displayed in the tower, it can be handily read to you during a tight approach, and takes precedence over all other forms of visibility measurement, except your own two eyes.

RVV: Runway Visibility Value—visibility at the approach end of the runway, measured by a transmissometer, and reported in statute miles and fractions thereof. (Gradually being replaced by RVR.)

Say Again: please repeat all of what you have just said.

Say Again All After. . . .: please repeat everything that followed a given word or phrase—implies complete understanding of whatever came before that point in the transmission.

Say Again All After ATC Clears. . . .: generally used by honest pilots when they miss an entire IFR clearance.

Say Again, You Broke Up: this is a good way to "keep your cool" when you don't have *any* idea what the man said—no one can prove that the transmission *didn't* break up!

SDF: Simplified Directional Facility—an instrument approach procedure that fits on the accuracy scale between a VOR and a localizer approach. Course width may vary from 6 degrees to 12 degrees among installations, with the final approach course offset somewhat from the runway heading.

SID: Standard Instrument Departure—a published clearance procedure designed to cut down communication time. Each SID is named and numbered and directs you to an enroute fix from which you proceed via the airways routing in your clearance.

Special VFR: an ATC clearance (sometimes called "poor man's IFR") to proceed into or out of a control zone under certain conditions.

Squawk Standby: when so directed, turn the transponder function switch to "standby" (or other relevant terminology), which will cause the transponder blip to disappear completely from the radar scope. Used for positive identification when the IDENT feature is inoperative or weak. Usually followed by "Squawk normal" when the Controller has positive identification. "Standby" should always be selected when taxiing.

Standard Rate Turn: a turn which results in the aircraft changing heading at the rate of 3 degrees per second. To approximate the angle of bank required, divide true airspeed (in knots) by ten and add five.

Stand by: the universal reply to a question from ATC when the answer is not readily available.

STAR: Standard Terminal Arrival Route—a published route into a terminal area, with the basic aim of reducing communications between pilots and controllers. Each STAR has its own name and number; for example, "cleared via the Fountainhead Four Arrival."

Star: a bright spot in the night sky, often mistaken for the lights of another airplane.

Stepdown Fix: an intermediate point between the Final Approach Fix and the Missed Approach Point, permitting a lower altitude when it can be identified by the pilot.

Straight-in Approach: a procedure which leads directly to the landing end of the runway, when that runway is aligned no more than 30 degrees from the final approach course, and a normal descent from the minimum IFR altitude can be accomplished.

TACAN: a military navigation system (TACtical Air Navigation) combined with a VOR to make a VORTAC, which supplies both azimuth and distance to DME-equipped civilian aircraft.

Tally Ho: say this when you spot the traffic that Center points out to you—"Barnburner 1234 Alpha, traffic at two o'clock, four miles, eastbound"—it's a wee bit melodramatic when you answer "Tally ho!" but it sure cuts down on communication time!

TAS: True AirSpeed.

TDZ: Touchdown Zone—extends 3,000 feet down the runway from the threshold; the highest elevation in the TDZ provides the point from which DH and MDA are measured for straight-in approach minimums.

Track: the path which an aircraft makes across the ground. When cleared direct from one point to another, that track is expected to be a straight line.

Track: parallel lengths of ferrous material secured to wooden crossties, and used for aerial navigation. Also used now and then by long lines of railroad cars.

Transmissometer: the electronic visibility-sensing device which povides the basic input for RVV and RVR measurements. It is installed beside the landing runway at the approach end, and is very accurate—the next-to-the-last word in visibility measurement.

Transponder: a device which responds to a coded radar pulse with a coded return, displaying a distinctive blip which provides positive radar identification.

Transponder Code: the specified sequence of numbers which, when selected on the transponder, provides a coded display on the radar scope.

Unable: the communication code word used to indicate your inability to contact a facility; for example, "Birmingham Tower. Barnburner 1234 Alpha UNABLE Approach Control on 123.8." Tower will then give you further instructions.

Vector: a heading assigned by a radar Controller; takes precedence over all other forms of navigation. You are expected to remain on vectored headings until advised "resume normal navigation."

Verify: when used by either a Controller or a pilot, means "did you really say what I think you said?"

VFR: Visual Flight Rules—conditions to which pilots are limited until they become instrument-rated. A non-specific term compared to IFR, which means "I Follow Railroads."

Visibility: what you need a certain amount of in order to legally land from an instrument approach. It may be measured and reported by a ground observer, a transmissometer (RVV and RVR), or the pilot. *You* become the official visibility observer on an approach—if the runway environment is in sight at a certain point, proceeding to a landing is completely legal.

Visual Approach: a short-cut to a published instrument approach procedure, treated in detail in Chapter 12, "Getting Ready for an Instrument Approach."

VOR: stands for Very high frequency Omni-directional Radio range.

What Am I Doing Here?: the question you will ask yourself in the middle of a thunderstorm.

X-ray Vision: what ATC expects you to have when the Controller says "the airport is at one o'clock, two miles; do you have it in sight?"

Yellow: the *other* half of the BLUE-YELLOW color arc on the bottom of the VOR display in the airplane.

Zulu Time: a military-spawned term which is easier to say than Greenwich Mean Time; means the same thing, and is frequently shortened to "Z."

3. Attitude Instrument Flying

THE PTERODACTYL, a lizard-turned-bird with huge leather-skinned wings who soared above the swamps and marshes of prehistoric times, may well have been the first creature to experience IFR flight. According to the geological history books, the earth was frequently covered with clouds of noxious gases from the volcanoes which dotted the landscape—it's a cinch that the pterodactyls on occasion ignored their VFR-only limitations, and flew into IFR conditions. Of course no one was there to prove it, but quite likely they had an instinctive reaction to counter the sudden loss of visual clues; they were probably able to set their wings for an optimum glide speed, maintain direction with some primitive vestibular gyroscope, and keep going until they broke out of the clouds. It's just as likely that some of them didn't make it; this theory is supported by the discoveries now and then of pterodactyl remains on or just below the summits of mountain peaks!

The blind-flying capabilities of our feathered friends extends to many of the birds we know today—ducks, pigeons, geese, and others have been known to successfully navigate through the clouds to safety. Man has not fared so well, requiring some sort of help from artificial references to maintain his spatial orientation. But anyone who has flown Cubs, Airknockers, and the like knows that if things really got bad, you could always close the throttle, roll the trim all the way back, keep the turn needle centered with the rudder, and at least come out of the situation right side up.

When aviation pioneers turned their efforts to making money with airplanes, they soon realized that they would have to figure some way to overcome what appeared to be the insurmountable problem of flying all the way through clouds—halfway just wouldn't do. A frightening number of our departed brothers tried it on guts and confidence, but it all boiled down to the necessity of substituting some kind of in-the-airplane instrumentation to replace the natural horizon when it disappeared. Early attempts included "playing it by ear," listening to the sound of the wind in the ample wires and stays which held those old airplanes together, watching the flutterings of pieces of cloth tied to the struts, and even Mason jars half-filled with oil which were supposed to indicate whether the airplane was banking, or in level flight.

None of these early methods worked very well, but with the advent of gyroscopic devices, a whole new world of airplane utility was introduced. When Jimmy Doolittle proved that man could take off, navigate, and land an airplane using no outside references, he introduced a system of instrument flight which we use, almost unchanged, to this very day.

Whether you took flying lessons yesterday or thirty years ago, one of the first things you learned was that when the cowling, or the top of the instrument panel, or some other reference showed a certain relation to the horizon, and when you had the engine wide open, climb airspeed resulted. You learned that when the center post of the windshield formed a particular angle with the horizon, some certain rate of turn happened. The substitution of a miniature airplane fastened to the instrument case and moving about a gyro-stabilized bar in the same direction and to the same degree as the actual movement of the real airplane merely transfers to an artificial horizon what you used to see outside. If you set up your old familiar climb attitude with outside references and at the same time notice what you see on the attitude indicator, you can forget the outside clues, and rest assured that anytime you put the miniature airplane in the same place, with the same power setting, you're going to get the same old familiar climb performance. That, in a very small nutshell, is attitude instrument flying—basic, reliable, and really very simple to accomplish.

But the attitude indicator can't do the job alone. Although it's the heart of the system, you must refer to the other instruments to determine what is happening when you select a two-bar-width nose high attitude, or a 20-degree bank, or a combination of the two. In other words, you must reason to yourself (or out loud, if it helps!) "I will place this little flying machine in the attitude that I *think* will produce a standard-rate climbing turn to the right, and then check the other gauges to see if I was right—if the needles and pointers aren't moving the way they should, I will change the attitude a bit to get the results I want." It's easy to see that if all the variables are held constant, the same attitude will give the same condition of flight every time. Now, in a manner of speaking, you *can* set your wings just like the birds, and have confidence that certain things will take place.

THE FUNDAMENTALS OF ATTITUDE CONTROL

Pitch, bank, power, and trim—the "Four Horsemen" of attitude instrument flight. When you get right down to it, there's not much you can do with an airplane except change the pitch, bank, or power, and how much you change what in which direction in concert with the others or all by itself determines what will happen. You may feel that this listing of the basics added trim unnecessarily, and left out rudder control; not so, because trim is of great importance in smoothing out your cloud-bound wanderings, and you are expected to maintain the ball in its centered position at all times in instrument flight. In general, you should always adjust pitch, bank, and power, then trim to hold the airplane in the attitude you want. The human machine is incapable of holding a constant, precise pressure for an extended period of time, but it can *recognize* that pressure and adjust trim controls until it disappears.

Now, you must become a believer. Raise your right hand, and repeat for all to hear: "I [state your name] do hereby solemnly affirm my belief in the fact that in all steady-state instrument situations [that is, any time a constant airspeed, constant altitude, or constant rate-of-change of altitude is desired], altitude shall be controlled by POWER and airspeed shall be controlled by PITCH." It's true! Believe! Go back in memory to those slow-flight exercises you went through early in your flying career—at a very-near-stall airspeed, if the altitude began to droop a bit, you didn't pull up the nose to correct, you added POWER. If the airspeed was somewhat higher than what your instructor felt was a good demonstration of slow flight, you didn't back off on the throttle, you applied BACK PRESSURE. And it works just as beautifully when you're under the hood or in weather—perhaps even more so than when you can see outside, because you have an exacting reference right there in front of you; it's called an "instrument panel."

When that gaggle of needles, pointers, gauges, and indicators is complete and everything's working properly, there is one instrument that must be considered THE primary one—the attitude indicator. It seems reasonable, in a context of attitude instrument flying, that the attitude *indicator* should be the most frequently consulted. It will tell you more at a glance than anything else on the panel. Changes in attitude on this instrument will be immediately reflected in the readings elsewhere—you are able to generate changes or keep them from taking place by referring to this gyroscopic manifestation of where-is-the-airplane-in-relation-to-the-horizon. Anytime it's not in the level flight attitude for the particular power setting in use, something is happening, or is about to happen. (Probably 99.9 percent of your instrument time will be spent scanning the indications of a so-called full panel, with all the instruments in working order, and doing their jobs. Mechanical devices being what they are, it's possible some day to find yourself operating in a "partial panel" situation, and you should know what to do and how to handle the airplane in this condition. See a good flight instructor for details.)

Your first step in becoming a good attitude instrument pilot is to find out what the gyro horizon looks like when you *are* in normal level flight. There are few attitude indicators in use today which are not adjustable; you should be able to move the miniature airplane up or down so that it is dead center on the artificial horizon in a straight and level, constant airspeed condition. Once you have found this attitude and adjusted the little airplane to show it, LEAVE IT THERE. This gives you a sound base from which to proceed. Now you can change the attitude as required—for a constant airspeed climb at full power, you may have to increase the pitch attitude two bar widths (raise the miniature airplane twice the thickness of its wings above the horizon bar), or perhaps you will recognize that a one-half bar width increase is required to hold altitude in a standard rate turn. Every time you make that little airplane move, the movement should be referenced to the level flight attitude as shown on the attitude indicator. (Slight adjustments for varying loads and atmospheric conditions may be required.)

Sources of qualitative information will change in various maneuvers. For example, when rolling into a standard rate turn, bank the miniature airplane until the turn needle moves to the proper indication, and then maintain the rate of turn as shown on the needle by minor changes in the bank attitude. The turn needle has become the primary source of information about rate of turn, but the attitude indicator remains stalwart in its indication of the bank required to sustain this condition. As you approach a predetermined heading, the heading indicator will tell you when to begin the roll-out, and it's back to the attitude indicator to return the airplane to level flight. When you're trying to maintain a precise rate of descent at a given airspeed (as in the final segment of an IFR approach), the airspeed indicator tells you whether or not the attitude you have selected is the proper one, and the attitude indicator is used to make any changes that may be required. Since you believe that power controls altitude (and altitude change), when it is necessary to increase your rate of descent, you will reduce power with reference to the engine instruments, but you need the attitude indicator to maintain the pitch relationship that will keep the airspeed constant. And of course, whenever straight flight is your target, keeping the wings level with the attitude indicator (and the ball centered as always with rudder pressure) can do nothing but make the airplane fly straight ahead.

APPLYING THE ATTITUDE TECHNIQUE

Some instrument pilots are sharper, smoother, and more precise than others—it's a fact of life, and is due partly to the physical and mental capabilities of each individual. But running through the performance of even the slowest, most plodding IFR aviator is an undeniable 1-2-3 sequence of events. Some are able to accomplish it faster than others, but you can't get away from (1) reading the instrument indications, (2) figuring out what they have to say to you, (3) doing something about it. This sequence is commonly known as cross-check, interpretation, and control.

INSTRUMENT CROSS-CHECK

Tirades from flight instructors, grueling sessions in ground trainers, and sophisticated eye-movement studies have failed to come up with a formula for cross-checking flight instruments. In addition to the fact that the amount of time spent on any one instrument must change subtly with every change in flight condition, cross-checking seems to be a very personal matter. The number of times per minute your eyes scan the entire panel, or how long they remain on the turn needle or the heading indicator isn't really important; the essence of cross-checking lies in the *amount* of information gleaned from each sweep of the gauges. You must develop your cross-check to provide enough inputs for meaningful decisions about what to do next, if anything. It stands to reason that the more complicated the maneuver, the faster your eyes must move, especially when you are introducing a change of attitude.

There is only one way to become a proficient cross-checker; force yourself to eyeball each of the instruments, with particular emphasis on the attitude indicator (you'll be amazed at the minute changes you can detect), and practice, practice, practice. Here's where the proficiency exercises described in Chapter 18 can be a big help—without the distractions of Approach Control, with no navigational load to divert your attention, go through these maneuvers if for nothing else than to speed up your cross-check. It's a skill, and as such must be practiced regularly and methodically if it's to stay sharp.

Later on, you must begin to include your navigational inputs in the cross-check. It's easy to develop instrument hypnosis, characterized by ignorance of navaid information. Pilots have been known to fly all the way to the missed approach point with great precision and beautiful timing, but at procedure turn altitude—right on course, but so concerned with maintaining an exact altitude that they forgot to descend over the Final Approach Fix!

INSTRUMENT FLYING FOR ANIMAL LOVERS

Having detailed the concept of attitude control, there is another method which you may prefer. For reasons which will become apparent, it is recommended for those pilots whose airplanes have large, easily cleaned cabins. Known as the "Cat and Duck Method" of instrument flight, it has received much publicity and is considered to have a great deal of merit by those who have not tried it. No reports have been received from those who did try it, and none is expected. Pilots are invited to assess its merits objectively.

Basic rules for the C&D Method of instrument flight are fairly well known and are extremely simple. Here's how it's done:

1. Place a live cat on the cockpit floor; because a cat always remains upright, he or she can be used in lieu of a needle and ball. Merely watch to see which way the cat leans to determine if a wing is low, and if so, which one.
2. The duck is used for the instrument approach and landing. Because of the fact that any sensible duck will refuse to fly under instrument conditions, it is only necessary to hurl your duck out of the plane and follow her to the ground.

There are some limitations to the Cat and Duck Method, but by rigidly adhering to the following checklist, a degree of success will be achieved which will surely startle you, your passengers, and even an occasional tower operator:

1. Get a wide-awake cat. Most cats do not want to stand up at all. It may be necessary to carry a large dog in the cockpit to keep the cat at attention.
2. Make sure your cat is clean. Dirty cats will spend all their time washing. Trying to follow a washing cat usually results in a tight snap roll followed by an inverted spin (flat).
3. Use old cats only. Young cats have nine lives, but old, used-up cats with only one life left have just as much to lose as you do and will be more dependable.
4. Beware of cowardly ducks. If the duck discovers that you are using the cat to stay upright, she will refuse to leave without the cat. Ducks are no better in IFR conditions than you are.
5. Be sure that the duck has good eyesight. Nearsighted ducks sometimes fail to realize that they are on the gauges and go flogging off into the nearest hill. *Very* nearsighted ducks will not realize they have been thrown out and will descend to the ground in a sitting position. This maneuver is difficult to follow in an airplane.
6. Use land-loving ducks. It is very discouraging to break out and

find yourself on final for a rice paddy, particularly if there are duck hunters around. Duck hunters suffer from temporary insanity while sitting in freezing weather in the blinds and will shoot at anything that flies.

7. Choose your duck carefully. It is easy to confuse ducks with geese because many water birds look alike. While they are very competent instrument flyers, geese seldom want to go in the same direction as you. If your duck heads off for Canada or Mexico, you may be sure that you have been given the goose.

4. IFR Flight Plans

IT'S AWFULLY NICE to have the flexibility of filing or not filing a VFR flight plan, being able more or less to come and go as you please, yet having the protection of a flight plan when you want it. When the weather slides downhill, and instrument flight is necessary, the rules change, and there is no longer a choice for the pilot operating in controlled airspace. Flight plans are a way of life for instrument pilots; they're an absolute necessity for IFR in controlled airspace. Whether it's filed formally by filling out the form and handing it across the counter to the Flight Service Specialist, or filed in abbreviated form by a radio transmission to Center, you must have a flight plan on file to be legal. Use of the proper filing procedures and a full understanding of what happens when you file can save considerable time, make your IFR operations more efficient, and enable the system to serve you better.

There are several ways you can file a flight plan with a Flight Service Station—in person, by telephone or radio—but they share one commonality: The form on which your request is recorded is as standard as peas in a pod. Whether you file IFR three times a day or once a month, you can exhibit professionalism and save a lot of time by studying the flight plan form and

FEDERAL AVIATION AGENCY

FLIGHT PLAN

Form Approved.
Budget Bureau No. 04-R072.3

1. TYPE OF FLIGHT PLAN: FVFR / VFR / ✓ IFR / DVFR

2. AIRCRAFT IDENTIFICATION: 1234A

3. AIRCRAFT TYPE/SPECIAL EQUIPMENT 1/	4. TRUE AIRSPEED	5. POINT OF DEPARTURE	6. DEPARTURE TIME PROPOSED (Z)	6. DEPARTURE TIME ACTUAL (Z)	7. INITIAL CRUISING ALTITUDE
BARNBURNER 408/A	170 KNOTS	BNA	1410		7000

8. ROUTE OF FLIGHT: V5E SUGARGROVE X, V243 BWG

9. DESTINATION (Name of airport and city): BOWLING GREEN

10. REMARKS: ROUTING REQUESTED DUE TO WX

11. ESTIMATED TIME EN ROUTE HOURS	MINUTES	12. FUEL ON BOARD HOURS	MINUTES	13. ALTERNATE AIRPORT(S)	14. PILOT'S NAME
0	20	3	30	STANDIFORD FIELD LOUISVILLE, KY.	J. DOE

15. PILOT'S ADDRESS AND TELEPHONE NO. OR AIRCRAFT HOME BASE	16. NO. OF PERSONS ABOARD	17. COLOR OF AIRCRAFT	18. FLIGHT WATCH STATIONS
ON FILE BNA FSS	5	FUSCHIA, MAGENTA & CERISE WITH BURGUNDY TRIM	

CLOSE FLIGHT PLAN UPON ARRIVAL

1/ SPECIAL EQUIPMENT SUFFIX
A — DME & 4096 Code transponder
B — DME & 64 Code transponder
D — DME
L — DME & transponder—no code
T — 64 Code transponder
U — 4096 Code transponder
X — Transponder—no code

FAA Form 7233—1 (4-66) FORMERLY FAA 398 0052-027-8000

Flight plan form, properly completed for the Barnburner's proposed journey from Nashville to Bowling Green. There is a flight log on the reverse side.

using its sequence every time. You can pick up a pad or two at any Flight Service Station, and you even get a bonus—if you like to use a flight log, there's one printed on the back side of the form. That's efficiency; one piece of paper doing two jobs and making for a neater cockpit.

This flight plan form is the same one the FSS specialist reaches for when you call and say you would like to file a flight plan. Notice that each block on the form contains a "question" to which you are going to supply the "answer," so there is no need to repeat the name of the item when filing. Recognizing that there will be times when you'll file without using the form, you should memorize the sequence, or carry a list of these items in the right order; a properly filed flight plan should consist of a series of numbers, abbreviations, and names—no questions, please, just the answers! Whenever you file and the specialist has to ask you to repeat something, you haven't done it right.

GET OFF TO A GOOD START

Assuming that you have received a weather briefing, decided on a route, and are filing with FSS by telephone, you can provide the information for the first two items right off the bat by saying slowly, "this is Barnburner 1234 Alpha with an IFR flight plan." When the man on the other end of the line rejoins with "go ahead," he will have inserted your aircraft number and type of flight plan in Blocks #1 and #2. (FVFR, or "Flight Following," is no longer used, and DVFR will be discussed later in this chapter.) You've blown your quest for efficiency if you repeat these items, so charge on, beginning with Block #3.

"Aircraft type" deserves some emphasis—Cessna or Piper or Beech by themselves don't tell the story, so make your description adequate. Use model numbers for most airplanes, i.e., Cessna 182, PA-28, BE-250. Everyone knows that a DC-3 is a Douglas, and nobody but Beechcraft has ever built a D-18, but who ever heard of a "Barnburner"?—it would be prudent therefore to refer to your flying machine as a specific model of Barnburner.

In this same block, an indication of special navigation equipment is requested; passed along to Center, it is vital information bearing on subsequent clearances and requests for position reports. Know which suffix applies to your airplane; if you fly several variously equipped birds, you might want to cut out the legend in the lower right-hand corner of the flight plan form. It will fit perfectly in one of your wallet windows—out of the way, yet handy for quick reference.

Four suffixes have been added to the list, but do not appear on the flight plan form. They indicate Area Navigation capability (Course Line Computers) and are defined as follows:

/C no code transponder and approved area navigation
/F 4096 code transponder and approved area navigation
/S 64 code transponder and approved area navigation
/W no transponder and approved area navigation

Moving on to Block #4, true airspeed, say only the numbers, such as "one seven zero." This figure may vary somewhat due to temperature changes aloft, but you should be able to hit it fairly accurately. Experience will provide a workable number for this block, but when in doubt, use indicated cruise airspeed plus 2 percent for each 1,000 feet above sea level, and you'll not be far off.

Block #5 should be given as an airport name or three-letter identifier, and Block #6 should be a reasonable estimate of the time you expect to be ready for takeoff. Always given in Zulu, or Greenwich Mean Time, it should not be less than 30 minutes from right now, the time you are filing. It usually takes that long for your proposal to filter through the system, from FSS to Center and back to Ground Control or Clearance Delivery, depending on the airport facilities. If you need to get airborne sooner, explain the situation and ask FSS to expedite your clearance—they'll do all they can to help, but it is ultimately up to Center to fit you into the traffic flow. The busier the terminal, the slower this process will be, but it's worth a try. Some very busy areas (Chicago, New York, Los Angeles, for example) would like to have your request at least an hour before departure. Since you're dealing with Zulu time, know what the conversion factor is and don't ask the specialist to do your arithmetic for you—time zones and the formula for each are found on IFR enroute charts.

If it appears that you will not be able to make your proposed takeoff time, you have a responsibility to let ATC know about it; as soon as your flight plan comes into the Center, tentative plans are made to accept it into the system. The computer will hold your request for two hours after the ETD, and you should amend this time if you can't possibly make it. It's simply a matter of calling FSS or Tower and asking them to revise your estimated time of departure—they'll appreciate your cooperation, and can then let someone else use the airspace they were holding for you. It's the old "golden rule" trick.

Your altitude request (Block #7) is based on a number of

factors such as winds, weather, and minimum enroute altitudes, and should be decided upon before filing. You should observe the hemispheric separation rules—eastbound, request *odd* altitudes; westbound, request *even* altitudes. The key word here is "request," because an IFR flight will always be assigned an altitude by ATC. Don't argue about "maintain niner thousand" on a westbound flight; the Controller has a good reason for it, and will probably amend your clearance later on. If you are filing in the High Altitude Route Structure (above 18,000 feet), the same general rules apply until you reach FL 290 and above—altimeter errors can really build up at these levels, and so 2,000-foot separation is required. "East—odd, west—even" falls apart. (Refer to chapter 5 in *Weather Flying* for a detailed analysis of what altitude to select with respect to the enroute weather.)

Block #8 can be either delightfully succinct or unnecessarily complicated, depending on your knowledge of what you can and cannot do when planning the route for your flight. (This chapter is concerned only with the language you should use when filing the flight plan; "Preflight Planning," Chapter 5, goes into detail about airways to choose, departure routes, etc.) The route for any IFR flight, no matter how short, must be made up of three segments: departure, enroute, and arrival. You leap off from one airport (departure), navigate to some radio fix (enroute), from which you can execute an approach to another airport (arrival). If you will keep this sequence in mind as you file, it will cut down the number of words required to communicate your request to ATC.

The departure phase can consist of a SID (Standard Instrument Departure), radar vectors, direct flight to a VOR, or immediate interception of an airway (if it's reasonably close to the departure airport). So, your initial response for Block #8 should be a concise description of how you intend to get to your first fix; for example, "Briefcase Two Departure to ALB" (identifier of the first VOR), or "radar vectors to ALB," or "direct ALB," or "Victor 14 to ALB."

If you harbor a suppressed desire to drive everybody in ATC right up the walls of their windowless control rooms, make it a habit to choose the most complicated, zig-zagging routes, using all the airways on the chart. Or make it easy on yourself and the system by picking out an established route, using wherever possible just one numbered airway to get where you're going. When you reel off the enroute portion of Block #8, use the Victor airway numbers and VOR identifiers.

More often than not, one airway will do the job—for example, consider a flight from Nashville, Tennessee (BNA), to Bowling Green, Kentucky (BWG)—Victor 5 runs straight as a die between the two airports, so why not file that way? "Victor 5 BWG" is all you need to say to tell the FSS man everything he needs to know about the departure and enroute segments. You've already mentioned the airport from which you're leaping off, and the next block is reserved for destination airport—the enroute portion should always wind up with the last radio fix you intend to use.

But suppose there is a line of thunderstorms showing up on radar along Victor 5, and you decide to take an eastern detour. File "Victor 5E Sugargrove intersection, Victor 243 BWG." Were Horace Greeley planning this flight, he would likely go west, and that's no problem, except that the airway change does not occur at a named intersection, so the flight plan should go like this: "Victor 7E, Victor 49 BWG."

There are times when it's advantageous to file direct, off-airways routes, and your flight plan should consist of the first and last VORs you intend using, with the identifiers of the ones in between that will serve as checkpoints—"LVT, BWG, CCT, MWA," for example. (The restrictions that apply to off-airways flight are detailed in Chapter 5.)

Having dealt with the departure and enroute phases of filing, turn your attention to the arrival portion. For planning purposes, an IFR flight terminates over the final approach fix at destination; the published approach procedure will get you from there

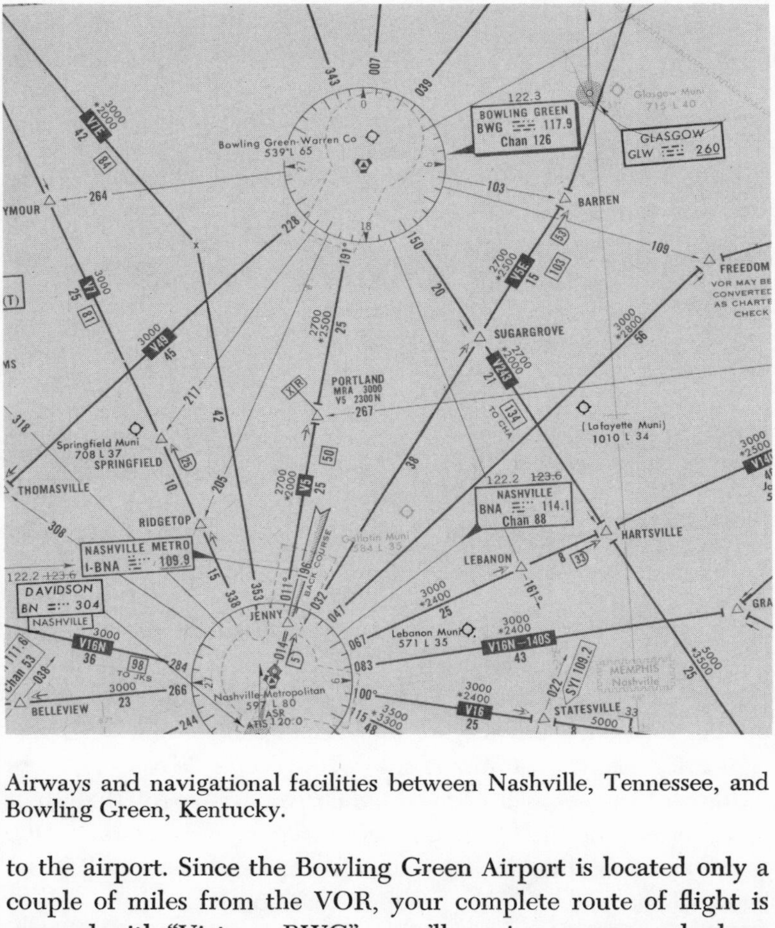

Airways and navigational facilities between Nashville, Tennessee, and Bowling Green, Kentucky.

to the airport. Since the Bowling Green Airport is located only a couple of miles from the VOR, your complete route of flight is covered with "Victor 5 BWG"—you'll receive an approach clearance before getting there, but in case your radios quit, ATC will know what you plan to do. If Glasgow, Kentucky (just east of BWG), were your destination, and Victor 5E did not exist, it would be proper to file "Victor 5 BWG, direct GLW." Of course, the sensible routing for such a flight would be "Victor 5E GLW," and have it over with—Glasgow is close enough to the airway to use the NDB as a termination fix.

Destination, like point of departure, is adequately identified by the name of the airport, unless there are several terminals in the area. "Bowling Green" would suffice here, since there are no other airports with which it might be confused. Whenever the aerodrome moniker is different from the city name, it's wise to include both in Block #9, so that Approach Control vectors you to the right airport—they'll assume you want to go to Big City Municipal unless you indicate some other airport as your destination.

Block #10 is a catch-all, and rarely used; however, there are times when it can save you (and ATC) time and trouble. In the previous example (Nashville to Bowling Green) you elected to detour to the east because of weather. But this is not the obvious airways route between the two cities, so Center would probably clear you on Victor 5 *unless* you indicated in the Remarks block "Requested routing due to weather." Or in parts of the west where higher altitudes are required, you may wish to impose a personal limit of 10,000 feet for physiological reasons; shortstop any haggling about the route you have chosen by inserting "unable higher than 10,000" in Block #10. This is also the proper place to insert "NO SIDs/STARs" if you haven't the appropriate publications on board. Flying into Canada and some other foreign countries, you can insert the code word "ADCUS" (ADvise CUStoms) so they will be there when you arrive. Anything that bears directly on the operation of your flight can be stated in the Remarks block, but don't try to have ATC let your girl friend know when you'll be on the ground—that's pushing a bit!

The reason for estimating your time enroute (Block #11) is not to see how accurately you can preplan an aerial adventure; it's something to hang your hat on when the radios fail and you're wondering when to come down from your lofty, silent perch to begin an approach. In the absence of a more relevant time, your ETE as indicated in the flight plan plus your takeoff time is the answer. (See Chapter 10, "Communications Failure.") When filing the flight plan, it is sufficient to use hours and minutes to the nearest five—just the bare numbers, no further explanation needed.

Block #12 (fuel on board) is a "nice to know" sort of thing for Flight Service, but it has no legal significance, since *you* as a pilot in command are responsible for having the proper amount of petrol in the tanks at the start of every IFR flight. (This rule is also discussed in Chapter 5, "Preflight Planning," and is a regulation which should never, never be broken, or even bent.) Having your endurance figure on record can help Flight Service in a search and rescue situation, since it will at least give them a rough idea of how far you might have flown. This block should also be addressed with hours and minutes to the nearest five, such as "four plus four five," or "three plus two zero." Max Conrad's flight plans for his long-distance record attempts in a single-engine, four-place lightplane with more than fifty hours fuel on board must have raised an FSS eyebrow or two!

The selection of an alternate airport (if indeed, one is required at all) is a rather complicated process, and is treated in depth in Chapter 5, "Preflight Planning"; the concern here is the proper way to express it to Flight Service, and Block #13 needs nothing more than the name of the airport. If it is something other than a self-explanatory name, include the city or town nearby.

Block #14 can have legal implications if there is more than one qualified pilot on board. The name that you use to fill this space will no doubt be the one tagged "pilot in command" should any court action arise as a result of this flight. If you're filing for someone else and he's willing to let you use his name, that's his business; but he should understand that the responsibility for the flight will probably be his—it's now part of the record. Initials and last name are sufficient.

You have a real opportunity to save time in the next block; right now, if you haven't done it already, pick up the phone and call the Flight Service Station serving the area in which you operate most of the time. Tell them you would like to put your name, address, phone number, and home base on file. Then, even if you are filing a flight plan from as far away as Coldernell, Alaska, all you need to say when you get to Block #15 is "on file at Hometown Flight Service." No matter where you roam in the IFR system, this will be enough to identify you, should the occasion arise.

"Number of persons aboard" (Block #16) is requested only for the customs people on international flights, and you are not really required to furnish this information for domestic trips. (Besides, there may be times when it's nobody's business how many people are on the airplane!) Tell FSS how many souls on board—just speak the number. "Souls on Board" is often abbreviated SOB, and there will be times when you list five SOB's on your airplane and *mean* it!

"Fuschia, magenta, and cerise with burgundy trim" is a rather wild color scheme for an airplane, and the FSS man would probably figure he had a real nut on the line if you indicated that for Block #17. What they want here are the predominant aircraft colors, useful information should you alight at some location other than the one you had planned—like a mountainside, or in the desert without benefit of an airport. When you stop to think about it, "fuschia, magenta, and cerise with burgundy trim" is not so strange for an airplane with a name like "Barnburner."

Flight watch stations are no longer used, so you can forget about Block #18, and you've named and numbered your way through an IFR flight plan. In total, using the eastern detour for weather, the trip from Nashville to Bowling Green should be filed like this:

FSS: Good morning, Nashville Flight Service, Hawkshaw speaking.

YOU: Good morning, this is Barnburner 1234 Alpha with an IFR flight plan.

FSS: [After a slight pause to write in Blocks #1 and #2] Go ahead with your flight plan.

YOU: [Take it from Block #3] Barnburner four zero eight slash alpha, one seven zero, Nashville Metro, one four one zero, seven thousand; Victor 5E Sugargrove intersection, Victor two four three BWG, Bowling Green; routing requested due to weather; zero plus two zero, three plus three zero; Standiford Field, Louisville [or "not required" if that is the case]; J. Doe, on file at Nashville Flight Service; five; fuschia, magenta, and cerise with burgundy trim.

FSS: [After recovering from hysteria over that color scheme] Roger, we'll put it on file; have a good trip.

If you have done your homework, thought out your statements, and filed the flight plan "by the numbers," the whole procedure will take about one minute; a definite time-saver for both parties, and you have invested yourself with an aura of professionalism.

SAME THING, BUT THIS TIME BY RADIO

Filing a flight plan from the air usually results from one of two situations: You have encountered unexpected weather on a route that appeared VFR from the forecasts, or you want to have an IFR flight plan ready for the next leg of your trip. Of course, you can file a whole series of flight plans with the original FSS, and they will pass your requests to the proper people along the route. But this is not always feasible, and opens another door to the possibility of your flight plan being lost in the communications shuffle.

An Air Route Traffic Control Center is not in the business of copying flight plan requests, so unless you're really in a bind, don't bother them—take your problem to Flight Service. Once again, having gotten your mind in gear, contact the nearest FSS (it's best to use 122.1 and listen on the VOR) and when he's ready, go through the names and numbers routine just as you did on the telephone. You should include the type of flight plan and your aircraft identification in the initial callup, such as "Broken Bow radio, Barnburner 1234 Alpha with an IFR flight plan, over." When he comes on the line (and it may be a minute or two if he's busy), he'll probably have his pencil poised, ready to copy—start right off with Block #3 when he says "go ahead with your flight plan." From here on, there's no difference in the filing procedure. FSS will tell you either to stand by for your clearance (if you need it shortly, he'll call Center on his direct line and probably get it in a few minutes), or he will tell you when, where, and whom to contact.

So much for getting a flight plan request into the system for a subsequent part of your trip—the other situation grows out of your need to obtain a clearance NOW! Not an emergency, but there you are, in absolutely beautiful VFR without a flight plan of any kind, and discover that your destination airport has just gone IFR. You can go from the ridiculous to the sublime, starting with a Unicom call to Irma at the FBO (Friendly Base Operator), and giving her the information to call to Flight Service. You'll be obliged to wait, remaining VFR of course, until she calls FSS, they call Center, who eventually returns the clearance to FSS, who calls Irma, who calls you back. Or you could contact FSS yourself, wait until they call the request to Center, wait until the Controller decides he can accept your flight, and wait until the Flight Service Station calls you back with the clearance. By the time all this has taken place, you might as well have landed, placed the call to FSS from the phone booth, and had a cup of coffee with Irma! The same lag in communications, though not so extreme, exists when you contact Flight Service by radio, and again "waiting" is the key word—why not contact Center directly, since you are only asking for clearance into the terminal area to make an approach? (Or if you can get into the terminal area VFR, call Approach Control.)

The first job is to find the proper frequency on which to call Center; your enroute chart provides this information. Each ARTCC area of responsibility is subdivided geographically, and the chart shows the coverage of these sectors. In the general area of the symbol, the Walnut Ridge sector of Memphis Center has control. You *always* use the Center name, never that of the sector. Flying in the vicinity of the Walnut Ridge VOR, the proper frequency for Memphis Center is 127.4. Make your first

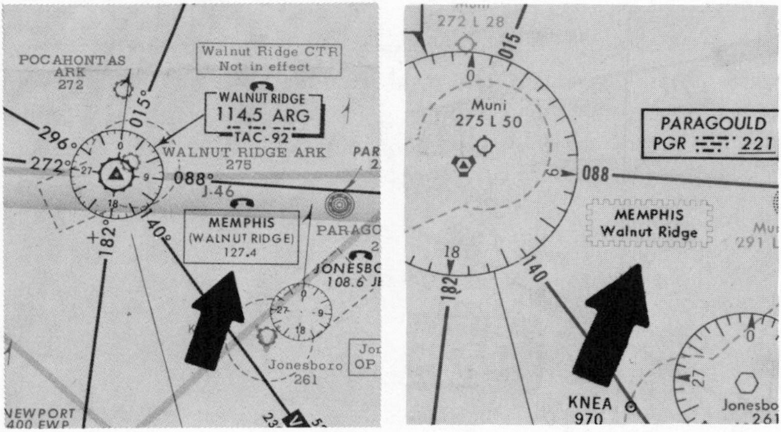

Symbols used to identify Air Route Traffic Control Center sectors (Jeppesen left, U.S. right).

call a short one, in case Center is busy—"Memphis Center, Barnburner 1234 Alpha." When they answer, the following dialogue might take place:

YOU: Memphis Center, Barnburner 1234 Alpha, ten miles east of Walnut Ridge, eight thousand five hundred, VFR, requesting clearance to Walnut Ridge Municipal. [If the Controller is too busy to handle your request, he'll tell you so, and ask you to contact the nearest FSS for clearance; but more than likely, he will come back with—]

CENTER: Roger, 34 Alpha, squawk ident; are you IFR rated and equipped?

YOU: [Pressing the ident button] That is affirmative.

CENTER: Barnburner 1234 Alpha, you're in radar contact, cleared from your present position direct to the Walnut Ridge VOR, descend to and maintain six thousand, say your aircraft type and true airspeed.

YOU: Barnburner 34 Alpha is cleared from present position direct to the Walnut Ridge VOR at six thousand; it's a Barnburner four zero eight, true airspeed one seven zero.

CENTER: 34 Alpha, Roger; expect a VOR Runway 27 approach at Walnut Ridge. By the way, is that the airplane with the weird paint job?

That's all there is to it; you're in the system, and can now proceed just as if you had been IFR all the way. A very efficient short-cut to the full-blown filing process, this method is much faster than going through Flight Service, although it is somewhat less preferable to filing IFR from the beginning. Don't expect this kind of service in one of the high-density terminal areas like Chicago or New York; they just don't have the time—in less busy parts of the country, your request will almost always be granted.

And if you're not in a hurry, stop in and see Irma anyway.

IFR FLIGHT PLAN TO A NON-IFR AIRPORT

There are literally thousands of small airports around the country which are used every day by general aviation pilots without the benefit of an instrument approach. Some of them lie in uncontrolled airspace, and are not subject to the IFR rules. But there are many in controlled airspace to which operations are conducted quite legally when the weather prevents VFR flight all the way. If there is an airport close by with a published procedure, you may be able to make the approach there, break it off when under the clouds, and proceed to your "little airport" destination. This is a good plan, but only under certain conditions: You must be absolutely sure that the weather will permit a safe VFR operation from the end of the published approach to the non-IFR airport; the approach used to get you down to VFR conditions should not lead to a "No Special VFR" airport if the weather is pushing visual minimums; you should be prepared to land at the IFR airport if things go down the drain.

Every bit as important as the other considerations is your responsibility to communicate to ATC your intentions as early in the flight as possible, preferably in the remarks block of your flight plan request ("will proceed VFR to Little Airport"). You'll earn the undying enmity of the Controllers if you wait until you're on final approach and fitted neatly into the landing sequence to let them know that you are going to "break it off" and go to some other airport. There is usually no problem if you will just make your desires known early in the game. It's a completely legal procedure and can work to your advantage under the proper conditions; it appears underhanded and less than professional when a pilot tries to "sneak" an approach for the purpose of proceeding to a non-IFR field. Unless you will present a traffic hazard for them, ATC will go along with you, sometimes even supplying vectors to the other airport.

IFR FLIGHT PLANS FROM A "NO-FACILITY" AIRPORT

Well, here you are, back at the airport after a day's work with your clients in West Showshoe, Montana. When you arrived this morning, the sun was shining from a clear blue sky, the weatherman promised a continuation of the same, and it looked like a perfect day. Now, preflighting the Barnburner in cold rain falling from a 500-foot overcast, you're not so sure. Besides that, the airport offices are closed and you have one thin dime in your pocket—thank the gods that look out for pilots there's a telephone booth outside the hangar.

All is not lost, because there is still a way to obtain a clearance under these conditions; the only requirement is that you are able to contact someone in ATC—a Flight Service Station, a nearby Tower, or perhaps Center. If you can take off and maintain VFR while you file your flight plan and receive clearance, that's the way to do it, but it will cost you some air time (that's another way of saying money) as you fly around waiting for permission to enter the system.

A more efficient way to get the job done is to call the nearest FSS on the phone (don't dial the wrong number with that last dime!), explain the situation, and file a flight plan, with the additional request for a "void time" clearance. (Choose the route and altitude to the first fix with great care, because you will be entirely on your own until ATC acquires you on radar. File so as to get on an airway as soon as you can, to take advantage of the guaranteed terrain and obstacle clearance. It may be necessary to refer to a sectional chart to make sure you know the elevations along your route to the first fix.) Under these conditions, Flight Service will likely ask you to stand by, and will call your flight plan request directly to the governing Center while you wait; bear in mind that this procedure is almost always undertaken from an out-of-the-way airport, and there will probably be little if any traffic in the immediate area. When a delay is probable, Flight Service will have you call back in a few minutes, or will take your phone number and call *you* back; the latter is especially important when you have no more dimes.

If Center can handle your flight at this time, your clearance will be issued with the stipulation that you take off no later than a specified time. Your clearance will end with "void if not airborne by such-and-such a time," and you can bet that the deadline imposed by the void time will not be very far from right now! If it is too close for comfort, tell the FSS specialist and it will be revised. In anticipation of this, figure how long it will take you to board your passengers, get the bird warmed up and taxied to the runway before you call for a void time clearance. Better yet, load the people in the plane, check the engines, and *then* go to the phone booth—when you get the clearance, make like an Olympic 100-yard dasher back to the airplane.

It is important to get ready for a five-or-ten-minutes-from-now void time, because Center doesn't want to hold airspace open any longer than necessary. If ATC hasn't heard from you shortly after the void time, they assume that you have taken off and suffered communications failure, and must therefore open up routes and altitudes for your entire proposed trip, just in case. This is one of those situations when a good pilot can exercise his judgment, and refuse a void time that is too close—remember that you will be taking off into IFR conditions (otherwise you wouldn't be bothered with the void time at all) and this is no time to be pushed by a pair of hands racing around a clock face. When you file your flight plan with FSS, let him know that because of the distance to the runway, or warmup problems, or whatever, you cannot possibly be off the ground in less than fifteen minutes (or a reasonable length of time according to the situation). He'll pass this on to Center, and they'll more than likely respect your problem. From the time you enter the clouds, this type of clearance is not a whit different than any other, and all the rules of IFR operations apply.

You can help yourself by anticipating the need for a "void time" clearance. Suppose that during the afternoon in beautiful downtown West Snowshoe you noticed the clouds beginning to thicken. If you suspect IFR conditions for your takeoff in the evening, call Flight Service and file your flight plan in advance, with the expectation of needing a void time. The FSS specialist may even be one step ahead of you (there's not much else to do in the Flight Service Station at West Snowshoe) and have a clearance waiting when you call.

Having received a void-time clearance, you must respect its limitations as if it meant life or death, which it might. Be sure your watch agrees with ATC time, and do all within your power to leave terra firma not one second past the appropriate mark. It's legal and proper to jump into the sky anytime between the time you receive your clearance and the void time, but very illegal and quite improper to do so later. If you can't quite cut it (and fuel-injected engines invariably choose a situation like this to not start), shut everything down, swear a lot, run through the rain to the phone booth, call Flight Service, and start all over again. It might be wise to toss a couple of dimes into the glove box of your airplane next time you fly; you never can tell when your passengers might be as broke as you are!

RESTRICTED, WARNING, PROHIBITED AREAS, ADIZS

When it comes to flying through restricted airspace, happiness is having the word "instrument" on your pilot certificate. As long as you plan your flight on the established Victor airways, you can rest assured that ATC will not let you traverse any airspace which is also being used by artillery shells, rockets, or the annual meeting of the United States High Altitude Kite Flying Association. When you ask for a direct, off-airways routing that will cross through restricted airspace, your request will not be honored unless and until the ATC facility with which you are working has coordinated with the using agency and made certain that it will be safe for you to pass. When operating VFR on Top in or near one of the Intensive Student Jet Training Areas, be aware of the high speed and small profile that make these training aircraft extremely difficult to see. The same caution applies to Alert Areas.

A PROHIBITED AREA is the most restrictive of all the limited-use airspace, and its label means exactly what it says. IFR routes pass through several Prohibited Areas, but a clearance is a clearance, and if ATC gives you the go-ahead, go ahead. (When you're on a VFR flight, trespass of a Prohibited Area might get you an audience with somebody in the FAA, maybe even the CIA.)

IFR AND ADIZS (AIR DEFENSE IDENTIFICATION ZONES)

National security is the only purpose for establishing ADIZs, and they are primarily concerned with aircraft approaching our shores and borders from the outside in. There is a part of the Federal Aviation Regulations set aside to describe this airspace and to lay down the laws for operating therein. Again, happiness is having an instrument rating, because your ATC clearance into or through an ADIZ takes care of all the reporting and filing requirements. There is a flight plan option (DVFR, Defense Visual Flight Rules) for pilots who wish to fly through an ADIZ without filing IFR, but once you have the rating, why not use it, whether there's a cloud in the sky or not? Of course, if you happen to be an aerial photography buff and would like to get some closeup shots of our Air Force's finest interceptors, fly out to sea a hundred miles or so, then turn around and head for shore, fast. You'll get your pictures, they'll get theirs, and in addition you will be given the opportunity to sit down for a friendly chat with representatives of several government agencies!

The ADIZ rules do not apply to any aircraft operating at less than 180 knots TAS north of 25° N. Latitude, nor west of 85° W. Longitude. But the same philosophy that kept you out of trouble in other types of restricted areas will work just as well here—when in doubt file IFR, get a clearance, and you're home free. ATC knows where you are, who you are, where you're going to and coming from, and when this information is passed along to the Air Defense Command people, everybody's happy.

5. *Preflight Planning*

IT WAS SPELLED OUT in letters a foot high, above the door to the flight line at a military pilot training base: "PLAN YOUR FLIGHT, AND FLY YOUR PLAN!"—a good piece of advice for any pilot. When you're flying IFR, there will be diversions and changes and non-standard procedures, and on occasion ATC may require you to go rather far outside the routing or altitude or timing you had planned for the flight; but having a plan puts you in the driver's seat right from the start. When changes come up, you have at your fingertips the information you need to make a decision; go or no-go, accept a clearance or reject it, try an approach or go directly to your alternate. You're asking for trouble when you leap into the clouds knowing nothing of the enroute weather or wind, or where you can go if everything turns sour.

A PREFLIGHT CHECKLIST

No one is going to double-check your preflight planning, so it's up to you to do it right every time. The easiest and surest way to accomplish this is to do it the same way every time—use some kind of checklist, or at least a routine information-gathering and decision-making process which leaves nothing out of the planning picture. Looking at the situation through real-world glasses, there will be many short IFR trips which don't require in-depth preparation of the sort you should go through for an extended aerial journey, especially into strange territory. However, when you form good habits, you will tend to include the critical items even though you're planning a short, uncomplicated flight.

CHARTS AND EQUIPMENT

Like an A&E starting a 100-hour inspection without his toolbox, you will be behind the power curve right away if you try to launch the planning process without the proper equipment. It's true that weather will be the most significant factor in planning, but how can you consider alternate routes around the weather or over more hospitable terrain unless you have the charts handy? The scope of your operations and the type of flying you intend to do determines how many charts you carry around—for basic IFR work, all you need are the appropriate enroute, area, and approach and landing charts. SIDs and STARs are nice to have, especially if you frequently fly into and out of airports where they are used, since they will save you and the Controllers a great deal of time.

The equipment that you have assembled to carry with you into the air is a matter as personal as the clothes you wear—some pilots carry more gear in a Cessna 172 on a thirty-minute flight than a 747 captain needs between New York and Paris! Whatever you settle on as minimum equipment, spend a few dollars for a flight bag of some kind to keep things organized; something that will hold what you need in flight, yet will not interfere with seating or control movement in your airplane. There are a number of specially designed cases on the market which will hold a couple of approach plate binders, your enroute charts, two ham sandwiches, and a paperback novel. There are also cases available which rival steamer trunks for capacity; you have everything you'll ever need, plus a lot of stuff you'll *never* need, and the weight may put you over max gross—leave these to the big-airplane pilots, who really need all that paperwork.

In addition to the charts, you should have a time and distance computer. As your experience grows, you will be able to estimate time enroute very closely by applying an average wind component to the true airspeed of your bird, but for the sake of accuracy, use a computer—especially when the proposed flight is long enough or the headwinds strong enough to generate concern about having sufficient fuel to get where you intend to go. The holding pattern plotter is a mighty handy device to have with you, and of course you will need a pencil or two. By all means, include a good strong flashlight and a couple of spare batteries—you never know when you might be caught out after dark, and a pack of matches or a cigarette lighter just won't do the job if the electricity quits.

CHECKING THE WEATHER

Without a doubt, the biggest single factor affecting your planning for an IFR flight is the weather, but you can drive yourself right up the wall worrying about it too far in advance of your trip. The very best the weatherman can do is to give you a general idea of weather conditions forty-eight hours ahead; at twenty-four hours the forecasts become more accurate, but in most cases, you can't really obtain a good picture until just before takeoff. (Of course, this is weather information for *planning* purposes—you should always be checking a tight weather situation right up until you walk out to the airplane, and continue checking it enroute.) Always be thinking of some alternate course of action in case the weather gets worse than you can put up with; if you *must* get somewhere at a certain time, and the forecasts are filled with doom and gloom, reserve an airline seat, plan to drive, or make arrangements to go another day.

When it looks as if the weather is going to put you between a rock and a hard place, get out the instrument charts to determine whether you can make it under the freezing level with respect to the minimum IFR altitudes, or whether there is a convenient detour available. Do you have the range to make it non-stop? Does the destination airport have an approach good enough for the weather they are expecting? Don't take for granted that all ILS approaches will bring you down to 200 feet and a half mile; there are a number of them that have much higher minimums because of terrain, and the same philosophy applies to all types of instrument approaches—check and be sure. (Chapters 3, 4, and 5 of *Weather Flying* will help you *interpret* the weather information you obtain before an IFR flight.)

Once you have decided you can get from here to there in one piece, there is another source you should consult to prevent an awkward, perhaps expensive situation. It is considered the last word in operational information (short of being there, of course) and bears the name NOTAM—governmentese for NOtices To AirMen. Whenever a radio aid goes out of service, or airport lighting systems fail, or parachute jumping is in progress (how'd you like to have a four-man star suddenly join you in the cockpit of a Cherokee?), or any one of a thousand things that could affect the operation of airplanes, it will be published as a NOTAM on the teletype circuits. It would be embarrassing indeed should you take off for Buffalo in the middle of winter with an airplane full of paying passengers, and find out halfway there that the only vehicles permitted on the runways today are snowplows! You can sidestep this sort of problem by asking the FSS briefer to check the NOTAMs for you while still in the planning stage.

ROUTE AND ALTITUDE

At this point, you should have enough weather information to make a choice of route and altitude. Unless a detour is indicated because of meteorological mischief (weather OR winds), you should be looking for the route that will get you where you're going in the shortest possible time—this usually means the nearest thing to a straight line between departure and destination. For long trips, you should consult an IFR planning chart, which shows the airways from coast to coast and border to border. (The Jeppesen service includes such a chart, or you can purchase one from the government.) You'll generally find an airway nearly parallel to the direct route. Unless you look at the big picture, you may miss the airway that goes all the way from point A to point B; filing one airway is so much easier than a bunch of short segments, and it eases the pain for ATC, too.

Listed in the Avigation section of the Jepp charts and in the AIM are the Preferred Routes, with major terminals and the airways that ATC would like you to use when traveling betwixt and between. Preferred Routes are the fastest, most efficient way to go—not always the *shortest*, but they are ultimately the *fastest* because that's the way ATC is going to clear you, so you are better off filing the Preferred Route at the outset. (See Chapter 4, "IFR Flight Plans," for the proper way to file a devious route because of weather or limiting altitudes.)

ATC's Preferred Routes can also be used to advantage when you plan a trip to a point short of the destination terminal mentioned in the route listing—use the Preferred Route as far as you can, and you'll get better service from ATC.

Standard Instrument Departures (SIDs) are really short-range Preferred Routes, limited to the departure phase of an IFR trip, and if you frequently fly from an airport with published SIDs, you'll find it worthwhile to have these charts in your flight kit. When SIDs are in use, plan your flight accordingly, by noticing the point at which the SID injects you into the enroute structure. Your enroute planning should begin at the VOR (or other fix) specified as the end of the SID, and use the Preferred Route, if applicable, from that point to destination.

The ultimate in preflight planning, at least from a routing standpoint, would see you departing under the guidance of a

SID, proceeding on your way via a Preferred Route, and winding up the flight with a Standard Terminal Arrival Route (STAR). The key is to realize that the air route structure is a huge system, and where the designers have identified channels (Preferred Routes, SIDs, and STARs) in the system, you are much better off to put yourself there as soon as possible after takeoff, and as early as possible in the terminal area. (If you don't possess SIDs or STARs, don't forget to make mention of that fact in the "Remarks" block of your flight plan. It's the best way to let ATC know of your limitations.)

When a SID isn't published, plan your departure by the most direct route that will get you to a VOR or an airway as soon as possible after takeoff. The outstanding advantage of choosing an airway, direct route, or radial to start your flight is that of definition—you know exactly which way to go in the absence of ATC instructions, or if your radios give up the ghost before you can receive further clearance.

Radar control on departure is the name of the game in IFR flying today—at most terminals, you will be picked up on the magic TV screen almost immediately after takeoff, and the Controller will vector you around other traffic and onto your airway route just as expeditiously as he can. If you're not at all sure of the best way to get from the airport into the enroute structure, there's one more way you can get help: Request radar vectors to the first VOR on your route, and Departure Control will lead you by the hand.

There are parts of the country which just don't have any airways headed in the direction you want to go, or which don't connect the particular point A and point B you had in mind. So why not devise your own route, direct from one VOR to the next on your intended line of flight? There are no rules against flying direct (off airways), but there are several very important limitations you must consider before undertaking such a course of action.

Right off the top, you may not file a direct IFR flight between omnis which are more than 80 nautical miles apart (this is a low-altitude limit; it's expanded to 260 miles for flights at 18,000 feet and above). Designed for frequency protection, the 80-mile minimum guarantees that your VOR receiver will not pick up a signal from another station on the same frequency.

Second, you must choose a flight altitude which will provide the same terrain clearance that is automatically taken care of by airway MEAs and MOCAs—you may have to consult sectional or WAC charts or other topographic references to be sure that your off-airways route is high enough.

Third, whenever planning a direct flight, use only those radio aids designated for use in the appropriate route structure (i.e., only (L) VORs below 18,000 feet and only (H) VORs above that level), and your course must be DIRECT—in a straight line between VORs—no doglegs on this trip!

When weather is a factor (turbulence, icing, wind effects), bear in mind that these situations will almost always be at their worst when the terrain provides additional mechanical lifting action. (See *Weather Flying*, Chapter 9, for a discussion of mountain weather flying.)

On the other end of the flight, your route should terminate at the navaid serving the airport (usually the closest VOR). At this stage in the planning process, you have no idea what approach will be in use when you get there (unless there is only one), so the nearest omni is usually quite adequate. Planning for the actual approach procedure cannot be accomplished until you're in the terminal area, so don't worry about it now. (See Chapter 12, "Getting Ready for an Instrument Approach," to find out when to start worrying about it.) Since you don't know what will take place approachwise at the end of the flight, just file direct from the final enroute VOR to the airport; Approach Control will give you further clearance when the time arrives. This preflight uncertainty about the tag end of a flight is one of the reasons the law requires you to carry a forty-five-minute fuel reserve on an IFR flight.

At an increasing number of airports, stars are coming into use—not heavenly bodies to be wished upon or used for celestial navigation, these are STARs, the acronymic way of saying *S*tandard *T*erminal *A*rrival *R*outes. They are just SIDs in reverse, and provide specific routings *into* the terminal area. When you are flight planning to an airport with a published STAR (the biggies may have several), end the airways portion of your route at the VOR that is the entry, or gate, to the STAR procedure. Using the STAR when you file your flight plan will save everybody time and trouble, because you won't have to be given a change of routing along the way.

In summary, you should consider the following order of routing priorities when planning a flight (disregarding deviations for weather):

1. The Preferred Route between departure and destination.
2. Victor airways which work out closest to a straight line between here and there.
3. A direct, off-airways route at an altitude high enough to provide *comfortable* clearance from terrain and obstructions. (1,000 feet above everything 5 miles either side of your course in the flatlands, 2,000 feet in those parts of the country which qualify as mountainous.)

ALTITUDE

Many pilots pay surprisingly little attention to the selection of an IFR altitude, even though it plays a huge part in putting the most miles behind you for the fewest dollars, or making the difference between a miserable experience and an aesthetic adventure. Of course there are some practical limits, like the minimum enroute altitude (MEA) and the optimum performance altitude for your plane; turbulence, icing, wind and weather problems cannot be ignored, but they'll be thoroughly hashed out later.

MEAs and optimum performance altitude provide the floor and ceiling for a non-supercharged airplane—you can't plan an

IFR flight at less than MEA, and unless there's a real whopper of a tailwind, you will probably lose money by climbing above your optimum altitude. (This is usually the highest altitude at which your engine can maintain 65 percent power.) Check the route for the highest MEA—that is eventually going to become your cruise altitude. Although you can file (and be cleared at) a lower altitude before you get to that particular airway segment, ATC will move you up to the MEA at the appropriate time, so plan on it. The abnormally high MEAs will occur over the mountains, because they *must* provide 2,000 feet of terrain clearance in those areas.

For normally aspirated (unsupercharged) engines, it sometimes comes down to a choice between less performance at high altitude and a much longer route to avoid the higher levels. There's almost always a westerly wind at altitude, so clawing your way up to 12,000 or 13,000 feet in an airplane with an optimum altitude of 7,000 is not necessarily a bad move if you're eastbound—the extra groundspeed on a long trip may easily make up for the time spent in the climb. There's only one way to decide, and that's to dig out the computer and compare the estimated time enroute for the high altitude versus a lower one.

In general, when weather conditions are not a factor, it is probably better to file just as high as practical, at or above the appropriate MEA, and at or above the optimum altitude for your powerplant. The benefits which accrue to high flight often overcome the extra five or ten minutes spent climbing; maybe it will put you above an icing level, or keep you out of turbulence, or treat you to groundspeeds you can brag about at the bar. And if nothing else, why not climb up above the choking brown gunk that is the rule rather than the exception over our country these days? Why not climb up into the only place left where you can see forever and, at least for a little while, treat your lungs to some really clean air? There's something to be said for the safety aspects of flying high, too. The very fact that fewer pilots use the higher levels means that there will be less people to run into at altitude; and given the usual situation of being in the clear (at least between layers) when you're operating in the upper reaches of the sky, you'll have much more time to observe and react to other air traffic.

At any rate, give "high-flight" a try on your next few trips, and decide for yourself—keep records of how much time is required to climb to higher altitudes, how much fuel is burned, and the difference in elapsed times for similar wind and weather conditions. Then, compare the hard facts with your memories of the smooth, crystal-clear air up there; remember the pleasant glow you experienced when that first-time-in-an-airplane passenger became a believer after flying high with you.

DISTANCE AND TIME ENROUTE

Now that you're settled on the route and altitude, add up the distance from departure point to the radio aid serving the destination airport (you don't know how Approach Control will handle you at the other end). If you are not in the habit of computing time enroute, or whenever your aerial steed is an unfamiliar one, take the time to figure it out rather precisely. You'll be loading the situation in your favor, but perhaps more importantly, you will be practicing so that as time goes on, you will be able to estimate the time very accurately with a minimum of paperwork. The basis of the computation is true airspeed, plus or minus a wind component, arriving at an average groundspeed. All three of these speeds will change during the climb, so you will have to add a time factor.

For most light, non-supercharged airplanes, a climb of less than 10,000 feet in still air will add just about five minutes to the time it would take if you were at cruise airspeed all the way. You can figure it out for your bird, but better yet, make a note of the time penalty for climbing to altitude on your next several trips, and you'll soon have a rule of thumb that will stand you in good stead.

Remember that you are asked to estimate your time enroute

for only two reasons: so that you'll have enough fuel on board, and to give you and ATC a descent time should the radios fail—nobody really cares how close your estimate is on a routine trip. One thing you *don't* want to do is be ultraconservative and estimate too much time for the journey; if the radios *do* fail, you're going to hold over the destination fix until that time elapses, and if you throw in a half hour "just to be sure," you may regret it on the other end. It's no fun going round and round in a holding pattern for thirty minutes in the clouds without radios, waiting for that ETA to come up—your nerves will be tied in double knots! Be as accurate as you can, but don't spend hours working out the ETE—it's just not worth that much of your time.

FUEL REQUIRED

Disregard for fuel requirements is an open invitation for BIG trouble. There's no other situation in aviation that leaves you so frustrated, so helpless, so upset with yourself as when you realize that you haven't enough gas in the tanks to get where you're going. It's bad enough VFR, but the pressure really builds when you're on solid instruments, and it will rapidly bring you to the PMP (Point of Maximum Pucker). The most sensible way to keep from painting yourself into a gasoline corner is to observe the forty-five-minute reserve fuel requirement on ALL flights, and when it appears that headwinds, holding, icing, carburetor heat, traffic delays, or route deviations are eating slowly but surely into your spare gasoline, DO SOMETHING, and do it NOW!

Whenever you are operating in IFR conditions, you must have on board enough fuel to travel from departure to the final approach fix at destination, and have forty-five minutes of fuel remaining, based on the normal cruise fuel consumption of your airplane. Regardless of the fact that you will reduce power whenever you are in a holding pattern, the forty-five-minute requirement at *cruise power* still exists, giving you a little additional cushion in a really tight situation. Compute the fuel you will use during taxi, takeoff, climb, and cruise at whatever power setting you intend to maintain. Subtract that total from the capacity of the airplane tanks, and if the resulting number doesn't correspond to forty-five minutes at the cruise power setting, you will be both illegal and foolish to start out on that flight. The alternatives?—plan a fuel stop, or wait for a day when the winds are a little less aggressive.

Provide yourself a solid planning figure with a little experimentation on your next short trip: Start up, taxi, take off, and climb to the highest altitude you normally use; do all this on one fuel tank (or set of tanks). When you level off, switch to a full tank and complete the flight. After landing, note the number of gallons required to top off the first tank—this figure plus the normal cruise fuel consumption rate will produce an accurate yardstick for future flights to make sure you have enough petrol.

ALTERNATE REQUIREMENTS

It's probably one of the most abused regulations in the IFR book, but treating the alternate rule lightly can get you into serious trouble. Even though Flight Service Station briefers are quite aware of the weather conditions at your destination, seldom if ever will they remind you of the need for an alternate when you are filing a flight plan; the responsibility rests only on the shoulders of the pilot. The regulation that covers IFR alternates is cumbersome, very wordy, and tends to drive pilots away from the consideration it deserves. There is a good rule of thumb which will *usually* do the job for you, and that is to get in the habit of filing an alternate for *every* IFR flight—pick the nearest airport with equal or better approach facilities within comfortable fuel range. Don't count on this procedure as an IFR panacea, but if everything goes down the drain, at least you'll have some place to go. The worst situation imaginable would see you arriving at destination in weather which prohibits a landing, with no alternate filed, followed by a radio communications failure—you don't know *where* to go, ATC doesn't have any idea where you *might* go, and the resulting traffic hysteria would certainly get you an audience with an FAA inspector, if you somehow manage to wander around through the clouds and get down safely without hitting anybody! You owe as much to the other airmen up there in the soup as you owe yourself—so always have an alternate airport planned before you climb aboard your flying machine.

Like most of the rules which govern your aviation adventures, the IFR alternate regulation is restrictive in nature, letting you know what you may *not* do; but it can be reduced to convenient operational terms by asking yourself two questions before every instrument flight. First, must I file an alternate airport, and second, what airport may I use for an alternate when one is required?

The answer to the first question depends on both the approach facilities available at destination and the forecast weather conditions for that terminal. If, as is usually the case, your planned destination has a published instrument approach (one the government has approved, not your personal procedure based on radio station WIFR!), you can go on to the weather situation, which will tell you whether or not you need an alternate. But if Destination Municipal Airport has no approved procedure, stop right there—an alternate airport is automatically required; no further questions to be asked!

In a conservative effort to keep you out of trouble, the government has decreed that either one of two weather conditions at destination demand an alternate be filed in your flight plan—one concerns the forecast ceiling, the other refers to visibility, and they both respect a four-hour time frame, from two hours *before* you expect to get there until two hours *afterwards*. Ceiling and visibility would not normally change that much for the worse during a four-hour period, and if this kind of rapid change were to take place, it would probably be adequately forecast.

Here are the weather limitations about which you should be concerned: The forecast CEILING (the lowest *broken* or *overcast* cloud layer) must be at least 1,000 feet above the lowest MEA, MOCA, or Initial Approach Altitude, and the VISIBILITY must be crystal-balled at 3 miles, OR 2 miles more than the lowest landing visibility minimum, whichever is higher. You've a bit of calculating to do here—determine which altitude applies (the MEA and MOCA will be found on the IFR enroute chart, but you'll have to refer to the approach and landing chart for the Initial Approach Altitude), add 1,000 feet, and there's your minimum ceiling forecast. The hooker lies in the fact that the altitudes you have picked off the charts are referenced to Mean Sea Level, but cloud height forecasts are based on the number of feet the clouds will be above ground level. So, you must find the difference between your manufactured minimum cloud height (MEA, MOCA, or Initial Approach Altitude plus 1,000 feet) and the elevation of the airport to arrive at the alternate-no alternate decision.

The visibility requirement (at least 3 miles, or 2 miles more than the lowest landing minimum) is a little easier to live with—a quick look at the approach plate for the destination airport will supply the lowest visibility minimum, and if it's more than 1 mile, start checking the forecasts with a sharper eye. The required visibility must also be forecast for the entire four-hour period. Particularly susceptible to the more-than-3-miles requirement will be those airports located in and around mountainous parts of the country, or those which lie a long way from the approach aid.

Now that you have all the regulatory impedimenta under your hairpiece, there's a short-cut which will keep you legal, and save at least some of the figuring. It involves an understanding of the chart altitudes used in calculating the lowest forecast ceiling—if all airports were blessed with a VOR right in the middle of the infield, MEAs and MOCAs would be universally satisfactory as starting points. But MEAs and MOCAs have to be established high enough to account for certain *enroute* minimums, not at all what you're concerned with here. Since the law allows you the *lowest* of three types of altitudes, why not forget the enroute minimums, and go directly to the Initial Approach Altitude, which is prescribed for a route leading to the approach aid for the purpose of executing an approach? Now you are cranking in meaningful information, dealing with the ceiling required *at the airport*, not miles away on a Victor airway. By using an Initial Approach Altitude as your base number for calculating the required ceiling height, you just can't go wrong—you'll always err on the high (safe) side, and it doesn't cost a penny to file an alternate.

Here, in tabular form, are the criteria you must consider when answering the first question: Must I file an alternate?

Condition	Must I File?
Destination has no approved approach procedure	Yes
Approach chart published for destination airport	No, unless weather is forecast below specified minimums
Ceiling forecast less than 1,000 feet above Initial Approach Altitude at any time during ETA $\pm$ 2 hours	Yes
Visibility forecast less than 3 miles at any time during ETA $\pm$ 2 hours	Yes
Visibility forecast less than lowest published landing minimum plus 2 miles at any time during ETA $\pm$ 2 hours	Yes

Notice that a forecast below *either one* of the conditions laid down by law (ceiling *or* visibility) requires an alternate. The complexity of the rule makes it even more sensible for you to form the habit of always filing an alternate when you're fixin' to go IFR. You'll have the comfortable feeling that comes with knowing all the bases are covered, and selecting an alternate automatically will keep you from forgetting it on those rare occasions when it's needed.

This leads to the second question: What airport may I use as an alternate? This one is not nearly so difficult to answer (it shouldn't be, with the built-in conservatism of the first question!). And it lends itself to a simple rule: If the airport you wish to use for an alternate is forecasting (at your ETA) a ceiling of more than 800 feet, and a visibility of more than 2 miles, it's OK; you can go ahead and file it in block #13 of the flight plan. Since you've already covered yourself for ETA plus or minus two hours on the destination airport, the alternate must have 800 and 2 at your ETA, period. There is some mumbo-jumbo in the regulation about whether or not the alternate airport has a precision or a non-precision approach procedure, but you will be on the safe side by always using the 800 and 2 rule.

In that rare (and not too sensible) situation when you might want to select for an alternate an airport that has no published approach procedure, you must be able to arrive over that airport at MEA (that's the lowest enroute altitude that ATC is going to allow) in VFR conditions, make your descent, approach, and landing in VFR weather.

When choosing your alternate, make sure that you can get from destination to alternate and still have forty-five minutes fuel at normal cruise power—more on this later.

On page 74 are the rules to be observed when selecting an alternate airport, including the precision versus non-precision mumbo-jumbo.

Now that you have gone through all the hoops, decided that you need an alternate, and have selected an appropriate airport, forget all about those minimums—they are just for planning purposes, and have nothing whatever to do with what must exist

CONDITION	MAY I USE THIS AIRPORT AS AN ALTERNATE?
No approach procedure published, but I can make it from MEA to the runway in VFR conditions	Yes
Non-precision procedure published, forecast at ETA at least 800 feet and 2 miles	Yes
Precision approach procedure published, forecast at ETA at least 600 feet and 2 miles	Yes

when you get there. When you arrive at the missed approach point, only the ability to see the runway environment and being in a position for a normal landing govern your decision to continue the approach or go around.

Through lack of weather observation facilities or local restrictions, some airports can't be used as alternates, or require higher minimum weather conditions. Jeppesen charts include this information on the back of the sheet, and the U.S. publications use a special symbol ▼A in the remarks block of the approach chart to refer you to a separate listing.

AIRCRAFT AND INSTRUMENT PREFLIGHT

A checklist within a checklist—that's the way to make sure that once you get into the air on an instrument flight, all the gauges and gadgets you need for aircraft control and navigation are doing their jobs, and doing them properly. An instrument checklist, if religiously followed every flight, will force you into two situations that can do you nothing but good. First, a preflight checklist will save your pride (ever tried to taxi away from the ramp with the airplane still tied to the ground?), and per-

WEATHER ANALYSIS

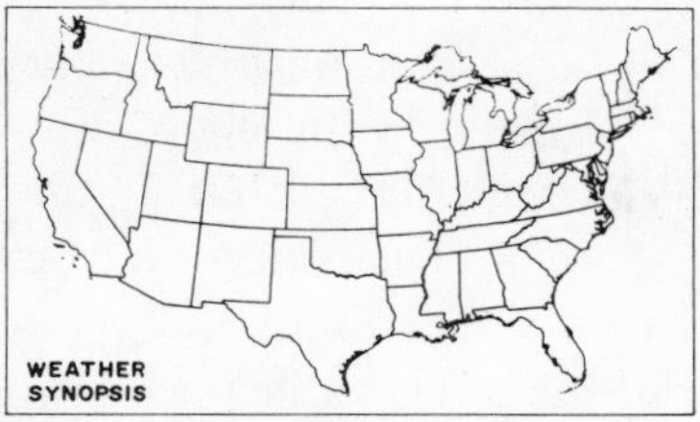

STATION	ENROUTE WEATHER TREND		

STATION	TERMINAL FORECASTS

STATION	WINDS ALOFT FORECASTS			

LOCATION	PIREPS/SIGNIFICANT WEATHER/NOTAMS

Weather organizer.

haps your neck; second, following a printed, orderly checklist will force you to slow down when preparing for an IFR trip. There's nothing wrong with hurrying, but there's a lot wrong with *being* hurried—the checklist will help you keep your head when all about you are losing theirs.

All the items on this instrument preflight are in-cockpit checks, except two which are of extreme importance. If you can't tell how high or how fast you are flying, you've got real troubles, so as you march diligently around kicking the tires and checking all the things you normally check, pay particular attention to these two—the static source and the pitot head. Most static ports are stainless steel discs set flush with the aircraft skin, drilled with several small holes to admit air pressure to the static system. If any of the holes are covered, deformed, plugged with paint, wax, or dirt, don't fly until you get it fixed. The pitot system plumbing must also be free of obstructions, including the cover you bought to keep ice and snow and house-hunting insects out of the tube. Even with a long red streamer with fluorescent letters warning the pilot to REMOVE BEFORE FLIGHT, the next pitot cover that is taken for a short airplane ride won't be the first one! For IFR flying, you should have a heated pitot tube, and the only completely reliable way to check its operation is to turn it on and feel the heat. (CAUTION: Let not thy sensing digits remain overlong in contact with the heated part, lest they come away medium rare!)

A general preflight item, which should become a habit so strong that you feel uneasy until it's done, is checking the fuel situation. Don't ever trust anybody but yourself to make absolutely sure there is as much gasoline in the tanks as you think there is, and that it's the grade you ordered. Gauges have been known to lie, and linemen occasionally get distracted and forget to fill the tanks on the other side of the airplane, so the last thing you should do before climbing up to the flight deck is CHECK THE TANKS. You may not always want them brim-full, but let your own two eyes gaze into the depths of the fuel cells and be sure you know how much is there. You'll realize a bonus from this last-one-before-getting-aboard check too, because you'll be certain that the fuel tank caps are replaced properly and securely (the same goes for oil dipsticks). When a lid works loose in flight (or maybe was never put on properly in the first place) and you suddenly realize you're venting 100-octane overboard, notice the color of the stain running back over the wing—it's green, the same as m-o-n-e-y, which is what it's costing you. There is also the problem of what-do-you-do-now? with half your fuel supply gone and no close-by alternate.

With engine(s) running and your normally-used radio equipment turned on, you should begin the operational part of the instrument checklist:

1. Suction and/or generators (alternators)
   Check for "in-the-green" or normal load conditions.

2. Alternate static source valve or switch
Check closed or normal. (If you haven't done so by now, open this valve in flight and record the difference in airspeed and altitude readings—they'll always be in error on the dangerous [high] side.)
3. Airspeed indicator
Check for normal "zero" indication. (Some never go all the way to zero.)
4. Vertical speed indicator (rate of climb)
Check for zero reading—if it's off, you'll have to apply that correction in flight. Try tapping the case lightly to get the needle on zero. If it's way off, have it adjusted to read properly.
5. Clock
Wind, and be sure that Mickey's hands are pointing to the right numbers.
6. Engine instruments
Check them all in the green or at least moving that way. (Of course you made sure you had oil pressure on engine start.)
7. Radio equipment (communications and navigation)
Turn on everything that can be checked at this point. If there's a VOR or VOT on the airport or close by, you can check the omni receivers and possibly DME. Tune and identify an ADF station and check for proper needle movement and relative bearing.
8. Publications, personal equipment
Before you leave the chocks, check once more to be sure you have all the charts and equipment you will need.
9. Altimeter
Set to field elevation, then put in the altimeter setting you get from Ground Control or ATIS—if the hands move more than 75 feet either way, you have an altimeter that is outside the legal limits of accuracy for IFR flight. If the error is less than 75 feet, don't attempt to carry the difference forward on subsequent altimeter settings—it is too easy to correct the wrong direction, and most of these small altimeter errors tend to cancel out over the duration of a flight.
10. Turn and bank indicator
As you taxi, check to see that the indicator shows turns in the proper direction, and that the ball moves freely in the opposite direction. If it moves in the *same* direction, call up the airport manager and thank him for banking the taxiways.
11. Attitude indicator (artificial horizon)

Normal taxi speeds will not affect the bank attitude of the airplane very much, but you will notice some displacement on the attitude indicator. If the bank exceeds 5° while turning on the ground, the instrument is probably unreliable for IFR flight. On those indicators which are adjustable up and down, leave the little airplane in the same place all the time—it should indicate the pitch attitude for level flight at your normal cruise airspeed.

12. Magnetic compass
While rolling straight ahead at a steady speed, check the reading against a known magnetic heading—a taxiway which parallels a runway, for example. If your deviation card shows some error, count that in your check.

13. Heading indicator (directional gyro)
Set this to agree with the corrected reading from the mag compass, and make sure the card remains stationary after you make the adjustment. DO NOT cage a DG on the runway heading with the intent of uncaging it just before takeoff—you will be forcing the gyros to work against the mechanical stops, and early replacement will probably be required. DO recheck the heading indicator when you are lined up on the runway; it's the most accurate check you can make.

14. De-icing and/or anti-icing equipment
Check for proper operation (visible check of boot inflation, loadmeter check for electrical devices, nasal check for alcohol).

15. Carburetor heat (or alternate air source for fuel-injected engines)
Your best friend in icing conditions—check to make sure it works as it should.

16. Clean-up and set-up
After checking everything, and you're satisfied that the bird will fly, take a moment or two to clean up the cockpit—put away all but the charts you'll need immediately after takeoff. Before you indicate your readiness to aviate, set up your radios for the task at hand. If the weather is really tight, you'll do well to have your primary navigation receiver tuned to the approach aid for the airport; if anything goes wrong right after you lift off, you'll have one chore already taken care of, and can transition to the approach situation smoothly. You should also have the approach and landing chart readily available for the same reason. Weather not too bad? Set your navigation gear on the proper frequencies and courses for your departure.

17. Before-takeoff check

Using a printed checklist or at least one of several mnemonic-type reminders, make sure all the little things are done, e.g., doors closed and locked, boost pumps on (if required), fuel on proper tank, etc. CIFFTR is an old standard—pronounced "sifter," it reminds you to check

Controls
Instruments
Fuel
Flaps
Trim
Runup

18. At the proper time, open the throttles, pull back on the wheel, and have a nice trip!

That's a preflight planning schedule that will keep you honest (if not busy) for any IFR situation. Change it to fit your airplane or the facilities you use, but remember that any one of these items could cause trouble if overlooked. To wrap it all up, here's the checklist in abbreviated form.

1. Charts and equipment.
2. Check weather.
3. Select route and altitude.
4. Check distance and time enroute.
5. Check fuel required.
6. Check alternate requirements.
7. Preflight aircraft and instruments.

6. IFR Clearances

THERE IS an all-encompassing rule in instrument flying, the "eleventh commandment" which says "Thou shalt not enter IFR conditions in controlled airspace without a clearance from ATC." A clearance, once accepted and acknowledged, is your authorization to proceed to a certain point, via a certain route, and at a certain altitude. With the majority of today's IFR flights under radar surveillance, the clearance becomes less a separation tool, and more a means of insuring continued safe operation when communications fail.

Clearances must conform to aviation's three-dimensional environment and therefore must always specify (1) *a point* to which you are cleared, (2) *a route* by which you are expected to get there, and (3) *an altitude assignment*. Amendments to previously issued clearances may change any or all of these, but prior to entering IFR conditions in controlled airspace, you need all three. If the point to which you are cleared falls short of your destination airport (and this is frequently encountered because of heavy IFR traffic), one more instruction must be added: a time to expect further clearance. The same holds true for any interruption (hold) in your instrument flight.

In general, ATC will deliver clearances to you when airborne in one of three ways—the big thing here is at what time do you make your move?—when do you climb or descend or turn? Suppose Center wants you to go to a lower altitude: "Barnburner 1234 Alpha, descend to and maintain four thousand." You are expected to acknowledge the new clearance, then begin descending—there's clearly no urgency about this change of altitude. But when Center says "Barnburner 1234 Alpha, descend IMMEDIATELY to four thousand," you'd better be on your way down even before you pick up the mike—he wants you out of your present altitude right away. When there's no traffic conflict and Center doesn't really care when you descend, you'll hear "Barnburner 1234 Alpha, descend to and maintain four thousand at pilot's discretion." Acknowledge the clearance, and when it suits your situation, start down. (It's wise to let him know when you commence the descent.)

So, when you hear:

"Descend to and maintain. . . ."	Comply upon receipt
"Descend immediately to. . . ."	Do it NOW!
"Descend to . . . at pilot's discretion."	Do it when you're ready.

COPYING CLEARANCES

Time was when a pilot had to have executive-secretary shorthand skills to copy a clearance like this, delivered at machine-gun speed by a ground controller with a warped sense of humor:

ATC clears Barnburner 1234 Alpha to the River City Airport via Victor 21 to the Maple intersection, Victor 418 Stone, Victor 25 West Lewis intersection, direct Elmville VOR, Victor 182 Downtown intersection direct, climb to and maintain niner thousand, cross the Hometown 23-mile DME fix at or above four thousand, cross the Smithville 120 radial at or above five thousand, cross Maple intersection at or below six thousand five hundred, expect higher altitude at Lewis intersection, contact Hometown Center on 123.8 when established on Victor 21, squawk one-one-zero-zero; read back.

There are several ways to handle a situation like this. You can develop a clearance shorthand (there are books and recordings available), or you can invest in a cockpit recorder which can be rigged not only to transcribe the clearance on magnetic tape, but to read it back to the Controller in his own voice. It would almost be worth the cost of the recorder just to hear a Controller try to correct himself! Or you can submerge your pride and say "ready to copy, *take it slow*." It seems the third alternative is the best, since it will result in fewer errors, less repetition, and, more importantly, will contribute to a safer operation; both parties will have a complete understanding of all parts of the clearance; mistakes of routing, altitudes, or frequencies will stand out like an oil leak on a new paint job. Before accepting an invitation to copy a clearance at a strange airport, take a few moments to listen to other clearances, and study the chart of the local area—you will lessen the element of surprise when the Controller reels off some obscure intersection or omni station.

There is no regulation that specifies a clearance readback, but the pilot must at least acknowledge receipt of a clearance before it is considered accepted. Remember that Ground Control, Clearance Delivery, Center, Flight Service Station, or any ATC facility from which you might receive a clearance is *people*, and subject to human error. If the Controller really wanted you to proceed via Victor 47 to Maple intersection but cleared you down Victor 21 through force of habit, the error might go unnoticed if you acknowledge the clearance with a simple "Roger"—perfectly legal, but not too smart. It makes good sense to read back all but the briefest clearances.

The nature of your IFR trips will have a bearing on the mechanics of copying clearances—if you frequently fly the same routes, your clearances will not deviate much from a pattern, and you'll know what to expect. But when you're trying to taxi your castering-gear taildragger in a 20-knot crosswind on solid ice, busier than a DC-3 co-pilot at gear-up time, and wishing you had another hand and foot to help, that's not the time to say "go ahead" when Ground Control has your clearance for a strange route! Tell him to "stand by," and when you have the airplane stopped and the enroute chart spread out on your lap, indicate that you are "ready to copy." Now you can devote yourself 100 percent to the business of copying the clearance correctly, noting changes in routing or altitudes as he spews them out.

And while you're at it, why not copy the clearance in soft, erasable pencil right on the chart? It gives you a record of the clearance in the handiest possible place, available for instant reference as you fly, and eliminating another piece of paper in the cramped confines of your "flight deck." You'll find plenty of blank space for this purpose on every chart. When the Controller comes to "contact El Paso departure . . . ," you know that the next item will be a communications frequency, and you can save more time by "writing" that frequency on the radio you're not using. The same technique can be put to use with transponders —if you have listened to the clearances issued to aircraft ahead of you, dial in the code they get, because chances are good you'll receive the same one. Writing on radio sets and transponders makes them the world's most expensive note pads.

Your clearance will usually come through with route and altitude just as you requested, and if you plan to fly that way again, make a note of the routing; you have probably hit on a combination that ATC will buy next time, too. But if the airways you have chosen don't fit the Controller's traffic situation at the time, he will "suggest" another route. Despite what you may on occasion feel is an attempt to see how much out of your way they can make you fly, variations from requested routes are necessary when those airways are full. It is the Controller's expression of the best he can do for you at the time.

Here's where it's good to have the enroute chart handy, to see if the route he suggests is compatible with you, your airplane, and the weather. Treating the clearance as a suggestion (a strong one, yes, but still a suggestion), if you don't like the looks of it, TURN IT DOWN! It may mean a delay, but that's immensely preferable to finding yourself loaded with ice, losing altitude, and headed toward a squall line on an airway with an MEA 5,000 feet higher than you can possibly fly—all because you accepted a clearance other than the one you wanted. ALWAYS REFUSE A CLEARANCE THAT WILL FLY YOU INTO TROUBLE! This philosophy assumes your complete knowledge of existing and forecast weather conditions along the route.

CLEARED AS FILED

On rare occasions, you will encounter a clearance as involved as the earlier example, but more than likely you will be "cleared as filed, maintain eight thousand, contact Hometown Departure on one twenty three point eight, squawk one zero zero zero." Used more and more, "cleared as filed" takes into account the destination and routing you requested in your flight plan, and does away with all the mumbo-jumbo of intersections and airways. It's a good idea to know what route you requested, since asking ATC "which way did I file?" can be a little embarrassing. And you'll have to ask if you're not sure, because the clearance is the only thing you have to hang your hat on if the radios quit enroute. "Cleared as filed" covers *only* destination and routing; you will always be assigned an *altitude*. It is your choice to accept or decline, but *every* IFR clearance will stipulate the height at which you are to fly.

Anytime that you change your intended route of flight after filing a flight plan, be very suspicious of "cleared as filed." Remember that there is a delay in getting a flight plan request from FSS to Center and back, and the route by which you are cleared "as filed" may be the original one. When in doubt, ask the Controller to verify which route he is talking about—it may take an extra minute or two, but it might save your life in the event of radio failure.

WHAT'D HE SAY?

Perhaps the best way to learn the jargon of clearances and sharpen your copying artistry is to buy an inexpensive VHF receiver, and listen to the "big boys" at work. (Besides, it gives you another excuse to drive out to the airport on those rainy Saturday afternoons when someone else wants you to move furniture or paint the living room!) Pretend you are receiving the clearances, and copy them down, using an old enroute chart for a note pad. Take heart as you listen and realize that even the most experienced professional pilots stumble over a routing now and then—when you're talking to a pilot who claims that he's never blown a readback, don't believe anything else he says.

And it's not always the frailties of homo sapiens that cause problems. Late one IFR afternoon, during the daily contest to see which Controller could issue the longest clearance, an airline crew got the winner. There followed a long silence which was finally broken by the Controller asking "Trans-Amalgamated 201, did you copy?" "You'll never believe this," said the captain, "but I think we've had a pen failure—say again all after ATC clears."

CLEARANCE LIMITS

Most of the time you will be cleared to the airport at which you intend to land, but now and then a traffic conflict will not permit enough separation to clear you all the way. If it appears the conflict can be resolved in a short time, the Controller may issue a clearance with a specified limit, and it might sound like this, for a trip from Kansas City to Oklahoma City: "ATC clears Barnburner 1234 Alpha direct to the Butler VOR, climb to and maintain 5,000, expect further clearance at 37." Although a traffic conflict has prevented the Controller from clearing you all the way to Oke City, he is telling you that he's willing to accept your flight in the IFR system, that he can guarantee separation to Butler, and that further clearance will be issued before you get there. The "Expect Further Clearance" time provides an emergency backup clearance if your radios (or his, for that matter) fail. Should that unlikely event occur, you would be expected to hold at Butler until 37 past the hour, then proceed along your route in accordance with the regulations. When there's no communications problem, Controllers will issue a new clearance approximately five minutes before you arrive at a clearance limit.

As always, you have the option to accept or decline this "short-range" clearance, but with the "we'll get you to Oklahoma City as soon as possible" implication, you're better off to accept, and trust ATC to clear you along the way. Should you turn down their offer of the short-range clearance, it is likely you will wait a considerable time until the conflict is resolved. Treat a clearance limit not as an indication of ATC snubbing your route request in favor of someone else, but as a sincere effort on their part to expedite traffic flow. If the probability of solving the aerial traffic jam is slim, Center will have you wait on the ground. With a short-range clearance, at least you're in the system, on your way, and that's far better than burning up gasoline on the ramp waiting for clearance all the way.

VFR ON TOP

In the beginning, the FAA created IFR and VFR. As time went on, it became clear that these two major classifications of flying conditions could be made more flexible, and "VFR on Top" evolved as one of several ways to make the airspace more useful to more people.

There are two distinct kinds of VFR on Top. There is *VFR* VFR on Top, and there is *IFR* VFR on Top. You have probably used the VFR type, where you were able to stay above all the clouds, complied with visibility and cloud clearance regulations, and were able to take off, climb, and land in VFR conditions.

Although there is some calculated risk (like an engine failure on top of an overcast with nothing but the Rocky Mountains below), this is a perfectly legal situation, and for the non–instrument-rated pilot, often the only way to get any utility out of his airplane.

The other VFR on Top is right out of the Instrument Flight Rules, and can frequently be used to advantage. It is *always* an *IFR* clearance, and as such, it's not something that you can do whenever you feel like it! Whether ATC actually says the words or not, VFR on Top when you're in the IFR system implies a clearance to proceed as in normal IFR conditions, but with a VFR on Top *restriction.*

Since it is a restriction, you should know the rules and conditions that apply to this type of clearance before attempting to put it to use. They are:

1. You must be *cleared* by ATC to operate "on top."
2. You must *follow the route* assigned by ATC.
3. You must *report* to ATC whenever required in accordance with IFR rules.
4. You must fly at *VFR altitudes*—eastbound, odd thousands plus 500; westbound, even thousands plus 500.
5. You are responsible (as you are at any time in VFR conditions) to see and avoid other aircraft.
6. You must be able to *maintain VFR conditions* above *all* clouds—flying between layers is *not* VFR on Top.
7. You should be reasonably certain you can continue your flight to destination in VFR-on-Top conditions.

So you're committed to a ball game that has two sets of rules—some IFR, some VFR. Rules 1, 2, and 3 come from the instrument book, 4, 5, and 6 are VFR-oriented, and number 7 is just plain old common sense.

When is an IFR flight plan with a VFR-on-Top restriction a good deal? Any time you have a need or desire to fly above the clouds, can maintain the altitude required to do so, and ATC is fresh out of available altitudes. But temper that need or desire with the limitations of your airplane, your passengers, and yourself; the next time a pilot gets into trouble from lack of oxygen while trying to stay VFR on Top won't be the first time.

Before you can make a rational decision about requesting VFR on Top, you should have some idea where those cloud tops are located—how high are you going to have to climb to clear all clouds by 1,000 feet? The most accurate answer is found in pilot reports (PIREPS), direct observations by the people who were there. (By the way, the more PIREPS that are made, the more complete the picture you can draw, so reciprocate by making reports of cloud tops, particularly when such information is sparse or non-existent. Early in the morning or late at night, when few other hardy souls are aloft, your reports will be of great benefit to your fellow fliers.)

The next best source of cloud heights is the Area Forecast, which will give you a general idea of the altitude at which the sky is expected to go from cloudy to clear. The information is not very specific, but it's a lot better than no information at all.

There are several situations which may prompt you to consider a VFR-on-Top clearance. Maybe there are cumulus buildups that you would like to avoid visually (ATC will allow you to deviate around them), or you might need to climb out of an icing level, or perhaps you would just rather fly high, where it's clean, clear, smooth, and cool. VFR on Top is a useful tool in your IFR kit when a higher altitude will help you, and ATC has run out of available "hard" (assigned) altitudes. If you can operate within the "on Top" rules, it is usually advantageous to seek a flight level which will reduce a headwind component or let you pick up a tailwind—that's using your knowledge to operate the airplane more efficiently.

At terminals where Special VFR is not permitted (and there are going to be lots more of these), your instrument rating can help you beat the system by obtaining a clearance to VFR on Top, then proceeding merrily on your way, especially if a full IFR clearance is not available. This situation frequently develops when a low-topped fog bank has the terminal all but shut down. CAUTION: If you leap off in below-landing-minimum weather, be sure there's a suitable airport close by to which you can go if things turn sour!

When a Controller suspects that the tops are rather high, and sees a traffic conflict developing above a certain altitude, he may clear you "to VFR on Top, if not on top at 8,000, maintain 8,000 and advise." If you're still in the clouds when you get there, or don't have the required visibility, you're stuck with that altitude until the traffic conflict is resolved or the weather conditions improve. Since you now have an assigned altitude, you have an out if the radios fail.

If the tops of the white stuff begin to rise under you, it is your responsibility to rise with them, maintaining 1,000 feet between you and the clouds. Higher cloud tops will force a minimum increase in flight altitude of 2,000 feet to be at the proper VFR level, and it is possible that a constantly rising cloud layer will soon have you trying to operate at heights that are untenable for you or your airplane, or both. At this point, when you need all the smarts you can muster, hypoxia may be robbing you of precious judgment, and in a manner that can only be described as insidious—you don't know it's happening, and worse, you don't care! As cloud tops rise, your concern should grow; it's probably time to request a hard altitude from ATC, and nine times out of ten they will grant it. "Denver Center, Barnburner 1234 Alpha, unable to maintain VFR on Top at twelve thousand five hundred, requesting one zero thousand." And the reply will usually be "Roger, Barnburner 1234 Alpha, descend to and maintain one zero thousand, report reaching."

But the man behind the radar screen cannot always assign an altitude—in a sense, you forfeit some of the ATC protection when you request VFR on Top, and the Controller is obliged to fit you back into the system only if it can be done without disadvantaging other flights under his control. If this happens (and it is rare), you must remain VFR on Top, either by climbing (seldom the best choice, especially if you are pushing your altitude limits at the time), or by holding as instructed until an altitude is open. Should you subsequently declare an emergency because of a fuel shortage or impending performance or physiological problem, be prepared to explain why you didn't comply with the regulation which makes the pilot responsible for "all preflight information affecting the proposed flight. In other words, you should have known about the higher tops enroute before takeoff. Sorry, but that's the law, and it underscores your responsibility to be reasonably certain you can make it to destination in VFR-on-Top conditions before you request or accept such a clearance.

SPECIAL VFR

Usually thought of as a crutch for VFR pilots, Special VFR is the simplest of ATC clearances, and can often be used to advantage by instrument-rated people as well. In contrast to the full-blown IFR clearance, Special VFR designates more a clearance "area" than a clearance limit, does not assign a "hard" altitude, and makes no provision for a specific route or for radio failure. You will be cleared into or out of a Control Zone, from or to a direction—north, east, southwest, etc. For example, "Barnburner 1234 Alpha is cleared out of the Fresno Control Zone to the east, maintain Special VFR conditions at or below 3,000 feet while in the Control Zone."

The heart of Special VFR is that airspace in the immediate vicinity of the airport (usually 5 miles in diameter with extensions for approach and departure paths) known as a "Control Zone." It extends from the surface to 14,500 feet MSL, and is there only for the protection of traffic executing IFR comings and goings at that airport. Since it is controlled airspace, you may not be there without a clearance when conditions are less than VFR.

Because a lot of non–instrument-rated pilots are inconvenienced on days when the ceiling is adequate but the visibility won't creep past the 2½ mile mark, or when they can see clear into the next county under an 800-foot cloud deck, Special VFR was developed. It is a *clearance* to proceed into or out of a control zone as long as you maintain 1-mile visibility, stay clear of clouds, and remain below the altitude specified in the clearance. The altitude limitation is usually imposed to protect IFR operations at higher levels. This is a "poor man's IFR" clearance, available to any pilot, instrument-rated or not.

A full IFR clearance supersedes Special VFR; that is, no Specials will be issued when IFR traffic is inbound or outbound and a conflict is possible. This means that Special VFR folks face long delays getting airborne or cleared into the control zone when IFR operations are heavy. Being instrument-rated puts you into the preferential group in this situation, and filing IFR will usually produce an earlier departure or arrival. At certain airports around the country, the flow of IFR traffic is so heavy and so consistent that these terminals do not permit Special VFR operations at any time, period. Know which airports are in this group, and don't ask a Controller for something he can't do.

It is at the less-busy airports that Special VFR serves all pilots most beneficially. Suppose you are waiting for your clearance at West Side Airport (tower-equipped) and the minutes as well as your gasoline are wasting away because continuous IFR approaches and departures are in progress at Downtown International, 10 miles distant. If the entire area is solid IFR, settle down, cool your heels, and wait—you've no choice. But if you can depart West Side in Special VFR conditions and *very soon thereafter* fly in "regular" VFR, you may be money ahead to request a Special for departure, and be on your way. (CAUTION: You will likely have to refile your IFR flight plan, as ATC will not allow you to cancel your IFR request, take off under Special VFR conditions, then pick up the same IFR flight plan in the air.) Conversely, you can sometimes get into a smaller airport with a Special VFR clearance when there's a long waiting list for approaches at a nearby "big" terminal. If conditions are favorable, it doesn't hurt to inquire.

An inbound Special is usually not much of a problem, since

you are flying toward a definite location (the airport) and various aids to navigation (radio facilities, city lights and/or landmarks, assistance from the Tower, etc.). It's the Special VFR *away from* the airport that is strewn with pitfalls for the unwary pilot; if traffic permits, you will be cleared out of the control zone, and that's as far as the Controller's responsibility goes. Should the weather outside the zone prove to be worse than expected, the Controller is under no mandate to let you back in, especially if he has other Specials or IFR traffic clamoring for his attention. And there you are, in IFR conditions without a clearance, can't get one, and trying to think up a good story to tell the FAA at your violation hearing!

Recognize the potential hazards of Special VFR and use it only when it can *safely* get you where you need to go. If you get in a bind and can't maintain the required conditions, don't press on, but contact ATC (Tower, Approach Control, anybody), explain the situation, and get a clearance as appropriate. Pride goeth before a fall, and when you are in an airplane, the fall usually hurteth a lot.

CRUISE CLEARANCES

Ask any ten instrument pilots to define a cruise clearance and you'll probably get ten different explanations, all the way from "maintain cruise airspeed" to "descend immediately to minimum altitude." A very useful tool of IFR operations, the cruise clearance carries a number of implications which bear on the efficiency and safety of getting to your destination, and it must be thoroughly understood to be used properly. Unlike the "Three Little Words" of musical fame, when an ATC Controller says you are "cleared to cruise," he doesn't mean "I Love You," but he *does* mean:

1. You are cleared DIRECT to the specified navaid.
2. You are cleared to fly at any altitude from that specified in the clearance down to the appropriate IFR minimum altitude.

3. You may leave the cruise altitude at your discretion for a lower altitude without reporting (unless requested, of course).
4. You are the only *IFR* traffic at cruise altitude and below between you and the navaid.
5. You are cleared for an approach of your choice on arrival at the airport.
6. You are responsible to advise ATC (the facility will be specified in the clearance) when your landing is assured or upon missed approach, depending on the situation.

And that's a lot of clearance for "three little words"!

Cruise clearances were designed primarily to accommodate the final segment of an IFR flight and are generally used at locations which have no Tower or Approach Control facility. A very flexible instrument of traffic control, this clearance allows you to begin descent at your discretion, choose an altitude best for the situation (turbulence, headwinds, icing, inoperative cabin heaters, or other fun things), and hopefully break out of the clouds sooner than you might otherwise. When you get to the appropriate minimum altitude, and find yourself in VFR conditions, there are several ways you can complete the approach.

First, if you want the practice, go ahead with the full IFR procedure (it will take a little longer, but there's something to be said for the IFR separation this offers, plus the fact that it will keep you from getting lost or landing at the wrong airport!). The second method, if *good* VFR exists in the terminal area, is to cancel your IFR flight plan, removing you from the system (although most Approach and Center Controllers will give you traffic advisories as long as their workload permits). The third and fourth possibilities are the Contact and the Visual Approaches, treated in detail in Chapter 13, "Instrument Approaches."

7. Communicating in the IFR System

THERE ARE A NUMBER of ways you can make your IFR communications more efficient, one of which is to get rid of the habit of prefacing every transmission with "uhhhhhh." There is no doubt some psychological theory underlying the several types of uhhh's, which range from the student pilot who truly doesn't know what to say and uses uhhh to fill a verbal void, to the 20,000-hour airline captain whose well-practiced uhhh is pitched at least two octaves below anyone else's and is his hallmark of accomplishment. There's nothing illegal, immoral, or fattening about using your own uhhh, but it takes time that can be better spent in meaningful communication. If you are a habitual uhh-her and somewhat condescending about your five-second tone which will get you the best DF steer in the country, don't try it out when IFR in the New York area—by the time you've finished uhhh-ing, New York Approach Control will have cleared three airline flights for approaches to JFK, handed off two Bonanzas and an Apache to LaGuardia Tower, and coordinated a Civil Air Patrol search for a sailboat missing on Long Island

Sound! As our terminal areas get busier, and until data link systems are in common use, it is incumbent on every pilot, and especially those using the IFR system, to become better managers of their communications.

Airborne communications problems have not escaped the attention of the wonderful world of research—someone studied it a while back with the aid of a number of in-cockpit recorders. In addition to taping the transmissions to and from the aircraft, pilot responses on the flight deck were also recorded. The researchers found that in almost every case, radioed instructions from the ground were followed by one of these phrases between pilots (listed in order of usage):

1. "What'd he say?"
2. "Was that for us?"
3. "Oh, shucks." (Cleaned up a bit so the book can retain its "G" rating.)

Practice communication management right from the start—when you turn the radio switch to the ON position, know ahead of time where the volume knob should be for normal reception. If there isn't some kind of mark on the knob, make one. Adjust the squelch control to a point just short of where the noise begins, and you've set up your transceiver properly for the first transmission. When Ground Control answers, adjust the volume for maximum clarity. Better yet, listen to other transmissions and adjust your radio before you talk to anyone.

TIPS FOR TALKING

Here are several things you should do (and some things you should *not* do) to improve the quality of your communications in the air:

- Always listen to be sure the frequency is clear before starting a transmission. You will often hear just one side of a radio conversation, so take that into consideration. If Center asks somebody else a question, but he's too far away for you to hear the answer, allow a reasonable length of time before you begin. You'll probably hear Center's acknowledgement of the other aircraft's answer—use that as your go-ahead signal.

- Before you transmit to anyone at any time, know what you want to say before you press the mike button. It's not necessary to abbreviate your words as they used to do in the movies, but do compress the message so that you get your point across with a minimum number of words.
- Don't make transmissions that are unnecessary. This should not preclude a friendly chat with the Controllers when they aren't busy and exhibit a willingness to pass the time of day.
- Don't click the mike button to acknowledge a transmission. To a Tower Controller, all clicks sound alike, and he will likely have to repeat his instructions to be sure the proper party understands. If you're too busy to acknowledge (and this is not an isolated circumstance, especially IFR), it's better to go ahead and fly the airplane in accordance with the instructions, and acknowledge a few seconds later, when you have the time.
- If you intend to fly a lot of single-pilot IFR in busy areas, invest in a boom mike and a wheel-mounted mike switch.
- En route, set your receiver volume so that you can hear Center's transmissions clearly. When another aircraft close by blasts through your speaker at an uncomfortable level, live with it for the moment. Recognize that the loudness is the result of his proximity—if you turn down the volume, you may set it below the level you need to receive Center, and you may miss an important message.
- Whenever you transmit, hold the mike close to your mouth, and speak in a normal tone and volume. This will eliminate engine and aircraft noise, making your transmission much more readable.
- When you're waiting in the number one spot at a crowded, busy airport and Tower clears you for immediate takeoff, if there's not time to acknowledge by radio, don't worry about it. The Controller will see you starting to roll, and that's the finest acknowledgement you could give him.
- After you have identified a VOR, turn off the audio side of the VOR receiver. The noise and occasional conversation on the omni frequency will serve only to distract you from more important business. Tune, identify, and turn off the sound.
- Never, never sacrifice the control of your aircraft for the sake of talking on the radio. If you didn't know better, you'd sometimes think that Tower Controllers were watching your takeoff with

binoculars, so they can ask you for your first estimate when they see you reach for the gear handle! The same philosophy applies to the required report on executing a missed approach—get the airplane on its way, and when everything is completely under control, let somebody know of your intentions.

BE A CONFORMIST

You must realize that when you file and fly IFR, you become part of a *system*, highly structured and organized to provide the fastest, safest service to all comers. You cannot be denied access if you are qualified, so your task is to fit into the system as smoothly as possible, going along with the established procedures, becoming a round peg when ATC wants to fit you into a round hole. Communication represents a key element in the systemizing process; no matter how distinctive you like to be on the air, there's only one way to do it, and that's "by the book." There are two parts to the problem: first, knowing exactly *what* to say (and no more), and second, knowing *when* to say it.

About this matter of your aircraft identification—except for those worshippers at the altar of distinction who obtain nonstandard registration numbers, nearly all civil aircraft in the United States consist of four numbers and a letter suffix. On your initial call to any ATC facility, the rule states that you should use all four numbers and the letter (spoken in the international phonetic alphabet). If the government man answers in kind, you are obliged to continue using the full ident in subsequent transmissions. The reason?—he may have another aircraft on his frequency with a similar call sign; if there are *two* Barnburners with numbers ending in 34A being worked by the same Controller, confusion can reign supreme if both parties insist on acknowledging with just "three four alpha." Use of the full identification completely eliminates this problem. However, if yours is the only one that comes close to three four Alpha, the Controller will shorten the call sign, and then you may respond with the abbreviated number.

Clearance amendments which involve rerouting, altitude assignments, and other major changes should be read back to insure complete understanding on both sides of the electronic fence, but "Barnburner 1234 Alpha, turn right to heading one five zero, intercept the Localizer course, cleared for the Runway 27 ILS approach" can be acknowledged clearly and efficiently by merely replying "Roger, 1234 Alpha." This and similar transmissions are rather hard to misread, and the shortened reply saves precious seconds, especially in a crowded terminal area.

The use of radar transponders introduces an opportunity to save time, too. When a Controller requests that you squawk "IDENT," you shouldn't even think about using the microphone; just press the "IDENT" button, and let the black box do the talking. There's no need to tell the Controller that you have responded, for he'll see the enlarged "blip" on his scope right away, and when he informs you that you are "in radar contact," all you need reply is "Roger, 1234 Alpha." The same is true of a code change; for example, ATC directs you to change your transponder to 1100, and your communication should be just that—flick the dials until the proper code appears, and wait for him to acknowledge. In those rare cases where he doesn't pick it up right away, he'll have you confirm that you have made the change; the important thing is that you didn't clutter the frequency with an unnecessary exchange at the outset.

In passing, it's interesting to note that the term "squawk" is an outgrowth of the World War II supersecret terminology which labeled the brand-new military transponders "parrots"; they replied to a coded electronic message just as the raspy-voiced green bird does. Some day when all has gone wrong, and you need an outlet for your emotions, a Center request to "squawk IDENT" provides the golden opportunity. Pick up the mike, and in the screechiest voice you can generate, make like a parrot—"IDENT! IDENT! IDENT!" (You should expect some sort of nasty reaction from ATC, but this little exercise is guaranteed to relieve your tensions.)

SAY ONLY WHAT'S NEEDED

There is a standard procedure for communicating when you are handed off from one Center sector to another, or from one Center to the next. You must realize that before a Controller requests that you "contact Cleveland Center now on 124.7," he has contacted the acquiring facility by telephone (all Centers and their sectors are linked by phone lines), confirmed that you are on his radar scope, and asked what frequency you should use. The subsequent sector (or Center) Controller therefore knows who you are, where you're going, and really only needs confirmation of your altitude, the most important ingredient of safe separation at this point. So, when you check in with the new Controller, you should say merely "Cleveland Center, Barnburner 1234 Alpha, eight thousand." If he wants to make absolutely sure, he may require you to squawk "IDENT," but he is not obligated to advise you "radar contact." You will assume that he has you on radar unless he advises otherwise—another case of the system eliminating needless conversation. If the handoff occurs while you are climbing or descending to a new assigned altitude, make this information part of your report: "Cleveland Center, Barnburner 1234 Alpha, five thousand six hundred, climbing [or descending] to eight thousand."

If it hasn't happened to you yet, it will—"Hometown Unicom, this is Barnburner 1234 Alpha; I'll be on the ground in ten minutes, will you call my wife and tell her to pick me up at the airport?" Followed by, "Roger, Barnburner 1234 Alpha, we'll be happy to make that call for you, but it will be long distance—this is Albuquerque Center." By switching back and forth from one radio to the other, you have transmitted on the wrong frequency! Using both radios can cause a great deal of confusion; eliminate it by using only one of your transceivers at a time. In addition to preventing you from talking to the wrong people, it takes one more monkey off your back, that of figuring out which radio is the right one to use. When you're in the IFR system, anything you can do to decrease your mental workload is good.

PLAY THE "NUMBERS" GAME

One of the most disturbing and time-consuming communications situations takes place on the ramp at any tower-controlled airport, where the Ground Controller reels off the active runway, taxi instructions, and altimeter setting to a departing aircraft, then hears "Barnburner 1234 Alpha, ready to taxi." Faced with this set of circumstances, the Controller has no choice but to go through the whole bit again, and the needless repetitions build into frustrating numbers in the course of a day. When you get the engine started, turn on the radio, monitor Ground Control, and listen; unless you're the only airplane getting ready to go, you can copy the appropriate instructions, and when you are ready to move out, save tempers and time by saying "Barnburner 1234 Alpha, ready to taxi *with the numbers*." (If you're on a large airport with several locations from which aircraft might taxi for takeoff, don't make Ground Control guess where you are; state your position with the original call: "Barnburner 1234 Alpha at Acme Aviation, ready to taxi with the numbers.")

When approaching for landing, the same principle applies; you can usually monitor the tower frequency from a considerable distance, learn what runway and traffic pattern is in use, and tell the Tower you "have the numbers" on the initial call, such as "Downtown Tower, Barnburner 1234 Alpha six miles northwest with the numbers, will call you on downwind for Runway 36." If the Tower Controller would prefer some other pattern entry or another runway, he'll let you know. The beauty of this procedure is that he will usually only need to acknowledge your thoughtful, preplanned transmission with "Roger, 1234 Alpha," again making the most of communication time.

Both of these situations, before taxi and prior to landing, have been improved immeasurably through the ever-increasing number of ATIS (Automatic Terminal Information Service) installations across the country. As a conscientious pilot, take a few seconds to look up the ATIS frequency and get all the information before reporting "ready to taxi." There's just no excuse for Ground Control having to spend time reciting the active runway, altimeter setting, and other pertinent information when it is waiting for you on a continuous ATIS recording. It's even more important for IFR operations, since the ATIS broadcast also includes weather, winds, departure procedures in use, and the frequency and transponder codes for departing IFR flights. At most large terminals Ground Control doesn't have the time to cater to uninformed pilots, and will refer you back to ATIS if you call for taxi instructions without the current information. "Kennedy Ground, Barnburner 1234 Alpha at Gate 4B, taxi clearance, please" would no doubt be rejoined crisply with "34 Alpha, information Bravo is current," and he'll go on about more pressing business, leaving you to find out for yourself what information Bravo is all about.

Inbound to a busy airport, solid IFR, Center keeping you as busy as a prize bull in mating season, there's still time to tune the ATIS frequency and get yourself set up for the approach segment of your flight. The busy airports don't have time to give you the good word; they expect you to be informed. Granted, it requires listening with each ear tuned to a different frequency, and ATC instructions certainly take precedence—but if you start listening to ATIS far enough out, you can pick up portions of the broadcast in between the calls from Center, and by the time you are handed off to Approach Control, you should have the complete message. The law says that you will inform Approach Control or Tower *on initial contact* that you have received "Information Foxtrot" (or whatever is current), so you must get this little chore out of the way as early as you can. To illustrate, when Center hands you off to Approach Control, you have listened to ATIS and the exchange goes like this:

CENTER: Barnburner 1234 Alpha, descend to and maintain five thousand, contact San Francisco Approach on one two five point three.

YOU: Roger, Barnburner 1234 Alpha cleared to five thousand, leaving eight thousand. [Unless you have some doubt concerning the facility or the frequency, there's no need to repeat that part of the clearance.]

YOU AGAIN: San Francisco Approach, Barnburner 1234 Alpha descending to five thousand, I have Foxtrot.

And the San Francisco Approach Controller will figure he's dealing with a pilot who knows which end is up.

GETTING AROUND ON THE GROUND

Proper communications discipline becomes more important as an airport becomes busier, and reaches its "ne plus ultra" at those terminals equipped with a Clearance Delivery facility. In addition to the requirement to listen to the ATIS broadcast, these fields insist that you have your IFR clearance before taxi. Besides the obvious rebuff you're going to get if you contact Ground Control sans clearance, consider the unruffled ease with which you can copy when you are sitting calmly on the ramp, nothing competing for your attention except getting that clearance right the first time. If you have a good strong battery (don't try this on a cold day when even the brass monkeys are heading south) and notice a long lineup at the departure end of the runway, you might consider switching on and getting your clearance before you even start the engines; if there is going to be an inordinate delay, you can save a lot of ground time on the motors. It's possible to get even farther ahead of the system by contacting Clearance Delivery as you taxi in after landing, when you have filed for an immediate turnaround.

Whether it's Clearance Delivery or Ground Control, you can help them dig your flight plan out of the heap by providing some basic information on the first call—"Washington Clearance Delivery, Barnburner 1234 Alpha, IFR to Saginaw at one zero thousand." The requested altitude and the destination gives the man something definite to look for.

Ground Controllers will set you up by asking "Barnburner

1234 Alpha, I have your clearance, ready to copy?" but knowing that you are monitoring the frequency, most Clearance Deliverers will just let 'er go, ready or not! The loudspeaker suddenly comes alive with "Barnburner 1234 Alpha is cleared as filed to the Saginaw Airport, climb to one zero thousand, etc., etc., etc., read back." Remember that a Clearance Delivery facility is there to relieve congestion and you wouldn't be on the frequency unless you were ready to copy, so *be* ready; have your charts spread out to visualize route changes and all the other good practices germane to clearance copying. (See Chapter 6, "IFR Clearances.")

Now that you have your clearance and are ready to drive the Barnburner to the other end of the aerodrome for takeoff, you may face a navigation problem that is more complicated than any airborne situation. As airports have grown in size and complexity, the number of taxiways, outerbelts, innerbelts, crossovers, and switchbacks has increased to the point where you are just about ready to concede that there is no way to get to the runway from here! An old adage of the flying business applies here: When in doubt, swallow your pride and ask. Sure, the airline captain who flies into a particular airport six times a day knows the taxi routes inside out, but Ground Controllers are quite aware that the "first-timer" is going to experience difficulty when he is cleared "to Runway 14 via Charlie and Mike, hold short of Juliet before crossing to the inner parallel, give way to the Shorthaul Beech 99 approaching from your right as you cross November." And Ground is more than willing to help you find your way, if you'll only ask. On a completely unfamiliar airport, the first thing to do is to break out the approach plate (or a separate taxi chart for the superlarge terminals) and from the airport plan view, figure the most likely taxi route; trace it as Ground Control reads it off, and you should be able to make it on your own.

But suppose you can't find the chart, or the taxi clearance is so confusing that you don't even know which way to turn as you

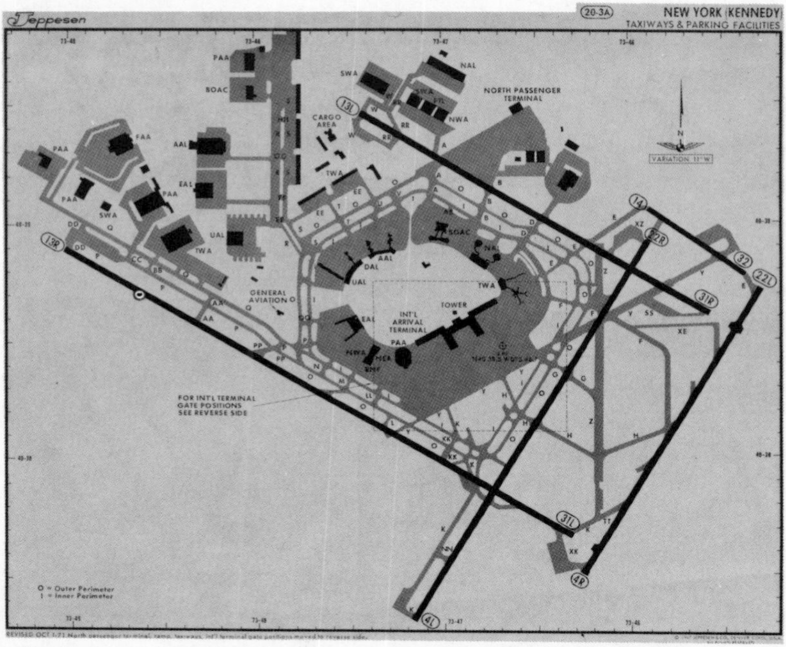

Taxiways and parking facilities at Kennedy International Airport, New York. © 1971 Jeppesen & Co., Denver, Colo. All rights reserved. Not to be used for navigation.

come off the ramp; here's where you admit to Ground Control that you are unfamiliar with the airport, and will he please give you directions? The answer may be humbling, because nine times out of ten, there just happens to be an airliner conveniently located so that you will hear (in a condescending voice): "Roger, 34 Alpha, turn right on the taxiway straight ahead of you and follow the United 747 to the active runway." So, tuck in under the tail of the big fella and it's "whither thou goest" from here to the end of the runway. Don't be chagrined, because the co-pilot is sitting up there with a road map, telling the captain which way to turn to make sure *they* are heading in the right direction.

Some air terminals are notorious for the curt manner with which their Controllers operate, and others are equally famous for the complete and willing cooperation that comes from Ground Control. In either case, you certainly have a right to ask, and 'tis a far better thing to find out from them which way to turn, than to taxi onto an active runway and find yourself staring down the intakes of a just-landed DC-9.

Once you are cleared by Ground Control to the active runway, you are obligated to remain on that frequency until you arrive at the runup pad. If you want to depart momentarily to listen to ATIS, or call Unicom, be sure to check off with Ground Control, and report back. Upon arrival at the end of the runway or the end of the line, whichever comes first, it is prudent to monitor the Tower frequency for takeoff clearances and restrictions being issued to other similar type aircraft—it's another way to stay one step ahead by getting ready for the next segment of your flight before you actually get there.

When the Barnburner is the only airplane waiting to leap into the blue (or the gray, as the case may be), the switch to Tower frequency should be made just as soon as you have all the knobs, switches, levers, and handles in the proper positions for takeoff, and all you need say is "Possum Kingdom Tower, Barnburner 1234 Alpha, ready for takeoff on one four." Especially at busy airports, including the runway number helps the Controller as he sorts out the departure requests. When he gets the word from Center that the system is ready to accept your flight, he'll advise "cleared for takeoff, maintain runway heading [or appropriate instructions], contact Departure Control on 124.3," and away you go.

Towers must always coordinate IFR departures with either Departure Control or Center, which means a communications lag, however slight. You can often circumvent this delay (assuming no lineup of waiting aircraft, in which case you must wait your turn) by advising Ground Control as you leave the ramp that you will be ready for takeoff when you reach the runway.

This gives Tower a much more positive departure time to pass on to the other ATC facilities, and your takeoff clearance will probably be waiting for you when you switch to Tower. If you do this, don't delay getting to the runway, because a phone call will have been made informing someone else up the line that Barnburner 1234 Alpha can be off the ground in two minutes.

POSITION REPORTS—A LOST ART

One of the most pleasant sounds to filter through your speaker on an IFR flight is the phrase "in radar contact." It will usually happen right after takeoff, when Departure Control acquires you on the scope, and in most parts of the country you will continue in radar contact right down to the deck on the other end of your trip. It is comforting to know that someone down there knows who you are, where you are, and where other traffic is; but there is an additional feature which has done more to clean up the communications clutter than anything else. When you are advised that your flight is "in radar contact," what the Controller politely means is "SHUT UP!" He doesn't want to hear from you, since he knows your position, groundspeed, and ETAs more accurately than you do. He doesn't want you to speak unless spoken to; as far as ATC is concerned, IFR pilots, like little children, should be seen (on radar) and not heard (on the radio).

Full-blown position reports are definitely taboo when in radar contact, but there are several other circumstances in which ATC would like to hear from you, mostly in confirmation of your actions which bear on safe separation from other IFR flights. Therefore, you should report without request when these situations exist (talk to the ATC facility with which you are in contact at the time, or as instructed):

1. Report the time and altitude reaching an assigned holding fix or clearance limit. (If you've been advised "in radar contact," you can forget this one.)
2. Report when leaving an assigned altitude. (Notice that a report is

not required or even desired when reaching the new altitude. If ATC wants to know when you get there, they'll ask for a separate report.)

3. When you leave an assigned holding fix or clearance limit, let ATC know what time you departed.
4. On an instrument approach, you must report when you pass the Final Approach Fix inbound to the airport. ATC will always let you know to whom you should report.
5. You must report when executing a missed approach—again, you'll be told whom to call.
6. If you have given ATC an estimate for a subsequent reporting point, and it appears that your estimate will be in error by more than three minutes either way, let them know. Not required when in radar contact.
7. You can fly at any altitude you choose (VFR altitude rules apply), but advise ATC if you make a change when you're operating IFR with a VFR-on-Top restriction.

In an effort to streamline the ATC system, the government has cut back the number of Flight Service Stations, and has increased the area coverage of the ones that remain. For example, the Millville Flight Service Station, located between Atlantic City and Philadelphia, handles the communications for several other VORs along this very busy IFR flyway. So, if you report over Millville, Woodstown, Coyle, Atlantic City, Sea Isle, or Kenton VOR, you're going to be talking to the man at Millville. Hung like a doctor's shingle below the VOR information box, the name "Millville" indicates that each of these is a remote site, and it is important that you identify your position when making the initial call. The proper way to do this is to call not "Millville Radio" but perhaps "Sea Isle Radio," which lets the Specialist know which microphones to select for his reply. After the first call which nails down your position, you can drop the facade and use "Millville Radio," which you knew it was all along.

Unfortunately, the widespread, almost universal coverage of enroute radar in today's ATC system breeds an insidious complacency. You'll probably fly IFR for a long time before it happens, but one dark night you will be advised "radar contact lost, resume normal position reporting." At the next compulsory reporting point (marked on the chart as a solid triangle) or the next fix that you named in your flight plan, whichever comes first, somebody will be waiting to hear from you with all the details of your flight.

There is one right way to do it, and as many wrong ways as there are pilots; the correct procedure begins with the initial call to Flight Service, "Goodland Radio, Barnburner 1234 Alpha at Goodland with a position report, listening on the VOR, over." By starting off the exchange like this, you will have accomplished several time-saving functions—Goodland FSS knows who is calling, what you want, and the frequency on which you expect a reply. Your mention of an impending position report gives the Specialist time to pull out a blank form listing the items in the report; he inserts your aircraft identification and then, broadcasting over the VOR frequency, tells you to "go ahead with your position." Just like filing a flight plan, there is a sequence to be followed which lets the Specialist copy your report in the most efficient manner; he wants just the answers, not the questions, so compose your report in terms of numbers and names.

An easy way to remember the proper order is PTA TEN, which you should commit to memory. It makes absolutely no sense like that, but if you will line up the letters vertically, they form a mnemonic, one of the best memory joggers of all:

P Position (usually a VOR, intersection, or airway crossing).
T Time (always given in minutes past the hour when you were over the reported fix).
A Altitude.
T Type of flight plan (IFR or VFR). (On that rare occasion when Center asks you for a report, use the same format, but omit "IFR" since they already know that.)
E Estimate at the next point you intend to report, again in minutes past the hour.
N Name of the next place you intend to report.

Of course, you would identify yourself as part of the report, so "Barnburner 1234 Alpha" would precede PTA TEN, and a typical IFR position report to a Flight Service Station would sound like this: "Goodland Radio, Barnburner 1234 Alpha, Goodland at four two, eight thousand, IFR, Thurman at one zero, Denver, over." A well-organized position report should not take more than ten or fifteen seconds using the PTA TEN sequence, and FSS will get it all the first time; if you've done it right, he will reply with "Roger your position, Barnburner 1234 Alpha, Goodland altimeter is two niner point seven six."

Some communications situations demand interpretation on the part of the pilot; ATC people use rather severely abbreviated phrases when time is at a premium. Such was the case one extremely busy morning when a Center Controller needed confirmation of the height of a particular flight, and transmitted "Trans Global two thirty-four, say altitude." The reply came back, "altitude." In a slightly more stentorian tone, Center tried again: "Trans Global two thirty-four, say *altitude*!" Two thirty-four was still feeling frisky, and replied again, "altitude." Taking the measure of his airborne adversary and displaying more than the usual amount of savoir faire, the Controller broadcast calmly, "Roger, Trans Global two thirty-four, say 'cancelling IFR.'" Only a few seconds separated that transmission from "Center, Trans Global two thirty-four, is level at one zero thousand."

On occasion, and particularly at lower altitudes over mountainous terrain, you will be asked to contact another ATC facility on a new frequency, and when you dial in the proper number, nobody answers. When this happens, wait a minute, and try again. If the third attempt elicits no response, return to the previously assigned frequency and advise the Controller of your plight. Nine times out of ten, the next man heard you calling, but was too busy with other traffic to answer; or perhaps you are just a bit outside the range of his transmitter.

Whatever the reason, don't go through a lengthy dissertation on what has happened, just say to the previous Controller, "Memphis Center, Barnburner 1234 Alpha, *unable* Kansas City on one two three point eight." The magic word is "unable," and tells him right away of the difficulty. After advising you to "stand by," he'll call Kansas City on the phone and ask if they heard you. Sometimes the new frequency is a bad one, and you'll be assigned another—but more than likely, Memphis will ask you to try again, maybe five minutes from now, when you'll be close enough to hear Kansas City.

Don't get up tight and call over and over and over—continue on your way, and after a reasonable time, try to establish contact. Even if your radios have quit, there are iron-clad rules to follow (see Chapter 10, "Communications Failure"); of course, before you launch into those procedures, try to contact a Flight Service Station, a Tower, or any handy ATC facility.

LETTERS AND NUMBERS

The International Civil Aviation Organization (ICAO) phonetic alphabet is the rulebook when it comes to proper pronunciation of both letters and numbers. Some of the letters may seem a bit unwieldy to you, but they've been chosen for their universality; theoretically, pilots from any country in the world can make themselves understood using these phonetics. But no matter how hard they try, our Oriental brothers-in-the-airspace will change Bravo to Blavo, Foxtrot to Foxtlot, and Romeo to Lomeo. The problems transcend geographical barriers within the U.S. also; you will seldom hear a pilot from the Midwest come through with OSS-CAH, as Oscar is spelled phonetically in the book—he's bound to drawl "OSS-CURR" from now 'til the end of time. His Downeast counterpart will likewise pronounce Sierra "SEE-AIRER," and the sod-buster who calls 'em like he sees 'em will always use "LI-MAH" as in beans instead of "LEE-MAH" as in Peru.

Numbers come in for their share of abuse, too, the most easily muddled combination being "five" and "nine." To eliminate confusion entirely, the communications experts would have us use "niner," which does the job very effectively. A man who suspected his wife of hanky-pankying with an airline pilot had his suspicions confirmed when, confronting her with the evidence, he demanded to know if indeed she had been indiscreet—"I've told you niner thousand times, NEGATIVE!" she replied.

Transiting the IFR airspace can be a trying experience for those who are not familiar with "what's happening," but we all had to start somewhere. If you are not a smooth communicator, able to become part of the system with a minimum of radio conversation, buy a VHF receiver and listen to the big boys; learn the jargon of instrument flying, anticipate the instructions coming up, and play the game of thinking ahead so that you can impart the most information with the fewest words. You'll endear yourself to ATC, save time for all the other airmen who have important things to say, and brand yourself as a "pro" in the process.

8. VOR Navigation

KEEPING THE NEEDLE CENTERED en route is a fairly simple task, and by always placing the airway course under the index, you can't go too far wrong. But when it's time for a VOR approach or a holding pattern, you've got to know what the receiver is telling you, and how to orient yourself to the desired radial.

All VOR receiver installations have this much in common: Each one is composed of (1) a Course Deviation Indicator (CDI) or, in everyday language, a left-right needle; (2) a TO-FROM indicator, which solves the question of ambiguity; (3) an Omni Bearing Selector (OBS), which sets the stage for interpreting the information from the other two. When the OBS is set on a particular course, the CDI will *always* tell you whether you are on, to the left of, or to the right of the radial that the OBS setting represents. The TO-FROM indicator furnishes additional information about whether that course (the OBS setting) will take you TO or FROM the omni transmitter.

Because of this orientation to a specific course, it is imperative that you begin interpretation of what you see on the panel by getting the airplane lined up on a heading the same as, or at least close to, the course you have selected. You can do this by physically turning the plane to that heading, or more likely, by imagining yourself flying in the proper direction. When this basic condition is met, the VOR receiver indications will always tell you a true story—if you fly a heading that agrees with the course that is set into the OBS, you will proceed toward the station if the indicator shows TO, or away from the station if it shows FROM. Should the CDI be centered when heading and OBS are close together, you can be sure that you are ON that particular radial; if it's displaced to the left, you must fly left to get to the radial, or fly right if the needle lies on the other side. Unless you are turning to intercept a radial, or just entering a holding pattern, the only difference between the OBS setting and your heading should be drift correction, and it will seldom be a very large disparity. (Technically, the "true story" on the VOR indicator exists on any heading up to 90 degrees either side of the selected course, but you'll do yourself a navigational favor by always imagining the airplane's heading in agreement with the OBS. If worst comes to worst, turn the airplane until the numbers agree and proceed from there—it's better than getting completely disoriented!)

RADIALS, RADIALS, RADIALS

If you don't speak, read, and write the language of radials, there's no time like right now to fix it firmly in your IFR thinking, because the entire VOR navigational system is based on courses *away from the station.* There is only *one* line on the chart for each numbered radial associated with a particular omni station; whether you are flying it outbound or inbound, holding on it or crossing it, a radial is always in the same place. The only possible complication lies in the reciprocity of the numbers—whenever you are proceeding *outbound,* your magnetic *course* (and *heading* when there's no wind) will be the same number as the *radial;* turn around and fly *inbound* and you must mentally reverse the numbers and physically reverse the

OBS setting so that your course is now the reciprocal of the radial. Be that as it may, you are still flying on a *radial*—it hasn't moved or changed one iota.

PUTTING VOR TO WORK

There are four basic problems you will encounter in everyday use of VOR; whether you're holding, making an approach, or navigating en route, a thorough knowledge of these four will enable you to handle any situation. They are:

1. Determining what course will take you *direct* to a VOR.
2. Determining your position in relation to a specific airway or radial.
3. Identifying an intersection (or crossing a particular radial).
4. Determining a wind correction angle that will keep you on course.

The first case is frequently put to use when you are cleared "from your present position DIRECT" to a VOR. The procedure is simple; after tuning and identifying the station (don't *ever* forget this step!), rotate the OBS until the left-right needle is centered, and the ambiguity indicator shows TO. The number that now appears under the OBS index is your course to the station (inbound, it will always be the *reciprocal* of the radial you are on); turn to and fly that heading, adding drift correction as necessary to keep the needle centered, and that's all there is to it.

Number two starts off the same way; when you are requested to "intercept and fly outbound on the 320 radial," make certain you have the right station tuned, and select 320 on the OBS (since you are outbound, desired course and radial are one and the same). If you're not on that heading or close to it, turn to 320 degrees, to satisfy the first condition of VOR orientation. Assuming that when you received the clearance you were already northwest of the VOR, the TO-FROM indicator should settle on FROM (located somewhere else?—keep flying on a 320 heading, you'll get a FROM sooner or later!). So far, so good; now to the heart of the problem, where are you in relation

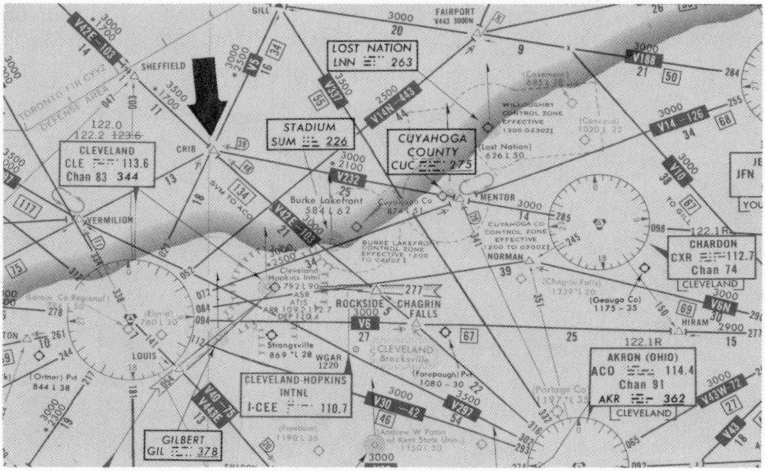

Navigational facilities forming the Crib intersection.

to the 320 radial? If the CDI centers, you're there; and since you have turned the airplane so that your heading agrees with the OBS setting, a deflection of the needle to either side will tell you which way to turn to get on course. Needle left? Fly left, and vice versa. The same procedure applies when you're cleared to fly a radial inbound (don't forget to reverse the numbers!), except the TO-FROM meter will read TO.

Situation number three comes up frequently, when you're checking groundspeed, temporarily out of radar contact, timing a holding pattern, or when asked by ATC to report at an intersection. Reporting points are usually the well-defined crossing of two or more airways or radials. Whether you're asked to report at a charted, named intersection or when crossing a certain radial, there's a technique that will work every time. For example, proceeding northwest from the Akron VOR on Victor 42E, Cleveland Center requests a report passing the Crib intersection—you have a choice of either the 027 radial of Cleveland or the Chardon 285 radial as your cross-reference (only those radials with arrows may be used). The Cleveland radial seems best, because you will be closer to that station, and the bearing will be closer to a wingtip position. When you tune and identify CLE, place the desired *radial* (027) in the OBS, and when the CDI centers, you have reached Crib intersection (maintaining the centerline of Victor 103 all the while, of course). Until you get to Crib, the needle will remain to the left of center, so here's the rule: When the "side" *radial* is set in the OBS, you have not arrived at the intersection as long as the CDI is deflected *toward the station*, or to the left in this case. (Prove it to yourself; before reaching Crib, mentally stop the airplane, turn it to a heading of 027 degrees—you'd have to fly *left* to get to that radial.) If you had tuned CLE and the needle came to rest on the side of the instrument *away* from the station (to the right), better let Center know about it right away—you've passed Crib.

And so to the fourth situation, the one you will use most frequently—figuring out the proper wind correction angle, or "bracketing the course." If you always take immediate corrective action when you notice the CDI drifting off center, you'll never get off course far enough to need bracketing; but a sharp turn over an omni, or vectors to a new radial where the wind effect is unknown, may find you chasing a CDI that's off-scale and still moving.

Assuming no knowledge of the wind direction or force, the first thing to do is turn 30 degrees toward the radial, and wait for the needle to center. For example, trying to track outbound on the 360 radial, you find yourself drifting off to the right (CDI moving left). When a heading of 330 degrees puts you back on course, you have established the maximum "bracket" within which the correct heading lies—at 360, you cannot stay on course, and 330 will take you back to the radial. Now, cut the difference in half; turn to 345 degrees, and again watch the CDI—if it stays put, 345 is the correct heading. But if the needle starts to the left again, immediately turn to 330, the heading you know will return you to course; it won't take nearly as long as the first time. Since 345 degrees has proved insufficient, take the next half-step and turn to 340 degrees; be practical, accept the nearest 5-degree increment. Before long you'll have a heading that will immobilize the CDI; this process works just as well in either direction.

This sounds like a terribly complicated, time-consuming process on paper, but in the air, it will take only a few minutes; as your experience increases, you will be able to tell roughly how much correction you'll need by observing the rate at which the CDI moves. Your target is a dead-center needle all the time—which may explain why a really good instrument pilot spends so much time checking his VOR receiver; the CDI remains so motionless, he has to make sure the set hasn't failed!

NO IDENT, NO GOOD

It stands to reason that the only stations which can be used for IFR enroute operations are those that are transmitting a usable signal. The designers provided a built-in alarm system to alert you when a VOR goes off the air, when it is shut down for maintenance, or when the signal quality drops below a certain level. It's a very simple scheme, and consists of either automatic or manual removal of the station's Morse code identifier when any of these conditions exists. So, your reaction is equally uncomplicated—whenever you tune a VOR and cannot identify it, DON'T USE IT! If an explanation of the outage isn't printed on the chart nearby, let someone in ATC know of the problem. They'll check their monitoring devices and take the appropriate action.

DISTANCE-MEASURING EQUIPMENT

If your airplane is equipped with DME, you'll probably have it turned on throughout the flight, so why not use it for identifying intersections? With the CDI centered, it's merely a matter of flying up or down the radial until the charted number of miles shows up on the DME scale. Establishing yourself at an intersection with the help of DME is valid *only* when you use a station directly ahead or directly behind—authorized DME intersections are shown on the Jeppesen charts by the letter "D" and on the government charts by an open arrowhead. (Check your legend for details.) The same ahead-or-behind limitation must be observed if you intend to derive accurate groundspeed readings from your distance measuring equipment.

VOR ACCURACY CHECKS

The odds are probably better than even that the next trip you fly IFR will be illegal, at least from a VOR receiver standpoint. Checking VORs is one of those things that almost all pilots know about, but somehow just don't take the time to accomplish at the required intervals. According to the book, you may not fly in the IFR system unless the VOR receivers have been checked for accuracy within the preceding ten days AND ten hours of flight time. Furthermore, the pilot in command is ultimately responsible for making sure this requirement has been satisfied. It matters not whether you're flying the same old airplane that you've owned for ten years, or the brand new Barnburner you rented for this one trip. You're the pilot in command, and you're the one the FAA will come looking for if they suspect an omni malfunction is involved in a mishap.

The way to stay current is to check the receivers on every flight. The system designers have made it easy for you, by putting a ground test station (VOT, in initialese) on most large airports, and designating certain spots on other fields where a nearby VOR signal can be received and used for testing. If time is running out and you are far away from either of these, there are designated airborne checkpoints—so there really is no excuse for flying with omnis that have not been checked. Look in the *Airman's Information Manual* for these facilities and checkpoints, and if all else fails, you may even designate your own airborne check—pick out a prominent landmark *on an airway* preferably 20 miles or more from the station, and get down low enough to fly directly overhead.

If all the electrons are behaving as they should, all these situations should result in a centered CDI when the OBS is placed on the appropriate number (radial or course). Should you have to turn the OBS more than 4 degrees either way to center the needle for ground checks, or more than 6 degrees either way for an airborne check, your set is out of tolerance, and IFR flight would be illegal.

Checking the VORs every time you fly is a fine habit to form, but all the effort and good intent will go for naught unless you make a permanent record of what you have done. As soon as you have checked the receivers, make a note of the date, the location, the bearing error (how much you had to rotate the OBS to make the needle come to center), and affix your signature thereto. Where you maintain this record of VOR checks is immaterial, as long as *you* know where it is, because it's one of the first things the inspectors ask for when looking into the whys and wherefores of an aircraft incident. By making *some* kind of a VOR check before *every* flight, in *every* airplane, you are effectively taking yourself off *that* hook, at least.

There is another way you can accomplish this check, but it must be placed in the last-resort category; if no other means is available within the time limits (and that's difficult to imagine—you can hardly fly ten hours anywhere in the United States and not have been *someplace* where there was a VOR checkpoint), you may legally check one receiver against the other. Tuned to the same VOR, the OBSs may not be more than 4 degrees apart with CDIs centered—but what if the first VOR is already 10 degrees off? Treat this check as something you will do only if there's no other way, and at the earliest opportunity, check the receivers properly.

9. Enroute Procedures

WHEN YOU'RE SETTLED at your assigned altitude and have the airplane trimmed for hands-off flight, when you're through with the sometimes demanding communications of the departure phase, an IFR trip becomes largely a matter of flying from one VOR to another. An occasional traffic advisory or sector handoff may be your only contact with Center; now and then you may feel like calling the Controller just to make sure he's still there. In the enroute portion, there is time to plan, check the weather ahead, and give most of your attention to flight management. On your first few flights, especially in weather all the way, you will no doubt hover over the gauges like a mother hen, but as your experience builds, you'll discover that the airplane does a very good job of flying itself. You should be more a navigator than a pilot at this point—more a manager than a manipulator. This chapter contains techniques and suggestions which should make your enroute operations less confusing, more efficient, and above all, safer. Once again, knowledge is the key—a thorough understanding of what you're doing now and what you may be doing in the miles ahead can have only one result: the making of a better instrument pilot.

FIRST, FLY THE AIRPLANE

At the head of the list is aircraft control—without it, nothing else counts. A key element is trim, and barring rough air, you should be able to set up your airplane so that it will fly for relatively long periods of time with only gentle nudges on the controls to maintain the desired altitude and heading. Most of today's aircraft are rigged so that rudder pressure is hardly required in turns, so "feet on the floor" is not at all a bad way to fly IFR; it will help you to relax on long flights when keeping your legs in one position for extended periods can cause a distracting amount of muscle fatigue. If you have invested in a wing-leveler or single-axis autopilot, by all means use it; that takes another load off your mind, and lets you devote attention to more important things.

An automatic pilot which not only maintains straight and level flight but is also equipped with various modes of heading and altitude control is your best friend on instruments. (It's even better than a co-pilot, because it won't drink your coffee or talk back!) Study the operating manual and find out what your autopilot can do and what it can't do. Use it most of the time—you're not going to increase your instrument skills a great deal by flying straight and level. At regular intervals, say, every third or fourth flight, fly the airplane manually through the departure and climbout, and make the approach yourself so you won't lose the touch. Autopilots have been known to malfunction; no superstition implied, but they always seem to fail when they're needed most!

LIKE A SCALDED DUCK

Climbing to your assigned altitude, or moving to a new, higher level when requested by ATC should be done at the best rate of climb speed for your aircraft. Your interest on the initial climb should be to get up there as rapidly as practical; out of the low-level turbulence, out of the icing layers, into clear air whenever possible. Your flight planning was no doubt based on the selection of an altitude as high as practical for you, the airplane, and the existing weather conditions, so get there as soon as you can. Cruise airspeed will inevitably be higher than that used for climb—since time is of the essence, spend as little of it as possible at low airspeed.

TRADE ALTITUDE FOR AIRSPEED

The low power, constant airspeed descent you use for the proficiency maneuvers should be reserved for your practice sessions under the hood—when descending in actual conditions, in the real world, the potential energy stored in the airplane as a result of climbing to altitude can be converted to airspeed on the way down. It will pay off in time saved, and that's the name of the game! The limitations to be observed are airspeed and "earspeed," the former a function of maximum speeds for the airplane structure, the latter concerned with the rate at which you and your passengers can clear your ears. There's absolutely nothing wrong with descending at as high an airspeed as possible, as long as you stay under the never-exceed speed, and carry enough power to keep the engines warm. (Of course, if you encounter anything more than light turbulence during the descent, you must slow down to stay out of the caution range on the airspeed indicator—corrugated wings went out with Ford Trimotors!)

Advise your passengers that "we're going to a lower altitude" —never use the phrase "we're going down"; some folks interpret this as advance warning of a crash, and will try to get out of the airplane. Remind them to keep swallowing or yawning as you descend. It's far better to put up with a grumbling passenger who resents being awakened for a descent than to have him cursing you and aviation in general for the pain in his ears the rest of the day. Most people can tolerate high rates of descent if they know what's happening and what to do about it; if you have doubts, take it easy.

Most supercharged engines have manifold-pressure limits built in, and you can come down through increasing atmospheric pressure without much concern; but normally-aspirated propeller turners are something else. Know the maximum manifold pressure for the RPM you have selected (or the limiting engine speed for fixed-pitch props) and let the pressure or RPM build up to that point, then make small throttle reductions to keep it there. You'll have longer-lasting engines, and will still be able to realize the high airspeeds that cut precious minutes from the total time. (Refer to the power chart in your aircraft handbook for maximum settings at various altitudes.)

When you have determined a comfortable rate of descent (experiment until you find the one that suits you best), divide it into the altitude that needs to be lost; this will give you the *time* required to descend. When you make an estimate of your groundspeed in the letdown, you can compute a *distance* from destination at which to request descent. In a crowded terminal area, this may be impossible because of other traffic, but plan ahead and ask—you've nothing to lose but time.

ENROUTE CHARTS MAKE GOOD FLIGHT LOGS

Your IFR route will usually be just what you requested, and maintaining a flight log is good practice; but it involves another piece of paper in the cockpit, and the most carefully-preplanned route of flight turns useless when ATC throws a change at you. Using a soft, easily-erased pencil to write your actual times of arrival and the estimates for subsequent fixes on the enroute chart puts the information you need right where you want it—in front of you, and available for quick reference. Put ATAs below the fix, ETAs above. (Mark down the times when you switch fuel tanks the same way.)

"In radar contact" is music to an instrument pilot's ears since it relieves him of any position-reporting responsibility; but it breeds a complacency that lurks in the shadows, waiting for the time when radar contact is lost, and you have to resume report-

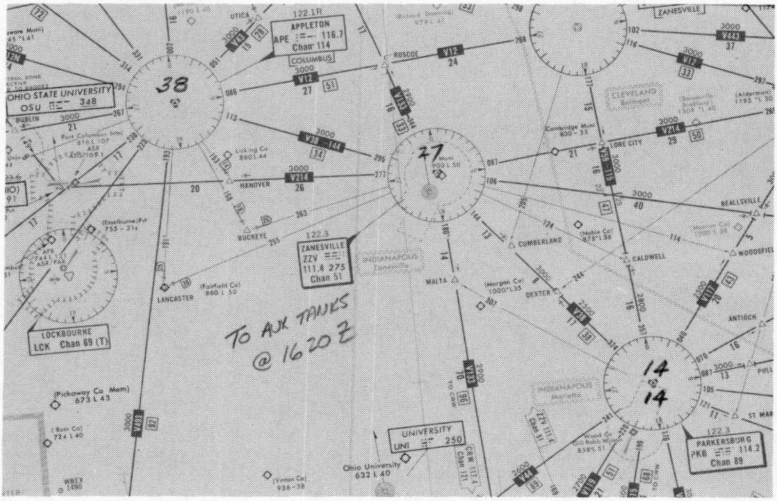

The enroute chart makes a good flight log and a handy place to keep a record of fuel management.

ing. This means figuring ETAs, keeping some kind of a log, and making all the navigational decisions yourself. Any system of aerial navigation requires that you know where you are now, where you have been, and at what rate you are moving across the ground. To forestall utter confusion, make it a habit to record the time you pass over navaids en route. When the day of reckoning arrives, at least you'll have some idea of *when* you were *where*—it's a place to start.

PILOT, KNOW THY FUEL SYSTEM!

The subject of fuel management on any flight deserves your careful attention, but it takes on greater import when you're IFR—there's not always an airport handy where you can put down to fill 'er up! Every airplane will be different in this respect, but two general rules apply to *all* flying machines: First, know what the range capabilities and fuel-burn rates are at various power settings; and second, fly by the clock—not by the indications on the fuel gauges. When you know the amount of gasoline on board at the start, and keep careful book on how much you burn, there should be no excuse for arriving at that frightening crossroads of not enough fuel for the distance you have to go. Running the tanks dry, to the point of engine stoppage, is not recommended as a continuous practice (passengers don't like to be awakened by a snorting, surging engine), but you should do it at least once for each tank under the proper conditions, keeping tab on the clock, so that you know *exactly* how long each tank will keep things going at cruise power. You may be surprised (pleasantly or unpleasantly) to discover the differences that exist between tanks; it can be twenty minutes or more on some models, and that knowledge might save your neck some day! (Chapter 6 in *Weather Flying* will add to your knowledge about fuel reserves.)

There is a plus associated with using all the fuel out of the tanks—it will keep the sumps as clean as a whistle. But remember that whatever finds its way past the fuel filter (dirt, water, bits of fuel-cell sealant) will be drawn through the engine when you try to run it on the fumes. It takes only a minute speck of dirt or a tiny crystal of ice lodged firmly in a fuel line or carburetor port or injector nozzle to shut off the power completely—you might want to limit your "dry tank" checks to conditions that will allow you to safely make like a glider.

STAND BY FOR THE LATEST CHANGE

The routing and altitude specified in your clearance are not sacred, and ATC will frequently make changes and amendments to suit the traffic situation as you proceed. It's possible that you may be asked to fly a different route, another altitude, or to hold at a designated point until a traffic conflict is resolved. You should treat any such change as a *suggestion* (just as you did when copying your clearance on the ground) and refuse *any* clearance that will fly you into trouble. This is not the sort of thing that should keep you awake at night, but remember that *you* are responsible for the safety of the flight, not the Controller. Don't be unreasonable about it, but if Center asks you to fly a route or altitude that you don't like, explain the situation to them and offer an alternative. If that doesn't work and they insist, exercise your authority and fly as you think you should to stay out of trouble—and be prepared to justify your actions. (Tell the Controller what you intend to do, of course.)

When ATC wants you to change altitude, they will let you know like this: "Barnburner 1234 Alpha, climb to and maintain eight thousand"—straightforward, right to the point. But you can almost always tell when a route change or a hold is coming your way, because the Controller will ask "Barnburner 1234 Alpha, I have an amendment to your clearance; ready to copy?" Your reply should be "stand by," which gives you time to break out the enroute chart so you can see if the upcoming change is compatible with the weather situation, terrain clearance, fuel remaining, and so on. With the chart spread out to cover the possibilities, you can tell the Controller to "go ahead with the clearance" and visualize his new routing or holding instructions to determine if you can comply.

SEE HOW THE OTHER HALF LIVES

If you haven't taken the time to visit an Air Route Traffic Control Center facility, by all means do so at your earliest convenience. In addition to gaining an appreciation of the monumental task facing the Controllers, you will also come away with a firm resolve to never again put all your eggs in one basket—you will forevermore keep a careful check on what ATC is doing with you *and* with other IFR flights in your immediate vicinity. ATC is *people*, and as such, they are subject to the human errors which have plagued us all in the past, which get us into trouble today, and which will continue to cause problems in the future.

A sharp instrument pilot knows what's going on around him. Witness a situation several years ago in which a pilot felt that Approach Control was issuing vectors to the wrong airplane; after several heading changes that just didn't seem right, he said to Approach Control "you're not sure *which* airplane you have on the scope, are you?" A long, embarrassed silence followed, as Approach Control tried to sort out its targets—everything worked out all right, but whenever you have that nagging doubt, check on it. A case of mistaken identity has no place in an IFR environment; it happens *very* infrequently; but it only takes once.

A PLACE FOR EVERYTHING

Be a good housekeeper whenever you are flying, and really work at it when you're IFR. Once beyond the terminal area, put away the SID or the area chart (put them where they belong, not on the cockpit floor!) and get out the enroute chart, folded to show the route you're flying. All the charts have information on the margins which indicates the frequencies, airway numbers, courses, and distances to on-the-next-chart facilities. When you fly off one chart, put it away and get out the next one; as you approach the terminal area, you are finished with enroute information, so put the charts back in the book, and break out the paperwork you need for the approach. Find a handy spot for your computer—perhaps the best place is on the end of a string or lanyard, with the airplane fastened to the other end—out of the way, but always in the same place when you need it. A boom mike and a control-wheel switch will pay for themselves many times over in convenience and composure. (You can buy rigs that are truly portable and can be used in any airplane you might fly.)

Your own personal short-cuts will develop as you gain experience in the IFR system—when you've done a good job of thinking ahead and staying ahead, you may find yourself with nothing to do. But when you're tempted to sit on your thumbs, look around; there's probably something that needs to be done. Recheck the fuel situation, or find out what the weather is doing up ahead, or make a correction to get the CDI on dead center. The more frequently you take inventory, the smaller your corrections and adjustments will be, and this goes a long way toward making the enroute portion of your flight smoother, more enjoyable, and safer for all concerned.

10. Communications Failure

IT DOESN'T HAPPEN very often, but when it does, complete communications failure can really loosen a pilot's psychological adhesive. If your radios are going to quit, they'll probably do it when you're fighting through a cold front, carrying an inch or two of ice, and wallowing around in moderate turbulence with a rough engine. This is no time to be digging through your flight bag, trying in vain to find the communications failure rules that you *know* are in there somewhere. You had promised yourself just last week you would review and really commit to memory those few simple regulations. And now it's happened, and you don't know what to do, you're in trouble, and there is always the chance that during your confused wanderings about, you may nail an innocent victim of your procrastination and lack of good sense. The point of all this should be unmistakable: Don't put it off, but learn (or maybe relearn) the rules that govern your actions when you lose communications.

Instrument pilots should toss a very large bouquet to the regulation-writers at this point, for the communications failure procedures are clearly spelled out, with no room for error or misinterpretation. Wizards those who laid down this part of the aviation regulations. An obvious pattern of common sense is woven throughout this section of the rules; you will find that they *require* you to perform as you would instinctively, given the considerations of your safety and the well-being of other pilots sharing the airspace with you.

These rules are rather discriminating—they apply only to a failure of *communications*; when you can neither transmit nor receive on any radio, you have suffered a bona fide communications failure, and the rules spell out exactly what is to be done. If everything goes (no communications, no navigation), it's an entirely different ball game, and sorry to break the news to you, but there are no rules for this situation. You're on your own, heaven help you, break out the common sense and good luck, and here's hoping you know which way to VFR. Should ATC suspect that you have suffered radio failure, they will try to contact you on several possible communications channels; for example, the first place they will try to get through is the VOR that they figure you are using for navigation at the time. So, if you think the communications radios may have departed for some electronic Valhalla, turn up the audio side of the VOR receiver, and listen—there may be enough power left for you to hear someone trying to help you. Of course, if you can hear, common sense tells you to listen, and do what you're told.

Here's where a transponder can be worth its weight in gold (a literal statement, if it saves you and the airplane!). Suppose you have one enervated receiver weakly informing you of ATC's efforts to make contact following loss of your transmitter. "Barnburner 1234 Alpha, if you read me, squawk IDENT," which you do, and then hear this: "Roger, Barnburner 1234 Alpha, radar contact, turn right heading one eight zero for radar vectors to a surveillance approach at Outhouse Municipal Airport." And you would do just what he says—as long as the transponder and one receiver hold up, you've got it made; you're communicating.

There are other radio facilities on which ATC will attempt contact when your transmitter goes out, and they include Localizers, Outer Compass Locators, some NDBs, and any other navaid they think you might be able to receive. You should know that any navigational aid shown on an IFR chart (enroute, area, or approach) can carry voice signals unless the frequency is *underlined*. The essence of all this is that you should try anything you can think of when you suspect a radio failure—reset circuit breakers, check fuses, kick the panel, listen on any set available. You might even put the relief tube to your ear. If you are completely unable to establish any type of communications, don't panic, because the rules will see you safely out of your predicament.

OUT OF THE CLOUDS, OUT OF TROUBLE

The first rule was written in recognition of the undeniable fact that breaking out into VFR conditions will go a long way toward solving your communications loss problem. If it happens in VFR, or if you fly into VFR conditions, it makes good sense to *stay* VFR, land as soon as practical, and let ATC know what you have done. Emphasis on that phrase "land as soon as practical" —the terrain over which you are operating has a lot to do with your decision, and as always, safe operation must be placed before anything else. If the VFR into which you have flown is a hole in the clouds with Pike's Peak sticking up in the middle, you might do well to keep right on flying.

But how about the situation when you are in IFR conditions, it's down to minimums all the way home, and as you prepare to acknowledge a clearance, the microphone falls apart in your hand? At the same time, you are hit on the head by the speaker as it falls out of the cabin roof. Friend, you have just lost communications! That reassuring voice from Center, your electronic umbilical cord to Mother Earth, has been cruelly severed, and you are on your own. What to do now? The answer is so simple: Just follow the rules. When the Controller suspects after several unanswered calls that you are experiencing Marconian distress (don't forget that you should announce your problem to radar sets far and wide by squawking 7600 on your ever-faithful transponder), he is bound by the *same set of rules* to clear out some airspace for you. It's obvious that he needs to know what route you'll be flying and how far you will continue, and at what altitude. The only way to accomplish safe separation in the absence of communications is for both parties, you and ATC, to operate under a set of common and inviolate conditions—that's why *every* IFR pilot MUST know the radio failure rules inside out before he ventures into the murky mists.

It's easiest to break the problem into its basic parts; when you're IFR sans communications, you will have to decide

1. How far you can go.
2. What route you should fly.
3. How high you should fly.

These three questions and their answers will provide the guidance that will get you safely out of trouble; the problem is whittled down to manageable dimensions with these solid guidelines. One at a time, then.

HOW FAR CAN YOU GO?

The first question has a most uncomplicated answer: Unless you get lucky and fly into some VFR, you're going to go all the way to the destination airport for which you filed! If your clearance at the start of the trip (or a later amendment) specified the destination airport as the clearance limit, just keep right on going; you are still cleared all the way. But suppose you accepted a short-range clearance so you could get started, and now the radios have quit short of that point. No big problem, as long as you were provided an Expect Further Clearance time. What has just happened to you is the only reason for these times being issued by ATC; in the event of a communication breakdown, the EFC is set far enough ahead to give the Controller time to clear out the airspace so you can continue on your way. This leads directly into the next phase of the procedure: You will remain at the clearance limit fix (holding in a standard pattern on the course on which you approached the fix, unless there is a holding pattern depicted on the chart) until the Expect Further Clearance time rolls around, then proceed.

There is another type of "radio failure" time issued by ATC, and it is an Expect *Approach* Clearance time, used in terminal areas to provide an envelope of protection in the event of communications loss while you are holding for an approach at destination. The same rules and philosophy apply; if communications fail, stay in the assigned holding pattern until the EAC comes up, then proceed with the published approach procedure. It should be unequivocally clear by now that any IFR pilot who accepts a "hold" without getting an EFC or EAC leaves himself wide open for a real problem. If ATC doesn't issue a time (and they very, very seldom miss on this one—it's as much for their protection as yours), DEMAND one; you're well within your rights. Picture the bewilderment on the ground and in the cockpit when the radios go out and no further clearance time has been provided; they don't know what you don't know they don't know, and it's a scramble to get everybody out of the way on all the possible routes you might take at any time.

So you were cleared all the way to destination, with no clearance limits, and the radios gave up the ghost soon after takeoff? In this situation, you will proceed to destination and hold at the appropriate altitude until your estimated time of arrival, based on the time enroute you put in your flight plan and your takeoff time, which, of course, you have forgotten. During a period of mental stress such as you will surely be experiencing following a radio failure, it may become very difficult to remember your own name, let alone what time you took off! Here's where you will be forever grateful for having formed a most useful habit—just before takeoff (before *every* takeoff, so you do it without thinking), set the red hands on your instrument panel clock, or on that 3-inch diameter, two-hundred-dollar wristwatch that does

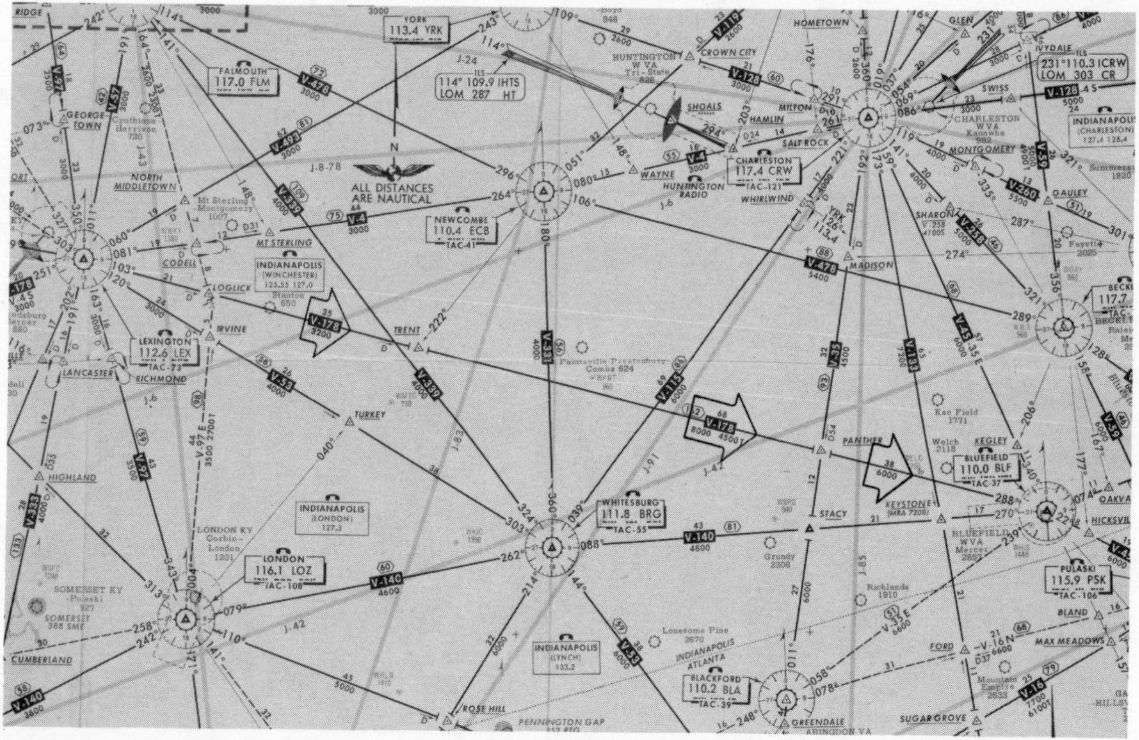

Airways and navigation facilities between Lexington, Kentucky, and Bluefield, West Virginia.

everything but compute your income tax, or write it down somewhere, but record the takeoff time. Obviously, it is also nice to remember the time enroute you filed in your flight plan.

WHAT ROUTE SHOULD YOU FLY?

The first part of the communications rule directs you to continue to your destination, respecting any holds or clearance limits along the way; now you are faced with the question of what route to fly. Equally sensible, this part of the problem is solved in one of three possible ways: You will fly via the last assigned route, or the route ATC advised you might expect in a further clearance, or in the absence of the preceding two, the route you filed in your flight plan.

To illustrate, suppose you plan a trip from Lexington, Kentucky, to Bluefield, West Virginia. Your flight plan requests Victor 178 to Bluefield, and your clearance comes through "as filed." If radio failure occurs anywhere along the route, you will continue on Victor 178 to the BLF VOR. So much for the first situation.

In the second case (same route, same clearance), you have just passed Loglick intersection when Indianapolis Center comes up with this little gem: "Barnburner 1234 Alpha, you are now cleared to the Trent intersection, maintain 7,000, and expect further clearance at 46 via direct Whitesburg, Victor 140 Bluefield, over." A couple of minutes after acknowledging this clearance, your radios give up. Combining your knowledge of the first two communications failure rules, you will hold at Trent until forty-six minutes past the hour, then proceed to Bluefield via direct Whitesburg and Victor 140—that's the clearance ATC advised you might expect, so it takes precedence.

Back up one more time, and copy the following clearance on the ground at Lexington: "Barnburner 1234 Alpha is cleared to the Trent intersection via radar vectors to Victor 178, climb to and maintain 7,000, and expect further clearance at 28, over." The implication is that your flight cannot be cleared all the way to Bluefield at this time, but ATC is willing to get you started with a clearance as far as Trent intersection, with the rest of the routing to follow. You accept, and as soon as Departure Control has vectored you onto Victor 178 10 miles from Loglick, the radios die. Proceed to Trent, hold until 28, then continue down Victor 178; in the absence of an assigned routing, without even a routing to *expect*, you'll fly just as you requested when you filed your flight plan.

ATC will frequently direct you around other traffic, or thunderstorms, or if they're not particularly busy, they will sometimes vector you right to your home drome. Should radio failure rear its ugly head at this point in an IFR flight, you will proceed direct to the fix to which you were being vectored (using your own navigational skills, of course). Good judgment once again prevails, as it would seem rather stupid to turn and fly into a thunderstorm in order to go direct to the next VOR, according to the rule; if you were advised of a storm cell 10 miles wide straight ahead, then were given vectors around it, common sense would dictate continuing the vector until you are reasonably certain you are past the storm. Don't ever let *anything* or *anybody* force you to fly through a thunderstorm. And don't worry about traffic separation if you wisely elect to continue around the storm after the radios stop radioing—you had to be in radar contact to get the vector in the first place, and the Controller would probably breathe a sigh of relief, watching you exhibit some "smarts."

In summary, you will fly one of these three routes when the thread of communication snaps (they are listed in order of precedence):

1. The route you have been assigned as part of a clearance.
2. The route that ATC advised you might *expect* in a further clearance.
3. As a last resort, the route you filed in your flight plan.

(When radar vectored, proceed direct to the fix to which you were being vectored.)

HOW HIGH?

Only one more question needs an answer to solve this three-dimensional problem of what to do when you realize you're talking to yourself, and that's the one regarding altitude. Your safety is the big concern here, and so the rules require you to fly at the highest, therefore the safest, of these altitudes:

1. The last assigned altitude.
2. The altitude ATC has advised you may expect in a further clearance.
3. The Minimum Enroute Altitude (MEA) for the particular airway segment in which you are operating.

To illustrate, consider the same Lexington-Bluefield trip; you are cleared "to the Bluefield Airport via Victor 178, climb to and maintain 9,000." If radio failure happens anywhere along this route, you will remain at 9,000 until reaching Bluefield (notice that there are no higher MEAs on this route), hold until your ETA, and make the approach. You are obliged to stay at 9,000 until your time runs out, then descend in the holding pattern prior to executing the approach. (By the way, in a situation like this, the approach you use is entirely up to you—anything published is legal.)

Had you requested 9,000 but ATC was unable to grant it in time for your takeoff, they might have cleared you "to the Trent intersection, climb to 4,000, expect 9,000 after Trent, expect further clearance at 36." You leap off the ground, climb to 4,000, and lose the radios before you reach Trent intersection. Hold there until 36 minutes past the hour, depart Trent climbing to 9,000, and maintain that altitude all the way to Bluefield. Again, you're above all the MEAs on the airway, and since you had been advised to expect 9,000 feet after Trent, that's the altitude you fly.

But maybe the airways are so congested that Center can only clear you to Loglick intersection at 4,000, gives you just an EFC time, and makes no promise of the necessary higher altitude at that time. Your task (after holding at Loglick until the appropriate time) is to determine if there are any MEAs *higher* than your last assigned altitude of 4,000. Sure enough, there are, and it is obvious that you will need to climb to 8,000 feet for the segment between Trent and Panther, then descend to 6,000 for the final segment into BLF.

You are expected to fly altitudes *as published* on the enroute chart when they apply; for example, in the absence of an assigned altitude, you would fly at 3,200 feet from LEX to the Trent intersection. East-odd, west-even, and the "nearest thousand" don't count here—fly 'em like you see 'em!

Summing it up, your determination of what altitude to fly is rather simple; it's the last assigned altitude or the MEA, *whichever is higher*. If ATC has advised you to expect a higher altitude en route, that's the one that applies. Whenever a route segment calls for an MEA higher than anything you have been assigned or advised to expect, climb to the high MEA over the fix that begins that segment, and descend to the previous highest altitude over the fix that terminates the segment. Airway segments are indicated by the little T-bars on the airway, every enroute VOR being automatically the beginning and end of a segment. In substance, when you see a T-bar or an omni on the airway, look for a change in MEA.

When dealing with a communications failure situation, pilots and Controllers must operate with mutual understanding of the regulations, and there's one more area in which the two parties must agree: You must not comply with the conditions of a clearance unless you are reasonably certain that ATC has received your acknowledgement. When radio failure occurs in IFR conditions, you'd best upgrade that certainty from "reasonably" to "absolutely." If you have any doubt that the man on the ground received your "roger" or your readback, proceed as if you had never heard his instructions—a clearance is considered valid only when it is acknowledged.

Here are the regulations in capsule form—when you lose two-way radio communications while in IFR conditions, you *will*:

1. Maintain VFR and land as soon as practical if the failure occurs in VFR conditions, or if VFR is encountered after the failure. (This rule is to be salted heavily with common sense and judgment.)
2. ROUTE—Continue to your destination on the last assigned route OR a route ATC has advised you may expect OR the route filed in your flight plan. On a radar vector, proceed direct to the fix.
3. DISTANCE—Proceed to the clearance limit, hold at the appropriate fix until the EFC or EAC time, then continue on your route. If the clearance limit is the destination airport, hold AT ALTITUDE until your ETA, based on takeoff time plus ETE.
4. ALTITUDE—Maintain the last assigned altitude OR the MEA, whichever is higher, OR at the prescribed fix, climb to the altitude ATC has advised you to expect. If subsequent MEAs are higher than assigned or expected altitude, climb to the higher MEA for the particular airway segment, then descend to the former highest altitude.

These rules work—don't expect to be treated like a hero at the completion of a radio-out IFR flight, because ATC knows what you will do, and makes the proper traffic adjustments ahead of you. But the rules work only if all concerned have these rules firmly established in their minds, and know how to employ them. You can bet that every traffic Controller has a bound volume of the regulations and procedures within arm's reach; but they're not always that handy in an airplane. Take time now and at frequent intervals to memorize and refresh your understanding of the communications failure procedures; when it happens, it's too late to learn.

11. Holding Patterns

"THIS IS MERCURY CONTROL; we are at 'T' minus 30 minutes and holding." Remember the voice of Colonel Shorty Powers, announcing a hitch in one of the early orbital flight schedules and enriching the public vocabulary with a space-age connotation of the word "hold"? It's about time the astronauts caught up, because holding has been with us in instrument flying for years, as an orderly way of suspending the progress of an instrument flight, either en route or in a terminal area. Since most aircraft depend on forward movement to keep from falling out of the sky, holding really becomes a matter of flying around in circles, but not going past a predetermined point. The reasons for holding are numerous, and sometimes apparently known only to heaven and ATC. But it provides an effective, if frustrating, way to "stop" the flow of IFR flights in the face of a traffic conflict, or to slow things down when terminal operations begin to exceed the capabilities of the system.

Being cleared to hold sooner or later is just as inevitable as automatic rough over the mountains at night, and with big brother watching on radar, you'd best know what you're about! In B.R. (Before Radar) days, you could enter and fly a holding pattern any way you pleased, as long as you stayed within the airspace limits; but on the very first day the radar sets were plugged in, Controllers observed a succession of pilots entering holding patterns, and were overwhelmed by the serpentine tracings of their entry procedures. So overwhelmed, in fact, that they were moved to call them "small intestine entries." This led to the development of the three ways you may enter a holding pattern today.

There are basically two situations in which ATC will require a flight to hold: one during the enroute portion of a trip, the other in the terminal area, in which case you will be holding in anticipation of an instrument approach to the airport. The rules are the same for both—they differ only in the procedures you use in the event of communications failure.

No matter where or when you are instructed to hold, there is a two-step method you must use to do the job properly. Step #1, decide where the "racetrack" pattern will be located in accordance with the instructions you have received (you can do this mentally, or actually draw it on the chart). Step #2, based on the direction from which you are approaching the holding fix, determine which of the three approved entry procedures you will use.

Every holding clearance must include either specifically or by implication these four components: a *holding fix*, the *direction to hold*, the *type of pattern* (standard or non-standard), and a time to *expect further clearance*. Each part of the holding instructions should be considered in turn.

THE HOLDING FIX

ATC can clear you to hold just about any place they want to, but the holding fix will always be one you can locate electronically; it could be a VOR, an NDB, an intersection, a DME fix. Most enroute holds will be at intersections or VORs along the airway, and terminal holding fixes are usually set up so that you will be in position to commence the approach when it's your turn.

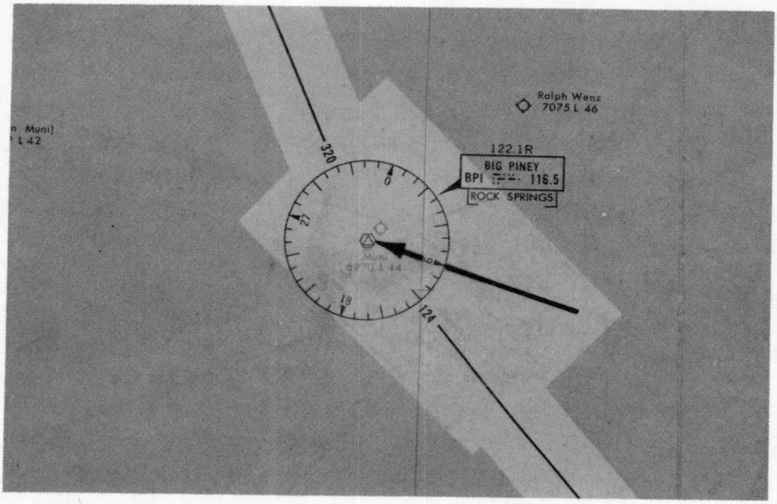

The holding course always lies in the direction you were cleared to hold.

DIRECTION TO HOLD

Before attempting to unravel the mysteries of "which way to hold," you must understand what is meant by the holding course. For example, the Big Piney VOR has been designated the holding fix, and you are cleared to hold EAST of the VOR (in the absence of more specific instructions, this means you are to hold on the 090 radial). Fundamental to solving the problem is the knowledge that the *holding course* lies EAST of the fix. Remember that the *holding course* always lies in the direction you have been cleared to hold, and once in the pattern, you will fly inbound to the *holding fix* on the *holding course*, every time you come around the racetrack.

TYPE OF PATTERN

With the holding fix, the holding course, and the direction to hold firmly established, determine the type of holding pattern to be flown—either standard or non-standard. For the time being,

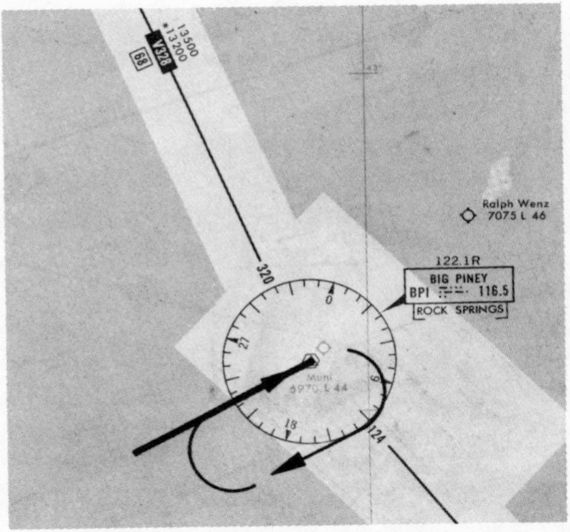

Standard (right turns) holding pattern southwest of Big Piney VOR.

consider right turns standard, and left turns non-standard. If the Controller doesn't mention the direction he wants you to turn, he expects you to execute a standard pattern, with right-hand turns. To complete Step #1, just "fly" your pencil inbound to the holding fix on the holding course, and turn in the appropriate direction. For example, to hold southwest of the Big Piney VOR in a standard pattern, find the holding fix and establish the holding course, "fly" inbound to the VOR on the holding course and turn right. Proceed one minute outbound, turn right again, and when you arrive over the VOR, you've completed one circuit of this particular holding pattern. If the Controller clears you for left-hand turns, fly inbound on the same holding course, and turn left—you're still *holding* southwest of Big Piney.

WHICH ENTRY TO USE?

So much for Step #1, establishing the holding pattern—now Step #2, deciding which of the three approved entries you will use. Fortunately, the one used most often is the easiest to ac-

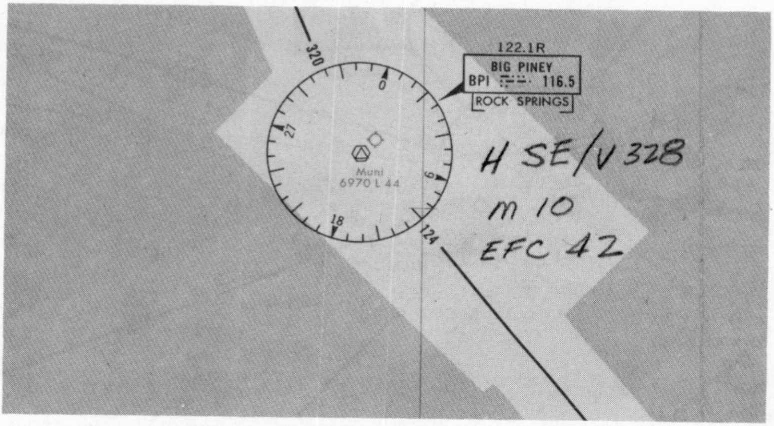

Copy your holding clearance right on the enroute chart.

complish. Suppose you are flying northwest at 10,000 feet on Victor 328 and are given this clearance: "Barnburner 1234 Alpha, hold southeast of Big Piney on Victor 328, maintain one zero thousand, expect further clearance at four two." If you want to copy the important numbers, do it right on the chart, and you'll have a permanent record of the clearance. The next thing to do is to break the clearance into its component parts:

1. The holding *fix* is the Big Piney VOR.
2. The holding *course* is Victor 328.
3. Since you will hold southeast of Big Piney on ictor 328, the holding *course* will lie southeast of the VOR on the 124 radial.
4. Absence of instructions to turn left or right implies a standard (right turns) pattern.
5. You will continue to fly at 10,000 feet while holding.
6. You should expect to be in the holding pattern until 42 minutes after the hour.

Now go ahead with Step #1, establishing the pattern. Draw (or imagine) the holding course southeast of Big Piney on Victor

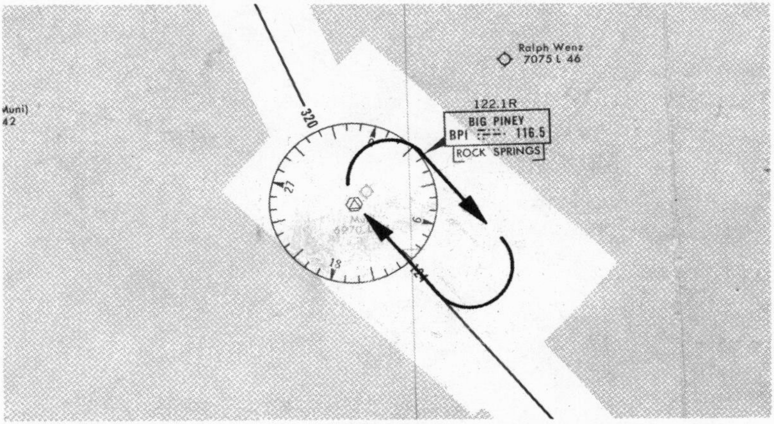

Holding in a standard pattern southeast of Big Piney VOR on Victor 328.

328, fly your pencil inbound to the fix on the holding course, turn right to 124 degrees, and you have the proper racetrack all set up—you're holding southeast of Big Piney on Victor 328.

THE DIRECT ENTRY

When you fly to the fix and turn to the outbound heading, you have accomplished a "direct" entry, which is always used when you approach the holding fix *on* the holding course. As a matter of fact, your approach heading can be somewhat off the holding course and the direct entry is still the proper one to use. If you will draw a line that lies 70 degrees from the holding course, then extend it beyond the fix, a direct entry is called for any time your heading puts you in the shaded half-circle. As soon as you pass the VOR, turn right to 124 degrees, and you have entered the holding pattern. That 70-degree line is the key to determining your entry procedure. It must always be drawn (or imag-

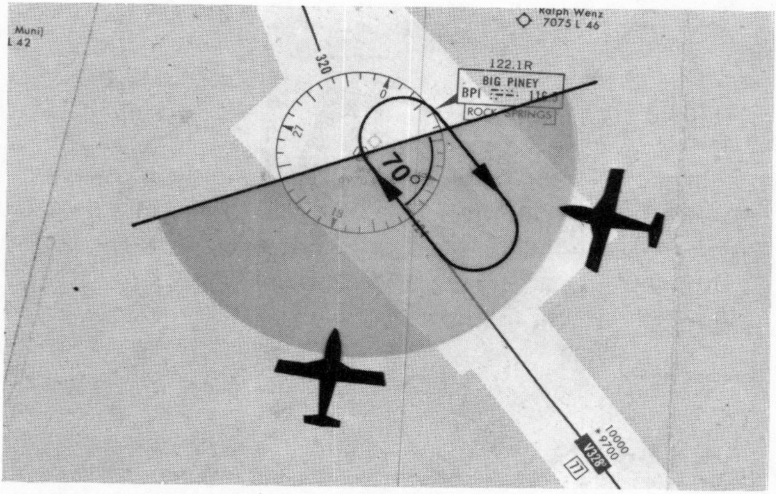

Approaching the holding fix on any heading within the shaded half-circle calls for a direct entry.

ined) so that it cuts across the racetrack, which you established in Step #1.

THE TEARDROP ENTRY

Keep the same holding instructions in mind (hold southeast of Big Piney VOR on Victor 328), but this time you are approaching from the west, on a heading of 080 degrees. Set up the racetrack again, draw the 70-degree line, and extend it through the fix. While you're at it, extend the holding course through the fix as well, which divides the unshaded half of the circle into two quadrants. The smaller of the two is of concern now, since you are approaching the fix on a heading that lies within that quadrant. When you reach the fix, a right turn to the outbound heading (124 degrees) would put you very close to the holding course, but going the wrong direction—so a procedure has been designed to get you into the holding pattern quickly, and well

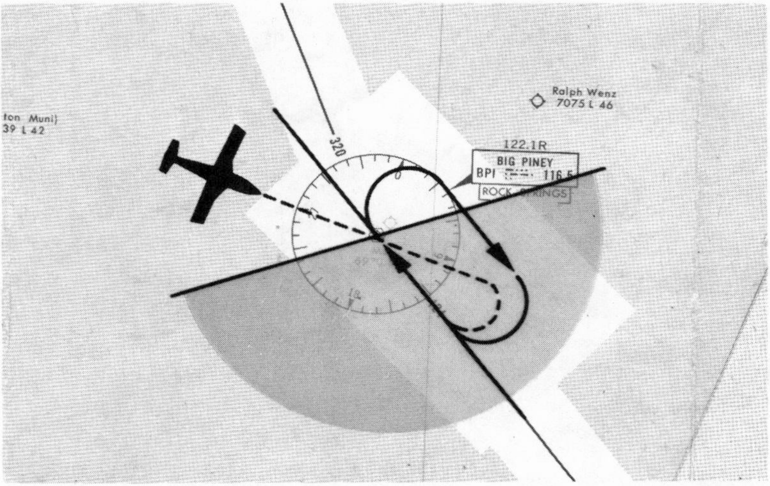

The teardrop entry is used whenever you are inbound in the smallest sector—turn no more than 30 degrees from the holding course.

within the limits of the airspace set aside for you. In this entry, turn to a heading no more than 30 degrees from the holding course (which in this case would be a heading of 094 degrees), fly for one minute, turn right again until you intercept the holding course, and return to the fix. (Don't forget to reset the OBS to 304.) This is the "teardrop" entry, the name coming from the flight path you describe.

THE PARALLEL ENTRY

The third entry is used when approaching the fix on a heading which lies in the larger of the two unshaded quadrants, and is called the "parallel" entry. Suppose you have received the same holding instructions, but you are approaching Big Piney from the north, heading 180 degrees. A parallel entry is called for, and here's how you do it: When you reach the fix, turn to the heading which *parallels* the holding course (in this example, a head-

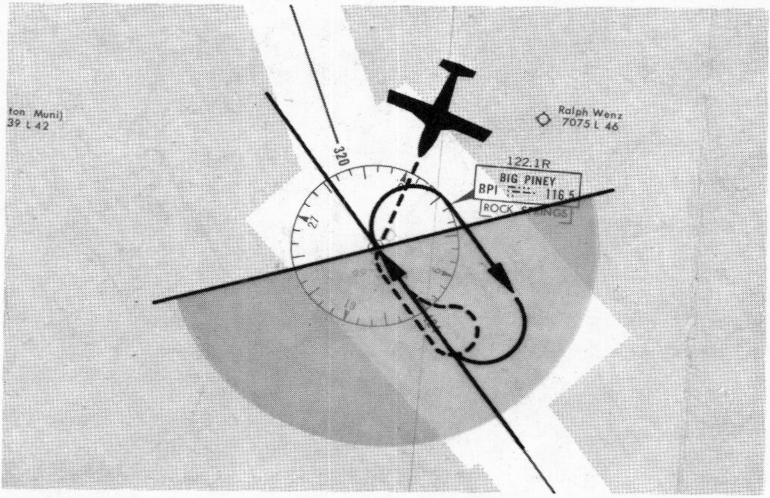

The parallel entry works when neither teardrop nor direct entry procedures apply. On station passage, turn immediately to the reciprocal of the holding course.

ing of 124 degrees), fly for one minute, then turn *left* until intercepting the holding course, or until you reach the fix, whichever happens first. A stiff tail wind as you turn inbound will often push you direct to the fix before you intercept the holding course.

HOLDING PATTERN LIMITS

When you are cleared to hold, the Controller assigns you a block of airspace large enough to separate you from other IFR traffic during your entry and subsequent pattern maneuvers. Airspeed limits are placed in the regulations to guarantee that aircraft entering a holding pattern would not go swooping past the airspace boundaries set up for them. For propeller-driven planes, the maximum speed is 175 knots indicated, and you must slow to this speed (or less) *within three minutes prior to crossing the holding fix.* Even with a strong tail wind, this maximum airspeed will see you safely through the entry and the holding pattern.

If your bird gets its "go-power" from a turbojet or two or more, you may increase the maximum speed: 200 knots up to 6,000 feet, 210 knots between 6,000 and 14,000 feet, and 230 knots above 14,000 feet (all indicated airspeeds, of course). In any event, be at or below the maximum holding speed before arrival at the fix.

There is one more variable in this airspace guarantee, and that is angle of bank. If all aircraft observe the maximum holding airspeeds, the lateral displacement during turns will depend on how rapidly those turns are accomplished. Therefore, during the entry and while holding, you should turn at either 3 degrees per second (a standard-rate turn), 30 degrees of bank, or if you are using a flight-director system, 25 degrees of bank, whichever requires the smallest bank angle. It's easy to figure out why this rule had to be, when you consider the direct relationship between true airspeed and the angle of bank needed to generate a standard-rate turn. You can approximate the bank angle by this rule-of-thumb: Divide the true airspeed (in knots) by ten, add five, and you're pretty close to the necessary bank. Applying this to an actual situation, a jet-liner flying at 600 knots TAS would have to be racked into a 65-degree bank to turn at standard rate. The airplanes can take it, but stewardesses complained—American industry builds 2g airplanes, but not 2g bras!

IT'S "FOUR T" TIME AGAIN

Approaching Big Piney VOR and with the Barnburner slowed appropriately, the CDI will begin to dance a bit, the TO-FROM indicator starts its reversal, and when it shows FROM, two things occur simultaneously: You have arrived at the holding fix, and for reporting purposes, *you are in the holding pattern.* Note the TIME as you pass the holding fix, TURN to the outbound heading, THROTTLE back to holding airspeed, and after all this is done, TALK—you owe ATC a report of the time and altitude entering the holding pattern. There's no need to rush this report to the Controller, since you're doing exactly what he expects you to, but when you are established on the outbound heading, slowed down, and everything is under control, report: "Salt Lake Center, Barnburner 1234 Alpha, Big Piney at three two [time you first crossed the fix], holding at one zero thousand." If you have been advised "in radar contact," forget the report—make it *Three* T's, since the Controller will observe your entry on radar.

Why slow down in the holding pattern? Because you're going to be flying around in circles for a while, and it's just not good sense to burn up more gas than necessary. Next time you're under the hood, try several power combinations and determine a comfortable holding airspeed for your airplane—make it a trade-off between ease of handling and economy.

In the time it has taken to read this, you will have turned outbound and accomplished all Three or Four T's, so in the piece of a minute you have left before turning inbound, rotate the OBS to the holding course (304 degrees), and you are ready to turn inbound to the holding fix.

Executing standard-rate turns during the teardrop and direct entry maneuvers in a no-wind situation should put you on the holding course when you roll out of the turn toward the station. The parallel entry sets you up for a 45-degree "cut" on the inbound course, which means you will fly on this heading until the holding course is intercepted. But the gods who rule the atmosphere have seldom been known to bless pilots in holding patterns with calm winds, and the disorientation caused by zephyrian displacement can be total. An excellent clue to your position and the wind factor you're fighting shows up during the turn inbound, when your heading is 45 degrees from the holding course. (In the example, 259 degrees.) If at this point the CDI has not begun to move from its full LEFT position, *stop the turn* and hold 259 degrees until it *does* begin to move. There is obviously a westerly component to the wind, and it has drifted you east while flying the outbound leg. Should the CDI start sliding toward center while you're turning through 259 degrees, *keep turning* and you'll roll out on course. Movement of the CDI *earlier* than the 45-degree point in the turn is a signal to *increase the rate of turn* (30 degrees of bank is *plenty*) and prepare to correct for an easterly wind.

You can formulate three situations and their solutions at the 45-degree point of the inbound turn. (The OBS must always be set on the inbound or holding course, which will cause the CDI to always be displaced toward the holding course.)

SITUATION (at the 45-degree point)	SOLUTION
CDI has not moved from full left or full right (depends on direction of turn)	Roll out, fly this "45-degree" heading until CDI centers
CDI starting to move toward center	Continue turn, you should roll out on course
CDI already centered, or well on its way	Increase bank to 30 degrees, prepare to apply correction to get back on course

TIMING THE HOLDING PATTERN

You are now on the threshold of the most important phase of holding pattern timing—the rules call for an inbound leg length (on the holding course) of one minute below 14,000 feet, and one and a half minutes from 14,000 up. You are given complete freedom to adjust your timing on the outbound leg so that the inbound requirement is satisfied. The moment the CDI centers on the inbound course (or when you complete the turn), start your timer and note carefully how long it takes to return to the holding fix. If it turns out to be exactly one minute, you've done it—you have hit that one-in-a-million combination of perfectly executed turns and absolutely calm winds. But suppose a minute and a half slips by before you arrive back over the VOR? You have encountered some tail wind as you flew outbound, and it's cut-and-try from here on. When you start outbound the next time, fly for only thirty seconds, head for the holding fix, and check the inbound time again; it should come out very close to one minute. There will be times when the outbound leg will be only ten, maybe twenty, seconds long; when the wind is *really* blowing, you may find yourself doing a 360 over the fix to keep the inbound leg at the proper length. On the other hand, you might have to fly outbound for two or three minutes, depending on the wind direction and force.

Once established in a holding pattern, your only concern with respect to timing is to make certain you're on that holding course *inbound* for one minute (or ninety seconds, depending on altitude)—no more, no less. Therefore you must know where to punch the stopwatch as you turn outbound. The solution is simple: Start timing when you are abeam (directly opposite) the holding fix.

WHERE IS ABEAM?

There are several holding situations which require different methods of determining when you are in that abeam position; the easiest is holding on a VOR, where the timing point is the TO-FROM reversal. Next in order of simplicity is a "square" intersection (VOR radials or a radial-ADF bearing combination crossing at or near a 90-degree angle), where you start the watch upon centering the side radial, or attaining the proper relative bearing. When the references are not close to "square," you must begin timing when you complete the turn to the outbound heading. This is also the best procedure when holding on an NDB; start timing when the outbound turn is completed.

It will likely require several circuits to nail down the exact

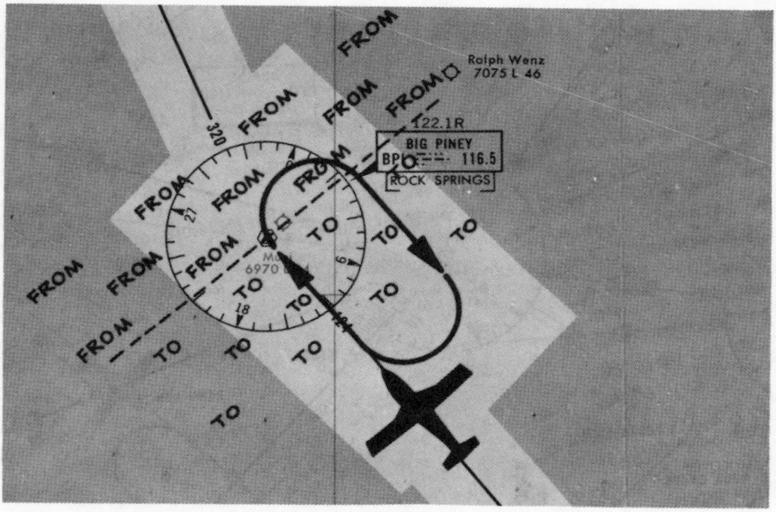

With OBS set properly, the TO-FROM indicator provides a good timing device in the holding pattern.

timing, so continue experimenting until you arrive at an outbound leg length which results in exactly one minute on the holding course.

DRIFT CORRECTION

A technique called "double drift" is an effective way to compensate for wind while going 'round and 'round in a holding pattern. When you have found a heading that will keep you on the holding course, correct *twice* that amount into the wind as you go outbound. Your pattern will look like this on radar, but you will intercept the holding course handily, and you'll stay safely within the airspace reserved for you. Combine good drift correction with proper timing, and your holding patterns will be just what the doctor (ATC) ordered.

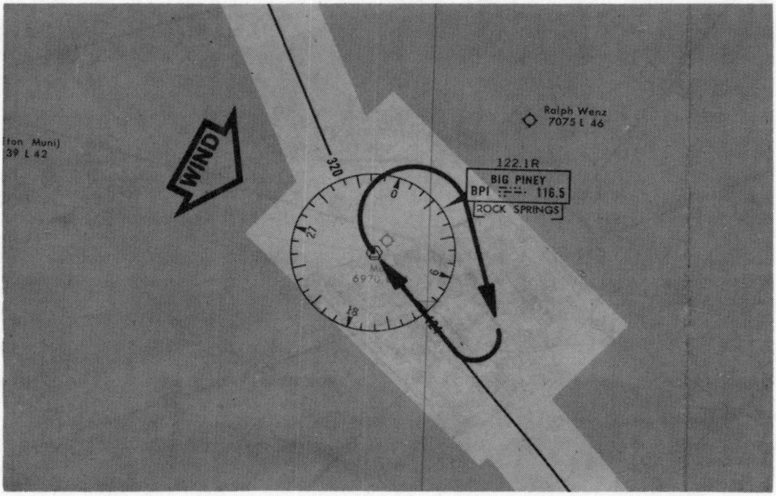

This is the track described by a holding aircraft using double drift to correct for wind.

HOW LONG TO HOLD?

The final portion of any holding clearance will consist of the time at which you can *expect further clearance* or *expect approach clearance*, en route or in the terminal area, respectively. Don't *ever* accept an interruption (a hold) in an IFR flight unless you receive one of these expected times; if a Controller forgets it, ask him—nay, DEMAND it! You will seldom have to hold until this time, since it is purposely set far enough ahead to provide a clear route for you if your radios quit. (See Chapter 10, "Communications Failure," for details.) However, you should plan to arrive over the holding fix (or at least be inbound to the fix) when the EFC or EAC time comes up on the clock. It is perfectly legal, and often necessary, to shorten the racetrack to do this. Bear in mind that a no-wind holding pattern (below 14,000 feet) consumes four minutes per circuit, so it is a matter of shortening the outbound leg to accomplish station passage at the proper time. Make a complete turn over the fix if your EFC/EAC is only two minutes away when you cross the fix, and be ready to go about your business on time.

Use the sometimes interminable minutes in an extended hold to listen to what's happening ahead of you. By paying attention to ATC's instructions to others in the holding pattern, you can get a good idea of whether you'll be cleared on your way or be held still longer. If your EFC or EAC is close (five minutes) and no word is forthcoming from ATC, give them a call and find out what to expect—you have a right to know, since continued holding doesn't improve your fuel situation even a little bit. You may want to divert to some less crowded route or terminal. *Any* hold should cause you to take a critical look at your fuel supply, and decide how much of what you have on board would be needed to fly out of trouble; remember that *you*, not the Controller, are responsible for not running out of gas.

An extended holding situation is a nuisance, a wearying exercise in making circles and going expensively nowhere; but sometimes it's unavoidable. When it appears that you're going to hold for a good long while and you tire of going 'round and 'round every four minutes, you might consider requesting a non-standard, longer-legged pattern of your own. This could be done by asking for two- or three-minute legs, or by using a convenient DME fix to stretch things out a bit. If it can be done safely, ATC will usually go along with you.

HOLDING WITH DME

"Barnburner 1234 Alpha is cleared to hold northeast of the Jack's Creek VOR, eight mile legs, maintain one three thousand, expect further clearance at one seven." This is the easiest holding pattern of all, because a DME reading replaces timing. Fly to the VOR, enter the pattern, and fly outbound until the DME reads 8; return to the holding course, fly back to the VOR, and do it all over again. It may require a bit more attention to drift correc-

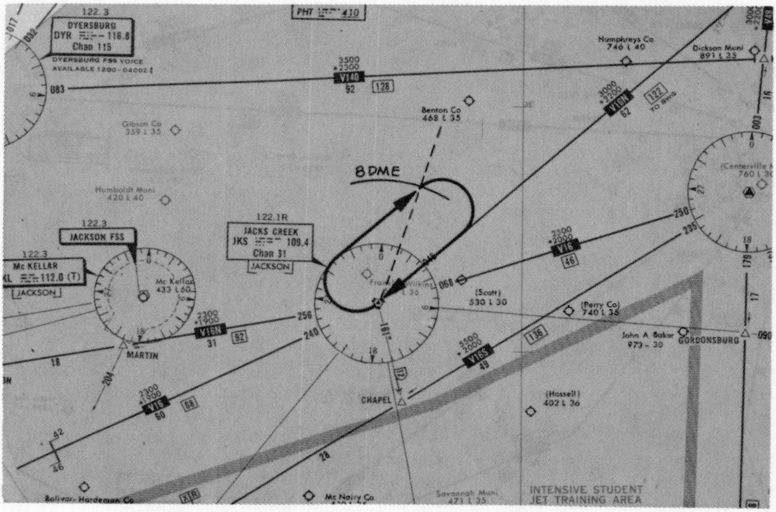

Cleared to hold northeast of JKS, 8-mile legs.

tion, since you are not basing your pattern on time, and the "double-drift" method doesn't always work; but the end of the outbound leg is very clearly indicated (8 miles northeast of the VOR), and you won't have to worry about timing.

DEPICTED HOLDING PATTERNS

On occasion, the nice folks who figure out the whys and wherefores of instrument enroute charts eliminate Step #1 of the holding pattern procedure, by depicting the racetrack for you. Published holding patterns will be found at intersections frequently used for these "IFR merry-go-rounds." They ease the workload of Controllers and pilots, because detailed holding pattern descriptions are unnecessary—if ATC clears you to hold at an intersection which sports a published pattern, the Controller has only to say "hold at the so-and-so intersection," and you will enter a pattern just as shown on the chart. All these are assumed to be standard as far as timing is concerned (one minute up to 14,000 feet; one and a half minutes above that level). If the Controller wants you to fly longer legs, he'll let you know.

HOLDING ON A LOCALIZER

When the weather is really lousy, and the inbound traffic is really heavy, Approach Control will frequently put you in a "stack," holding on the localizer at the outer marker, waiting your turn for an approach. You couldn't ask for a more easily-defined holding pattern—the fix is the marker (dah-dah-dah, flash-flash-flash, and a 180-degree swing of the ADF needle when a compass locator is installed), and the holding course is the localizer itself. Round and round you go, and each time someone breaks out of the clouds and hollers "runway in sight," Approach Control shakes the box and moves everybody down a thousand feet.

IT HAPPENS TO EVERYBODY

Drawing a holding pattern and the proper entry on a piece of paper and actually flying it are two different things, to which every honest IFR pilot will bear witness! The first few times will likely leave you wondering where the heck you are, and fortunately there's an easy way out of this situation—when disorientation strikes, level the wings (no matter what direction you're headed), rotate the OBS until TO appears, then turn to that heading and fly to the station. On the way, orient yourself to the radial you're on, and when FROM shows up, start all over again. Should you have to do this several times in succession, don't worry—at least you're staying close to the holding fix! If you become utterly and genuinely lost, holler for help, and ATC will come to the rescue—they're perhaps more anxious than *you* are to straighten things out.

12. Getting Ready for an Instrument Approach

THERE ARE A NUMBER of instrument procedures in use today, with more just over the horizon; but before beginning *any* approach, there are several things you can do to make the entire operation easier and safer.

In the interest of constantly being one step ahead of the airplane, begin to develop your approach frame of mind when you're still many miles from the terminal area. There are clues to tell you when things are about to happen. For instance, enroute transponder codes fall into a pattern, and you will notice that approach control requests the same squawks time after time when you are inbound. So, when Center asks you to set your transponder to what you recognize as an Approach Control code, expect a subsequent hand-off to that facility, and get ready for vectors and an altitude change to start the approach procedure.

In a non-radar environment, Center will frequently hand you off to a Controller at the airport, but since he doesn't have the advantage of seeing your flight on a radar scope, he'll request that you report passing an intersection or a DME fix as you fly inbound. When you reach the specified point, expect an approach clearance, or a hold, if there is traffic ahead of you. Listen to other clearances on the Approach Control frequency, and you'll have a good idea *what* to expect, and *when* to expect it.

Find out as early as you can what approach is in use at the destination, especially if it is an airport or an approach that is a stranger to you. If you're bound for an airfield with only one published procedure, there's no problem, but the larger terminals may have several types of approaches to three or four different runways. Chicago's O'Hare Field at one time had twenty-four procedures, plus radar approaches to eight runways!

There are several sources of approach information—at the top of the list is Automatic Terminal Information Service (ATIS), broadcast continuously on a VHF frequency listed on your approach chart. If two ATIS frequencies are given, choose the one that is *not* the localizer frequency—you'll find that the reception will be much clearer, and receivable from a greater distance. The localizer is somewhat directional, and is not powered for long-range transmission.

When you're headed for a non-ATIS, multiple-procedure terminal, Approach Control will usually spill the beans something like this: "Barnburner 1234 Alpha, you're in radar contact; expect vectors to the final approach course for the Runway one six VOR approach."

The Center Controller can get terminal information for you, but it's a bit outside his bailiwick, and such a request really shouldn't be made unless you need to know a long way out. ATIS or Approach Control notification should give you plenty of time to get set up for the approach.

What about the airport that has no ATIS, no Approach Control, and you don't want to bother Center? Do the logical thing, and monitor the tower frequency for a while on your other radio; you'll likely find out what procedure they're using. Or ask

Center if you may leave the frequency for a moment (a request almost always granted) and call the Tower, who can also give you the weather situation first hand. If there is not even a tower at Boondocks Municipal Airport, there's likely to be a Flight Service Station close by that can supply you with weather and winds, and you can make up your own mind about how to get to the runway.

As soon as you are in the terminal area, put away your enroute charts, notepads, computers, coffee jugs, and whatever else might divert your attention from the approach chart. Clean up the cockpit so that you can devote all your talents to flying the approach.

GOOD PRACTICES MAKE GOOD HABITS

As you study the published procedure, there is a method you should use for maximum efficiency, standardization, and safety. Done exactly the same way every time, it will soon become a habit, and will prevent missing some vital bit of information on that dark, stormy night when the engine's running rough, you're picking up a load of ice, and the gear won't go down. In a predicament like this (or any stress situation) your well-practiced system of chart study will come booming through.

Here's the way to do it: The first two items (and at this point the *only* two) to be memorized are the *first heading* and the *first altitude* of the missed approach procedure. Allow those two numbers to burn themselves into your mind, because the next item on the approach agenda is to convince yourself that you will definitely have to execute a missed approach, even though you *know* that the airport is VFR. With this attitude, no major shift of mental gears is required on those very rare occasions when you are forced to pull up and go around because of weather. And what a pleasant surprise when you break out of the murk, and there is the runway, straight ahead! (It may be the wrong airport, but in lousy weather, *any* runway is beautiful!)

This leads directly to the next part of your approach preparation: What will the airport look like when you make visual contact? Approaching the home drome, you can probably handle this admirably; but an approach to a strange airport, in weather all the way to minimums, or when cleared for a circling approach to some runway other than the one on which you're lined up, can introduce considerable disorientation. Prevent embarrassment ("Tower, this is Barnburner 1234 Alpha, if you have me in sight, *please* tell me which way to turn") by studying the airport plan view on your approach chart. Turn the chart until you're looking at the airport layout just the way you will see it when you break out of the clouds; find the landing runway, and decide which way you will turn if necessary. It's also an excellent way to make yourself aware of trees, power lines, grain elevators, high-rise apartments, and other obstructions that people insist on building in approach airspace.

Next item for the study system is the approach itself. All published procedures have one thing in common: They proceed step by step from the initial approach through various segments to the landing or missed approach, as appropriate. At this time, make a "big picture" study of the entire procedure: headings, altitudes, distances, times, etc. When you actually get into the approach, always let your mind fly one segment ahead of the airplane.

Now tune, identify, and orient yourself to the navigational aids you will use. (If you are being radar vectored to the final approach course, use this opportunity to set up all the approach aids. Your only responsibility while inbound is to follow the instructions from Approach Control.) When the weather conditions promise a tight approach, it's not a bad idea to tune two radios to the approach aid, so you can check one against the other. If the missed approach is an involved one, you would do well to set up your radio equipment so that there will be a minimum of knob-twisting when you are busy with a go-around.

After all this, you have one more number to memorize, and it's really an important one: the MDA or DH, depending on the type of approach in use. In either case, it's the lowest altitude to which you may descend until the runway is visible. Picture in your mind's eye how the altimeter hands will appear when you get to that altitude, and keep it in mind. If you have a co-pilot familiar with the altimeter, have him holler when you are 100 feet above that altitude.

Approach charts are published on single pages and kept in loose-leaf binders for good reason; they are intended to be removed and placed somewhere in the cockpit for ready reference during an approach. The best possible location is in the jaws of a spring clip firmly attached to the control wheel, where you don't have to move your head to look at it. Next time you are under the hood with a well-qualified pilot in the other seat, put your approach plate on the floor between the seats; just as you begin your turn back onto the final approach course after completing a procedure turn, lower your head and look down at the chart for ten seconds, then rapidly back to the panel. This will probably induce vertigo such as you never believed could happen to you, and should convince you that the best place for the approach plate is right straight in front of you!

By the numbers, here is the approach study system:

1. Clean up the cockpit.
2. Find out what approach is in use, remove that chart, and put it in the spring clip.
3. Memorize the missed approach procedure (at least the first *heading* and *altitude*).
4. Convince yourself that you will have to make a missed approach.
5. Orient yourself to the airport layout as it will appear when you break out of the clouds.
6. Study the entire approach—the "big picture."
7. Set up the radio gear for the approach.
8. Memorize the DH or MDA, as appropriate.

Although it seldom happens, be ready for a missed approach every time. This includes a quick mental review of the mechanics of "going around," as well as an early decision concerning your intentions immediately thereafter. Remember that Tower Controllers have a standard response to a missed approach report—"Roger, Barnburner 1234 Alpha, what are your intentions?" Compose your answer well ahead of time, *every* time you start an approach, and on that rare occasion when you need it, the words will come flowing forth just as if you knew what you're doing.

13. Instrument Approaches

FROM A "DO WHAT YOU'RE TOLD" radar approach at the low end of the simplicity scale, to the Instrument Landing System where the entire job of navigation is up to you, every instrument approach is just a means to an end. When enroute navigation has brought you through the clouds to that fabled "point B," the approach and landing charts take over to guide you to a point from which you can land the airplane—it's that simple! Whenever you are able to position yourself more accurately on the final approach segment of the procedure, that point gets closer to the runway. It will be at its maximum distance on a typical NDB (ADF) approach (because of the inherent inaccuracy of the system and the great amount of pilot navigational inputs required), moves closer with VOR, gets even better on a Localizer approach, and gets right down to the runway with the most accurate of all, the ILS.

You may have personal opinions about the accuracy of the various types of approaches, but when it comes to precision, there is a major classification already laid down for you: ALL approaches are put into one of two general categories, precision or non-precision. (The semantics can be argued, since some of the so-called non-precision procedures lead you right down the

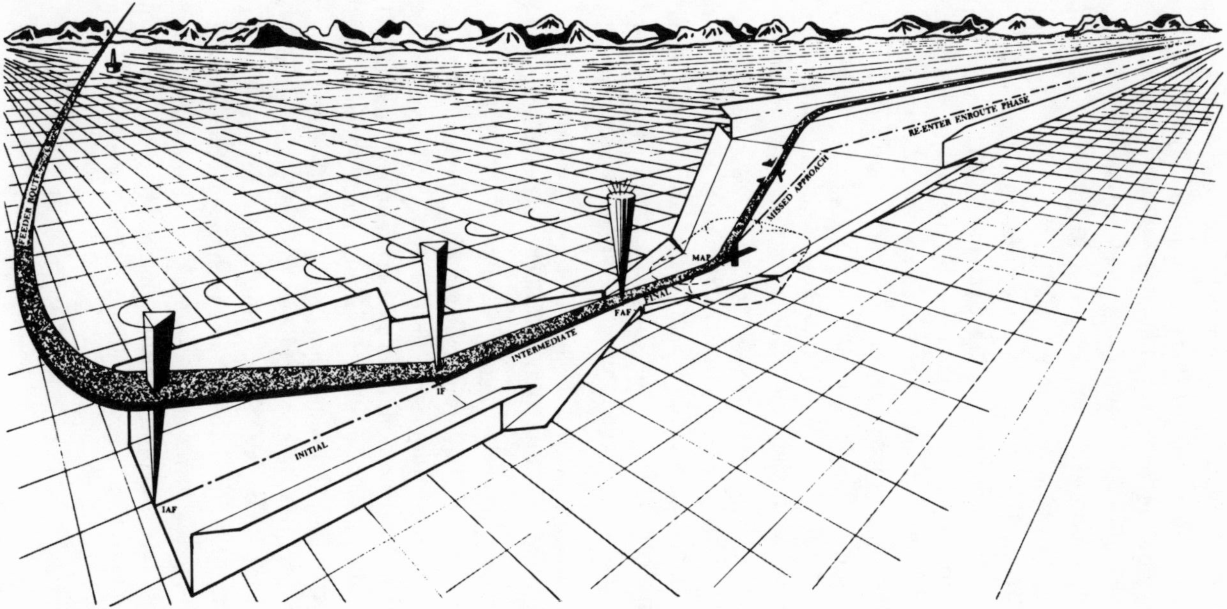

Segments of a typical approach procedure, showing how terrain and obstacle clearance "funnels down" toward the runway.

paint stripe in the middle of the runway; but there are important implications stemming from these descriptions, basic to a complete understanding of instrument approaches.) If the installation transmits glide slope information electronically, it's known as a "precision" approach; a procedure without a glide slope falls into the "non-precision" category.

For all practical purposes, the only precision approach in use today is the Instrument Landing System (ILS), in which the glide slope is displayed to the pilot in the form of a moving pointer or indicator of some sort which enables him to adjust the flight path of the airplane to conform to a prescribed path leading to the runway. There is another system which qualifies, Precision Approach Radar (PAR), but these facilities exist at only a few civil airports in the United States. When it's in operation, the PAR glide slope is observed on radar and corrections are made by the pilot at the Controller's direction. This means that the approach can be accomplished with only a radio receiver and basic instruments operating in the aircraft—a good deal if the weather and your navigation radios fail at the same time!

HOW MANY BLACK BOXES DO YOU NEED?

The least complicated situation would be a radar approach, for which you need only some means of receiving voice communication—no navigation gear at all. For a VOR procedure, it's obvious that at least one omni receiver is required, and an NDB approach cannot be accomplished without an ADF on board. In order to get to the Decision Height on an ILS approach, you must be able to receive the localizer, the glide slope, and two marker beacons. (The law allows you to substitute radar for the outer marker, or ADF if the system includes a compass locator. Be careful here, as locators are being phased out gradually all over the country, and with neither marker beacon, radar, nor ADF, there's no legal way to identify that point on the approach.)

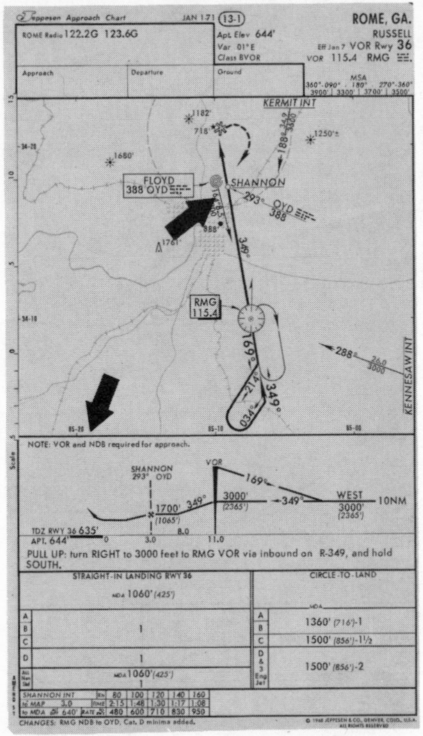

Approach and landing chart for Runway 36 at Rome, Georgia. © 1968 Jeppesen & Co., Denver, Colo. All rights reserved. Not to be used for navigation.

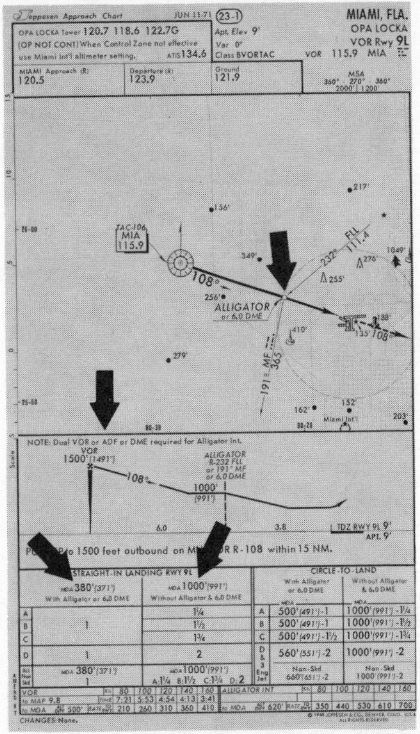

Approach and landing chart for Runway 9L at Opa Locka, Florida. © 1968 Jeppesen & Co., Denver, Colo. All rights reserved. Not to be used for navigation.

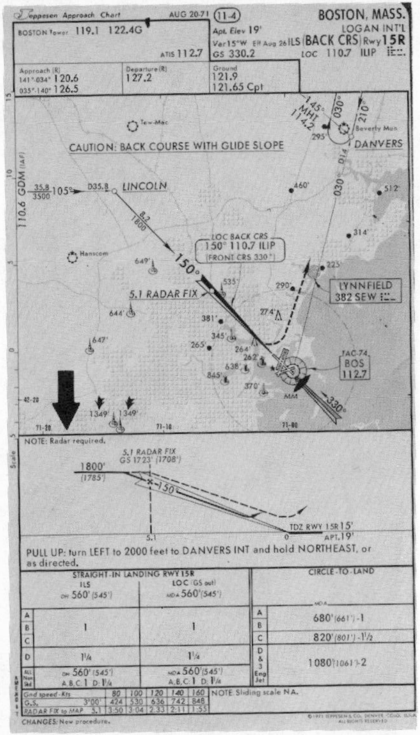

Approach and landing chart for Runway 15R at Boston, Mass. © 1971 Jeppesen & Co., Denver, Colo. All rights reserved. Not to be used for navigation.

Some VOR approach procedures include DME fixes which allow you to position yourself more accurately on final approach, and lower Minimum Descent Altitudes are therefore authorized; if you don't have DME, or if it's not working, you're stuck with a higher MDA.. On the other hand, an approach procedure which is specifically titled "VOR-DME" requires BOTH receivers—if either is inoperative, you're out of business.

A few procedures require more than the basic navigational aids because of local conditions. They fall into two groups: those that *absolutely require* additional equipment, and those in which lower minimums are *available* for aircraft with more radio gear (or radar service). At Rome, Georgia, both VOR and NDB receivers are needed for the VOR Runway 36 approach, since the final approach fix (Shannon intersection) cannot be identified without ADF. The VOR Runway 9L procedure at Opa Locka Airport in Miami can be executed with just an omni set, but you can descend 620 feet lower if you can determine the Alligator intersection; this requires dual VOR, or ADF, or DME. On a rainy, scuddy day at Miami, that 620 feet could easily be the difference between a successful approach and a go-around. Boston's Logan International Airport exhibits still another unusual situation, in that the back course approach to Runway 15R can be executed only when radar service is available. (Notice anything else different? *This* back course is also a full ILS; glide slope and all!)

With radar approach control, more often than not you will be given a vector to the final approach course, and so the procedure turn is slowly going the way of the position report. But you must know how to fly the complete approach as published, because there'll come a non-radar day when you will have to fly the whole thing by yourself. Accordingly, the first subject in this chapter is "procedure turns."

Once you've learned the basic segments of an approach procedure, and the principles underlying pilot actions at various times, you can fly any approach in the book. Each of the most-used procedures (ADF, VOR, Localizer, ILS) is discussed using this format:

Description
Setting up the radios
Initial approach
Station passage and tracking outbound
Procedure turn
Final approach

Straight-in approaches (those that lead directly to the landing runway with no maneuvering) are the first order of business, followed by circling approaches, and the next logical step when the weather is lousy, the missed approach. (In the Air Force it's a "go-around," in the Navy it's a "wave-off," and in the airlines it's "co-pilot error.")

An instrument approach doesn't have to follow the printed directions right to the letter, but if you're going to take advantage of the legal short-cuts, you must know what you're doing. A pilot who accepts a contact approach but has no idea what he is expected to do can become a hazard in the airspace. So, contact and visual approaches are discussed, followed by radar approaches and several other procedures you should know about to make the most of your IFR abilities.

PRACTICE IS A *MUST*!

Pilots aren't the only egomaniacs in the world. A famous musician once said "if I practice four hours a day I am the world's greatest pianist; if I practice *eight* hours a day, I am Paderewski!" Practice improves performance in any endeavor, but it becomes more significant when you're talking about instrument flying skills.

Going 'round and 'round the flagpole at your home drome is commendable, since you'll probably make most of your down-to-minimums approaches there, but this kind of practice doesn't do much for your versatility. The time that you set aside for instrument practice (and you should do this unless you fly IFR regularly and frequently) can be more productive if you will have your instructor or safety pilot pick an instrument approach procedure at random from the chart book—give yourself a few moments to study it, using the method in Chapter 12, and then fly it. Of course you can't practice ILS or Localizer approaches this way, but if you can receive a signal from any VOR or NDB, you can use that signal to simulate an approach procedure; the local standard broadcast station is often convenient for ADF practice.

To make these exercises as realistic as possible, reset your altimeter to an indication that will put the MDA for the approach at a safe level. Under the hood, you should be concerned only with the numbers you can see—it makes no difference to you what your actual altitude is, or where the navigation signals are coming from; keeping you clear of things is your safety pilot's job. After a few of these randomly-selected-approach sessions, you'll have convinced yourself that approaches are generally the same; different altitudes, different headings, but you won't be surprised when cleared for a procedure you've never seen before.

Instrument approaches are the command performances of the flying business; the ones you make when the weather is right down on the deck are the ones you practice for, so when you have the opportunity, get under the hood and really *work*—don't bore expensive holes in the sky.

PROCEDURE TURNS

It's refreshing, in this overregulated aeronautical world, to have one instrument procedure which a pilot can legally execute just about any way he pleases. To be sure, there are limitations on the airspace you may use for a procedure turn, but by and large, how you reverse course during an instrument approach is up to you. (The real gutsy pilots could even Immelman or Split-S their way through procedure turns if it weren't for the restrictions on aerobatics in a control zone!) A procedure turn is the instrument pilot's modus operandi to get turned around and headed back the way he came, and on a specific course.

Three types of procedure turns have evolved over the years, and they are best classified in terms of their relative difficulty. (Not to imply that any one is actually harder to perform than the others, but the elapsed time from start to finish grows shorter as you move up the scale, and this means that you have to be very much on top of the entire situation when using the most rapid reversal.) The "old standard" is the 60-second procedure turn, and requires at least three minutes from the time you leave the outbound course until you're back to where you started the maneuver. The 40-second type (really just a modification of the 60-second turn) cuts the total time somewhat depending on the wind, and the fastest one of all is the 90-270—you'd better be ready for your inbound chores shortly after reversing direction. (Standard-rate turns are assumed in each case.)

These IFR turn-arounds have several things in common: They must be executed at or above a specified minimum altitude (although *maximum* and *mandatory* procedure turn altitudes are not unknown); you may not go beyond a specified limit from the approach facility as you reverse course; and your maneuvering must be accomplished on the specified side of the course. The restrictions are designed to allow plenty of room, yet keep you clear of obstacles as you turn.

The maneuvering side of the course (indicated by a barbed arrow on the U.S. charts or Jeppesen's full depiction of the turn) and the procedure turn altitude (shown on the profile view of the approach procedure) are quite variable, but the maximum distance is 10 nautical miles from the approach fix on almost every chart. And therein lies a trap for the unwary pilot who always allows himself the full 10 miles—some approaches cannot guarantee terrain or obstruction clearance for this distance, and a shorter mileage is quoted. "Non-standard" procedure turn distances are not emphasized on approach charts, and it's easy to count on 10 miles, only to find yourself in trouble. Pay close attention to the maximum procedure turn distance on *every* approach, with airports in the mountainous sections of the country most suspect.

All three types of turns are safe procedures if you remain at or above the procedure turn altitude *until established on the approach course inbound*, when you may descend to the next lower altitude, if the published procedure permits.

THE 60-SECOND PROCEDURE TURN

Used by some pilots because of its simplicity and the fact that it gives you a "breather" on the inbound leg, the 60-second procedure is commenced by a standard-rate 45-degree turn away from the outbound course (headings are given on the chart), and flying for one minute on the new heading. When the minute is up, turn at standard rate 180 degrees IN THE DIRECTION OPPOSITE THE FIRST TURN, or always turn AWAY FROM THE AIRPORT, whichever is easiest for you to remember. In a no-wind situation, you'll have about half a minute to fly on this heading before you reintercept the inbound course. It's a good time to refresh yourself on the MDA or DH, or your missed approach procedures, or your anticipated circling maneuvers, depending on the kind of approach you are flying. When your navigation displays show that you're approaching the inbound course, lead the turn a bit, and track to the fix.

The only timing you need worry about is the one minute outbound—when starting the procedure turn from an on-course position (which is where you should be!), activate your timing device as soon as you level the wings after the 45-degree turn. This rule also holds for those times when you find yourself *slightly* off-course on the maneuvering side—start timing when you level the wings. However, should you begin the maneuver from the *other* side of the course, you mustn't start timing until your instruments indicate that you have crossed the course.

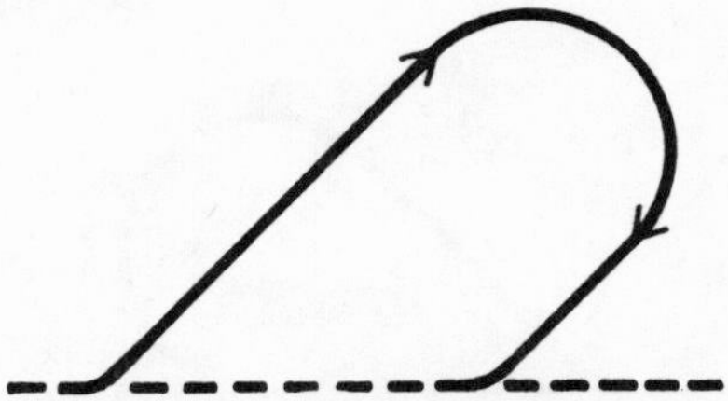

The 60-second procedure turn.

In a situation where you have no idea of the wind conditions, the 60-second procedure turn will probably give you the best break—if there's *no* wind, it will show up as a normal 30-second trip from completion of the inbound turn to the final approach course. If the zephyrs have pushed upon the tail of your flying machine while outbound, you may need a box lunch to survive the journey back to course. And in the worst situation, a strong headwind outbound, you will see the navaids indicating course interception during the inbound turn; in this case, steepen the bank and turn directly to the inbound heading.

Safe, simple, and sure, the 60-second reversal is a good one to use when in doubt. But don't get the idea that it's just for beginners and those who have time to spare. There are occasions when it becomes necessary to lose a lot of altitude during a procedure turn, and that full minute outbound, another in the turn, and a chunk of a minute before intercepting the inbound course can mean several thousand feet, even at a comfortable rate of descent.

THE 40-SECOND PROCEDURE TURN

Here's a way to make the procedure turn more efficient by controlling the effects of the wind, instead of accepting whatever displacement it may cause. It's a modification of the turn just discussed, and involves changes in the time outbound as well as the point at which you will reintercept the course. The 40-second turn will obviously cut down the time you spend reversing

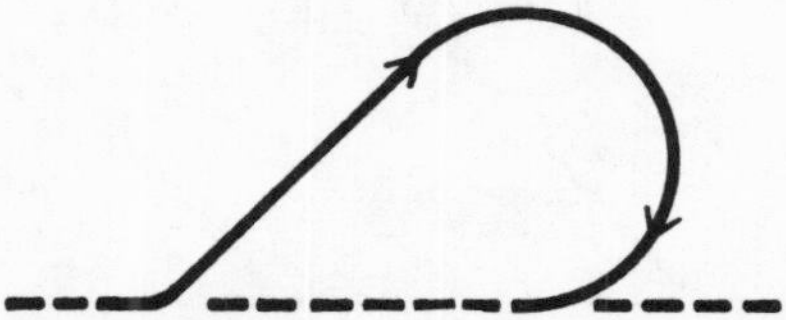

The 40-second procedure turn.

course, and can be your contribution to speeding up the flow of traffic during rush hour at the local airpatch. But it requires a little more of the pilot, since you must calculate roughly the effect of wind, apply the correction, and perhaps more importantly, be prepared to cope with the faster return to course that results—there'll be no breather after you turn inbound on this one; if properly done, you will roll out *on course,* and you must be all set to proceed with the remainder of the approach.

The 40-second turn begins the same as its 60-second brother, with a standard rate 45-degree turn away from the outbound course, and timing also starts at the same place. The duplication stops right there, because now you will add or subtract from the 40-second base figure a time factor to correct for wind. The calculation puts together the number of degrees of wind correction which was required to keep you on the outbound course, and in which direction. If your procedure turn takes you downwind, *subtract* one second for each degree of crab required on the outbound course—when turning into the wind, *add* one second for each degree. Thus, you will shorten or lengthen that first leg, and change the radius of turn as you head back for the inbound course. If this is done properly (and "properly" includes all turns made at the same rate), you should find the appropriate needles centering as you roll out on the inbound heading, plus or minus drift correction, of course. A well done 40-second procedure turn should conclude with a smooth, sweeping standard-rate turn onto the approach course, and even if you are off a few seconds in your calculations, you will have saved some time.

This is also a good one to use when there is no wind and you wouldn't mind getting on the ground a little sooner. It's a difference of only half a minute or so, but when the terminal area is saturated with IFR traffic making procedure turns, those half-minutes add up.

THE 90-270 PROCEDURE TURN

Maybe it all started with an indecisive IFR pilot not being able to make up his mind after the first 90 degrees of turn, but whatever the origin, the 90-270 will get you turned around in the minimum time, and with the minimum outbound displacement, of any of the procedure turns. You will also find it very helpful as a low-visibility approach procedure, when you are forced to

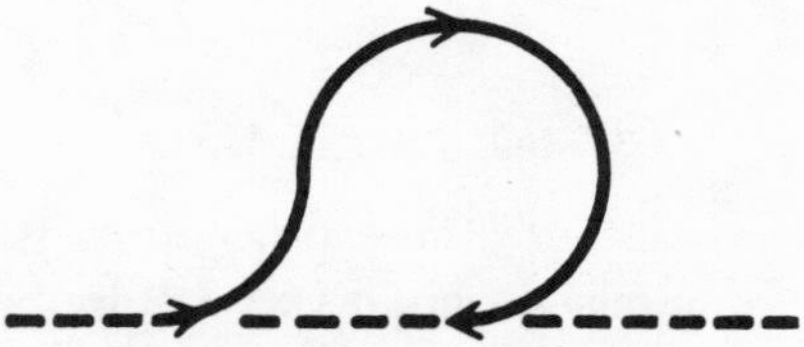

The 90-270 procedure turn.

fly the length of the runway, then reverse course to land. (See the section below on "Circling Approaches.") There is no timing involved, and it will work in all but the strongest winds—the key is to make your turns at a uniform rate, and to change heading a FULL 90 degrees on the first turn.

Choose carefully the point from which you begin a 90-270, because you will come back onto the inbound course not very far from where you left it. If you have more than a thousand feet to lose in the turn, you're going to be plunging earthward at a rapid rate, which will speed up the whole approach to the point where things may be happening so fast you can't keep up. Having to execute a missed approach because you started a rip-snorting 90-270 too close to the fix is hardly a laudable demonstration of efficiency!

When the distance out and altitude-to-lose are compatible, start the Rapid Reverser with a 90-degree turn in the appropriate direction, and *immediately* on reaching the 90-degree point, roll smoothly into the identical angle of bank in the opposite direction. Depending on the wind condition, you will probably begin to center the nav-needles about 45 degrees from the inbound heading—keep turning, and as you roll out, you'll be "right on." Remember that the accuracy of this maneuver depends on uniform and constant rates of turn, and a 90-degree heading change at the outset—if you're holding 15 degrees of crab as you proceed outbound before starting the procedure turn, count 90 degrees from that heading, not from the course you are on. (Some pilots like heading changes of 80 degrees and 260 degrees; it's a matter of personal preference.)

OUTBOUND TIMING

No matter which of these three procedures you elect to use, you must decide how far outbound you will fly before beginning the procedure turn. Bearing on your decision will be the maximum distance allowed, the amount of altitude you have to lose, and how much time you figure you will need (or would like to have) to get squared away on the final approach course. When the weather is hovering around minimums and you want everything going for you, give yourself plenty of time. Within reason, the distance you fly outbound before beginning the procedure turn should increase as the ceiling and visibility decrease. A generally accepted figure for light planes is two minutes, which will supply that comfortable time pad (unless there's a terrific head wind outbound), yet keep you well within the mileage limit. Of course, you should slow down as soon as you cross the fix outbound—there's no reason for high airspeeds during the procedure turn; you'll use up more fuel, increase your radius of turn, and fly farther away from the fix. At a reasonable airspeed and two minutes outbound, you needn't worry about a 10-mile limit; a groundspeed of even 180 knots will keep you inside the envelope of airspace reserved for you as you maneuver.

NO PROCEDURE TURN, PLEASE

There are two situations frequently encountered which preclude the use of a procedure turn. The first occurs when you are issued a radar vector which the Controller states will take you to

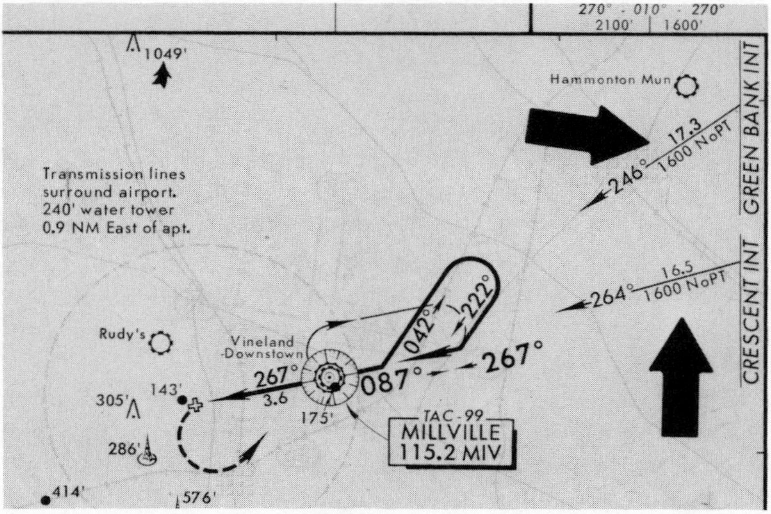

Initial approach routes which do not require a procedure turn (NoPT). © 1969 Jeppesen & Co., Denver, Colo. All rights reserved. Not to be used for navigation.

the final approach course for the appropriate instrument procedure. The second involves an approach clearance via a route on the approach chart which bears the notation "NoPT," meaning of course "No Procedure Turn." In these cases, the routing (either by vector or charted directions) will result in your intercepting the final approach course at a distance sufficient to allow you to line up and descend if required before reaching the Final Approach Fix.

A PROCEDURE TURN IS NOT THE *ONLY* WAY

When is a procedure turn *not* a procedure turn?—when it is omitted from the published approach, or replaced by some other maneuver, as at Parkersburg, West Virginia, where lead-in headings from two intersections provide adequate guidance to get lined up on the localizer course. On occasion a holding pattern is substituted for a procedure turn; perhaps to limit the outbound distance, or to guarantee that pilots turning around will be doing so in a prescribed manner, instead of the several options available for a regular procedure turn.

One of the smoothest, least complicated procedures is the teardrop turn. (When the over-the-fix altitude gets up to 20,000 feet or so, and the rate of descent required is 5-6,000 feet per minute, it's called a "jet penetration.") You'll find one leading up to the localizer approach to Runway 31 at Dothan, Alabama. Over the VORTAC at cruise altitude and cleared for the approach, head out the 150 radial, descend to not less than 2,000 feet, and when you figure you can turn onto the localizer comfortably, do it. If you want to cut the elapsed time right down to the bone, watch the DME readout during the teardrop turn, and you can put yourself on the localizer right at the outer marker.

Another variation of the procedure turn is well illustrated by the situation at Oak Bluffs, Massachusetts, where Martha's Vineyard VOR provides the course guidance for an approach to the Oak Bluffs Airport. On an IFR day when the airborne vacationers are swarming, you may be obliged to hold at the VOR, waiting your turn for an approach. As you move down in the stack, a question comes up regarding your actions when you are cleared for the approach: Do you execute a procedure turn or not? Take another look at the chart, and notice that the holding pattern uses the same airspace as the charted procedure turn.

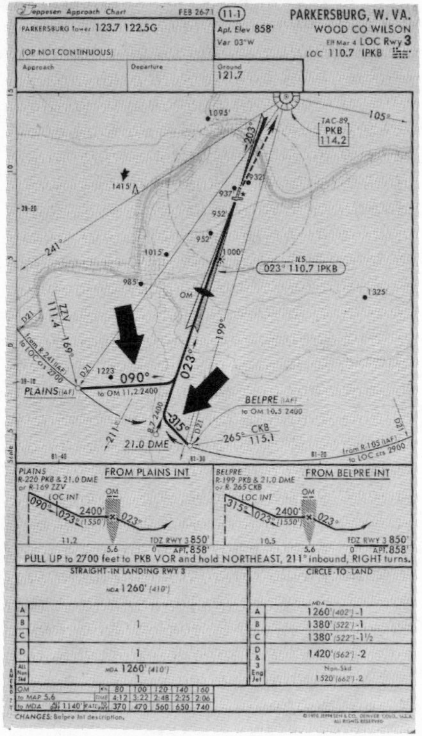

Lead-in courses at Parkersburg, West Virginia, which take the place of a procedure turn. © 1970 Jeppesen & Co., Denver, Colo. All rights reserved. Not to be used for navigation.

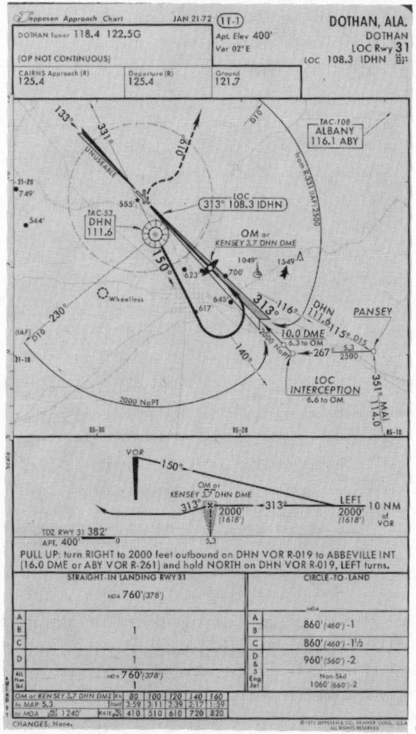

Approach and landing chart for Runway 31 at Dothan, Alabama, showing the teardrop turn in lieu of a procedure turn. © 1971 Jeppesen & Co., Denver, Colo. All rights reserved. Not to be used for navigation.

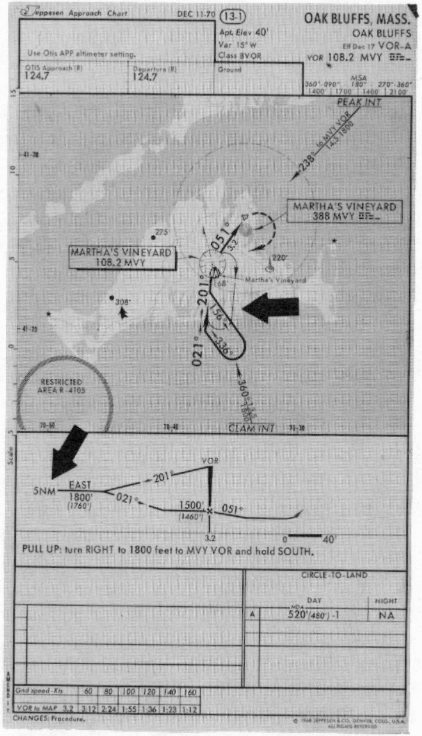

VOR approach for Oak Bluffs, Massachusetts (Martha's Vineyard). © 1968 Jeppesen & Co., Denver, Colo. All rights reserved. Not to be used for navigation.

The only restriction you must observe here is the non-standard distance of 5 miles, so be sure you stay within that limit, descend to 1,800 feet during your final circuit of the holding pattern, and go ahead with the approach. Otis Approach Control would surely aim a word or two in your direction if they observed you making a tight turn over the station, proceeding outbound on the 201 radial, and into a beautiful procedure turn—no matter how well executed, this maneuver would be unnecessary, ill-advised, and rather thoughtless of the pilots above you in the stack. Whenever possible and practical, continue in the holding pattern when cleared for an approach IF THE HOLDING PATTERN AND PROCEDURE TURN ARE COINCIDENT ON THE CHART. If time versus altitude loss becomes a problem, you can always extend the outbound leg of the holding pattern for two minutes or so before turning inbound.

Referring to the *NDB* approach procedure for the Oak Bluffs Airport, it appears that the same philosophy would apply, and when cleared for the approach, continued descent in the holding pattern would be the most practical thing to do. But there's one drawback—in the profile view, "NOTE: Final Approach from holding pattern not authorized." With this restriction, it is incumbent on the pilot to return to the beacon when cleared for the approach, execute a complete procedure turn, and do it within 5 miles of the beacon!

APPROACHES INTO NO-CONTROL-ZONE AIRPORTS

Notice how thick your books of approach and landing charts have grown over the past few years? It's the result of more and more airport operators and users being able to convince the government that an instrument approach procedure is justified, and it has increased the usefulness of small airplanes many times over. The multitude of instrument-accessible landing places is certainly to be welcomed, but there is a trap of complacency which you should know about.

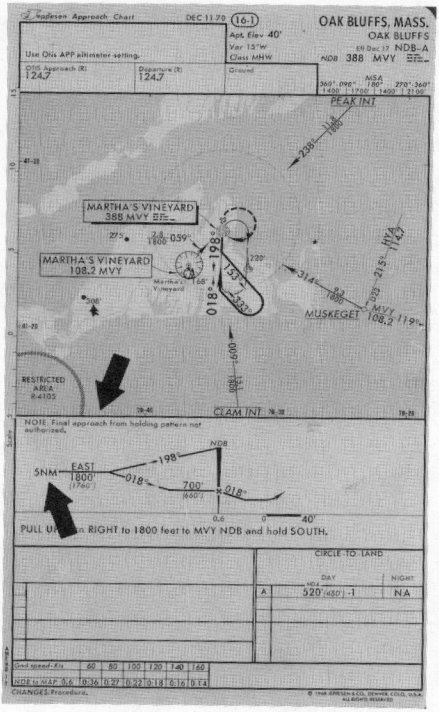

NDB approach for Oak Bluffs, Massachusetts. Not to be used for navigation.

If an approach procedure and the airport for which it is intended meet specific requirements, a Control Zone is established for the protection of aircraft arriving and departing under IFR conditions. But many of the smaller airports, while qualifying for an instrument approach, do not meet the criteria for a Control Zone. A Transition Area is usually set up, but it doesn't do a complete job—instead of protection from the ground up throughout your approach, *you are in Controlled Airspace only during the time you are 700 feet or more above the ground*! This means that you can be cleared for an approach, fly the proper procedure, hold your track precisely and make good your timing to within a gnat's eyelash, and wind up *in uncontrolled airspace*! When the altimeter hands slide below the numbers that represent 700 feet AGL, you have gone from one world to another—from the *complete* protection of ATC to *no* protection except your own eyes.

This situation is not a fault of the system, but is the sort of thing you should know about so that you can increase your vigilance. Just because you have been cleared for the approach, don't get the mistaken idea that you are the only one who is allowed to be there. In uncontrolled airspace, the only requirements to fly VFR are 1-mile visibility and clear of clouds, so there is nothing to prevent some dedicated pilot from going out to the airport for a few touch-and-go's even though the weather is perfectly horrible. And it's not just the VFR types you have to worry about, because there could even be an intrepid soul approaching the same airport IFR—without a flight plan, a clearance, or any notification to ATC. He, too, is completely legal as long as he remains clear of controlled airspace; not necessarily smart, but legal.

There are three ways you can lessen the danger when inbound to a no-control-zone airport in IFR conditions. First, ask the Approach Controller (or Center) to check for targets in the vicinity of the airport. Second, get on Unicom and broadcast your position and intentions as soon as you are able, continuing this broadcast in the blind as often as you think necessary. Third, get down to the MDA early and keep those eyeballs moving! Remember that the minute you descend below 700 feet AGL, you must share this uncontrolled airspace with whoever else may be using it—you're in the arena with the scud runners, obligated to see and avoid, just as you hope they are doing.

CIRCLING APPROACHES

"Barnburner 1234 Alpha is cleared for the Runway 28 ILS approach, *circle to land Runway 14.*" If you operate into airports where only one approach system is installed, you can bet that you'll hear clearances similar to that one many times, since the winds don't always favor the primary runway. A circling approach increases the flexibility and utility of the airport, but like anything else, it costs something; in this case, the price is higher minimums, and some rather stringent additional requirements to keep you out of trouble while you're circling.

The criteria which make an approach a circling approach are quite straightforward; whenever the landing runway is aligned more than 30 degrees from the final approach course, or when a normal rate of descent from the minimum IFR altitude to the runway is considered impossible, a circling approach is indicated.

You may be cleared for a circling approach at the tag end of *any* published procedure, from NDB to ILS; the Controller's motives are honorable, and he won't ask you to circle unless wind and weather conditions are such that landing straight-in would present a hazard. "Cleared to circle" does not mean that you are *required* to maneuver—if you have the active runway in sight in time to make a normal, straight-in landing, by all means do so, keeping the Tower (or whatever ATC facility you're working) informed of your plans.

No matter how your circling approach begins, it is going to turn into a non-precision procedure—there's no way to provide a circling glide slope for some other runway. Even if you are cleared for an ILS approach with a circling maneuver on the end, you may not go lower than the circling Minimum Descent Altitude; in addition, you will find no circling approaches in which the required visibility is less than one mile. The designers of the procedure must provide you with at least 300 feet vertical clearance from all obstacles in the circling area, which is the

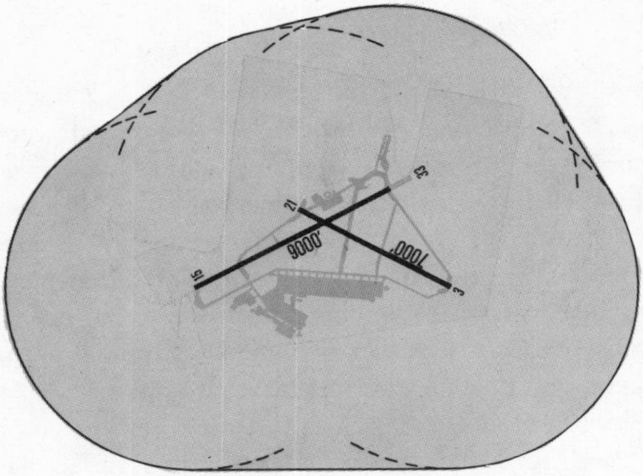

Circling area around a typical airport. You are guaranteed at least 300 feet obstacle clearance within this area. The radius of the circle is 1.3 nautical miles for Category A.

connected radii from the ends of all the airport's runways. For Category A circling, the area in which you are cleared to maneuver is described like this, at a typical airport. When you are cleared for a circle-to-land maneuver, you should shift mental gears as you prepare for the approach, and when studying the chart, don't even look at the straight-in minimums, but let that circling MDA burn itself into your mind.

The legal requirements you must observe while maneuvering to land in this situation are: (1) you must not descend below the circling MDA until descent is necessary for landing (practically, this means when turning base or final for the landing runway); (2) you must keep the airport in sight throughout your circling maneuver; and (3) you must remain clear of all clouds. Should you lose sight of the field because of reduced visibility or flying into a layer of scud, you are bound by law to execute an immediate missed approach.

Obviously, it would be unwise to begin circling before you have the field in sight, so fly the final approach course right

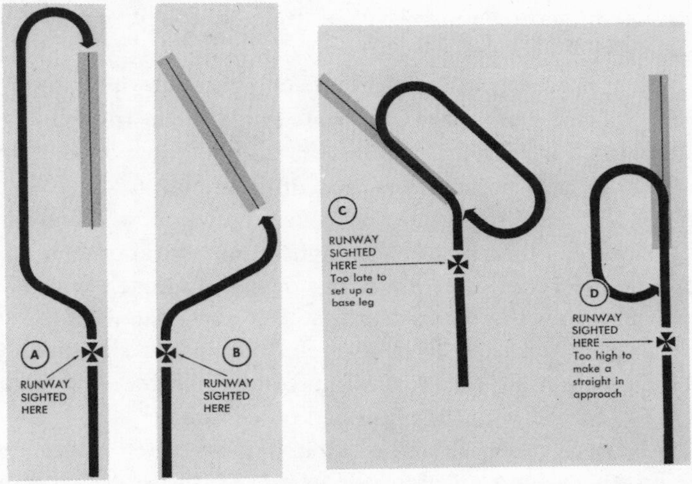

Suggested maneuvers for circling approaches in low-visibility conditions.

down to the circling MDA; if the field doesn't show up, go around. But suppose that you have eased down to the MDA well ahead of time, and at 1 mile, the airport begins to take shape ahead of you. If you have done a good job of studying the airport layout during the preparation for the approach, you will know just how it will look, and more important, you will have decided which way you are going to circle for landing. Always check the remarks section of the approach chart before commencing a circling approach; there may be some surprises waiting for you if you maneuver where you shouldn't.

How you get lined up with the runway is completely your business, as long as you comply with the restrictions mentioned above. There are several generally-accepted patterns suggested for the low-visibility approaches, and it's rather difficult to imagine a situation which would require a maneuver much different than one of these. The important thing is to decide way back at the beginning of the approach what you're going to do when the field comes into view, and then stick to your plan; 1-mile visibility and only 300 or 400 feet of altitude doesn't give you much room to change your mind.

Every approved instrument approach procedure includes a set of very specific instructions for your guidance in the event you see nothing but clouds outside the airplane windows at the missed approach point. This procedure is also to be followed after an aborted circling approach, but now you will find yourself someplace other than the straight-in missed approach point. There's a special rule for a *circling* missed approach which will keep you within the allotted airspace. It says that when executing a missed approach from a circling approach situation, you will start a *climbing turn* that will take you back *over the airport* and *then* proceed with the published procedure.

The successful completion of a circling approach under really tight weather conditions depends in great measure on your ability to maneuver your airplane in close quarters, and to do it safely. Since radius of turn increases quite rapidly with airspeed, it behooves you to slow down as you enter the final phase of the approach—when the weather is near minimums, it's a good idea to pull back on the reins a bit anyway, so that things don't happen quite so fast. Power-off stall speed times 1.3 (plus 10 knots for the wife and kids) is a good, safe speed at which to maneuver around the airport on a circling approach. Above all, don't try to bend your airplane around a tight turn to final. Remember that wind direction is probably the reason you're circling in the first place, and as you make the turn to final, the wind will be trying to blow you away from the runway—steepen the bank and pull back to tighten the turn at this low altitude in less than favorable ceiling and visibility conditions, and you just may pull yourself right into the ground. Since stall speed goes up alarmingly as you increase bank, you're setting yourself up—most stall-spin situations that close to the ground provide grist for the headline mills! If you feel uncomfortable while circling, if you get that "gut" feeling that things just aren't what they ought to be, go around and come back for another try.

When you are flying a high-performance airplane, it is possible to get into an unusual situation on a circling approach; suppose your aircraft has a computed approach speed (for Category purposes) of 89 knots, which allows you to make the approach under Category A minimums. If it is necessary to *maneuver* at an airspeed that puts you above the 91-knot maximum for this category, you should circle at the MDA prescribed for Category B—it's the circling *speed* that counts. You probably won't make your low-visibility approach with full flaps (part of "landing configuration"), so adjust the airspeed accordingly. (The legend for your approach charts explains "Approach Categories" in detail.)

Here are the points you should remember about circling approaches:

1. Your circling clearance will always specify the landing runway, so you can plan ahead.
2. You must always observe an MDA on a circling approach, no matter what type of approach you started with.
3. You must remain at or above the *circling* MDA for your category until further descent is necessary for landing.
4. While maneuvering, you must keep the airport in sight and remain clear of all clouds.
5. If a missed approach becomes necessary, make a climbing turn that will take you back over the airport, *then* proceed with the published missed approach instructions.

SHORT-CUTS TO AN INSTRUMENT APPROACH

When ATC gives you the "go ahead" for an instrument approach, you are cleared all the way to the missed approach point, and you're guaranteed safe separation from all other IFR aircraft while in the process of getting there, if a Control Zone exists at the airport. But an approach clearance is not ironbound; it does not mean that you must fly to the MAP in strict accordance with the published procedure. There are some very efficient ways of short-cutting the involved and time-consuming maneuvers you accomplish flying the full approach, and they're legal, safe, and sensible WHEN FULLY UNDERSTOOD AND PROPERLY PERFORMED.

All three of these short-cuts are contingent on breaking out of the clouds at some point well before the MDA or DH is reached. Be familiar with them and put them to use when you can save yourself some valuable time, and vacate a chunk of airspace for your brother airmen waiting in line behind you. ATC will be happy, too, because as soon as the Controller can get you out of his electronic hair, he can let someone else in, and in general speed up the flow of traffic. This way, he gets no ulcers, doesn't beat his wife and kids when he gets home, and everybody is happier. See how far a little professionalism can go?

"CANCEL MY IFR"

The first method of short-cutting an approach clearance is to terminate it with a straightforward directive to ATC: "New York Center, Barnburner 1234 Alpha, cancel my IFR." This usually elicits an equally straightforward response from the ground: "Roger, Barnburner 1234 Alpha, cancelling your IFR at one six three two." The only difference between this and any other ATC response is the tone in which it is delivered; the Controller's voice will be so beautifully articulated, each word so perfectly pronounced that his elecution teacher would bust her buttons with pride. There's only one reason the Controller makes his reply so clearly understood: He wants the cancellation, the time, and the aircraft number on the tape which records every radio conversation. Later, if any "discussion" of the flight were required, the evidence is right there; the world (or at least the FAA inspector) will know without a doubt that the pilot of Barnburner 1234 Alpha removed himself from the protection of the IFR system at 1632 Zulu time on the day in question.

Never, never cancel an IFR flight plan and give up all that protection unless you are absolutely sure you can get where you're going in healthy VFR conditions. ATC looks with understandable scorn on pilots who cancel IFR, then return sheepishly for a clearance after finding out that they can't maintain VFR. Although the people in the Center are there to help, they don't like to duplicate their efforts, and such a request is frequently answered with "call the nearest Flight Service Station and file a flight plan." Now you must go back through the system, maintaining VFR all the while, and it's going to cost you minutes on the clock, gallons on the fuel gauge, maybe a missed appointment. Anyway you look at it, an unwise IFR cancellation is spelled M-O-N-E-Y!

You must be especially cautious about cancelling after the sun ceaseth its labors for the day. The next pilot who is lulled into a false sense of "I've got it made" when he can see the rotating beacon at Destination Municipal won't be the first. He cancels, maybe even with the airport itself in sight from afar. Nothing is so reassuring as those flashes of white and green beckoning to you out of the darkness after a long trip, and the feeling of security grows as you pass over the airport, able to see the windsock and all the familiar landmarks. Now onto the final approach, and just about the time you flare, the whole world turns white; you've flown into one of those insidious shallow fog conditions. Visibility was unrestricted when you were looking straight down through the fog, lying in gossamer sheets just above the runway, but when you flatten out to land, you're looking through the fog endwise, and the visibility is something else! Not only is this situation embarrassing if you have to return to ATC for the clearance you gave up so confidently a while ago, but there is also an instinctive reaction to push the nose over when encountering suddenly lowering visibility—that close to the ground, it may be all she wrote.

"HOW ABOUT A CONTACT APPROACH?"

The second short-cut is very much like a Special VFR clearance, using the same basic weather and navigation criteria. Known as a "contact approach," it is unique in that it must be requested by you, the pilot, when you feel you can navigate to the airport by ground reference, thereby eliminating the need to fly the complete published procedure. It's a real time-saver—whenever you can lop a few minutes off the time you spend in the air, you're using the airplane more efficiently, and opening up the airspace for other pilots in the bargain.

Since it is a deviation from the instructions you have received, you *must* receive a clearance for a contact approach. The rest of the way to the airport, it's up to you to navigate, to look out for other aircraft, and to stay at a safe (and legal) altitude. ATC will not turn you loose unless you are safely separated from other aircraft on contact approaches, regular instrument approaches, or those operating under Special VFR clearances. The Tower will probably clear you to land on the first communication and you have just saved yourself the trouble of going to the navaid and flying the complete published procedure, which may have taken you another five to ten minutes.

The specifications for a contact approach call for you to be "reasonably certain" that you can get to the airport on your own—what happens if you are unable to maintain the 1-mile–clear of clouds restriction? You must let the Tower know (or Approach Control if a frequency change has not been given to you) and they will advise you to climb to the appropriate minimum altitude and continue with the published approach procedure. You are still under the protective umbrella of the IFR system, and may continue just as if you had never requested the Contact Approach in the first place.

In summary, then, the conditions for this short-cut are:

1. The *pilot* must request a contact approach.
2. ATC must come back with specific instructions, i.e., "cleared for a contact approach."
3. You must be able to maintain at least 1-mile visibility and remain clear of all clouds.
4. You must be able to navigate to the airport by means of ground reference.

As always, you are expected to avoid other aircraft whenever you are able to see them.

THE VISUAL APPROACH

It is possible to cut down your time in the terminal area through the use of a third deviation from the published procedure, the visual approach. Although it accomplishes the same thing, there are significant differences from the other short-cuts; in the first place, a visual approach is *always* instigated by ATC. You will be radar vectored to a point at which one of two things will happen: Either you'll see the airport or you will be directed to follow another airplane. The Controller will aways ask you to verify that you have the other fellow or the airport in sight. More closely controlled than a contact approach, and obviously a feature of radar-equipped terminals only, the visual approach is intended to lead you directly to the traffic pattern for the destination airport, and short-cuts the "full" approach at the discretion of ATC. It's a "VFR only" short-cut, since the Controller's minimums for issuing such a clearance are 3 miles visibility and ceiling at least 1,500 feet above the ground—when it's honest-to-goodness IFR, you should expect the complete approach.

On occasion, the visual approach clearance is issued when you are behind another IFR flight approaching the same field. When the Controller sees that you are 3 miles from that airplane, he will ask "Barnburner 1234 Alpha, do you have the Trans-Lunar 727 in sight, one o'clock and three miles?" When you answer "yes," he can tell you to "follow the 727, cleared for a visual approach" and your responsibility is to do just that, hoping all the while that the Trans-Lunar pilot is headed for the right airport.

The visual approach presents ample opportunity to cheat, since you can answer "Roger, have the airport [or Trans-Lunar] in sight" when you don't; but you're just cheating yourself, because ATC is expecting you to provide your own separation when in VFR conditions. There may be a considerable number of VFR pilots out there, milling around in the 3-mile murk (in busy metropolitan areas you can *bet* on it!). You are a definite hazard if you accept a visual approach clearance when you're not really "visual."

Here are the requirements:

1. Always instigated by ATC.
2. Visibility minimum 3 miles, at least 1,500-foot ceiling, altitude assigned by ATC.
3. Will not be issued until you have the airport or a preceding aircraft in sight.
4. Puts the "see and avoid" monkey on *your* back after the clearance is issued.

ATC will never ask you to cancel your IFR flight plan—after all, handling instrument traffic is their job, and they are obliged to provide all the services of the system to any pilot who operates IFR. But they sometimes make a request like this: "Barnburner 1234 Alpha, will you accept a contact approach?" It's the Controller's way of trying to tell you that a good purpose can be served by having you fly a short-cut to the full procedure. Never construe this as a goad, but make certain that you are in a position to comply with all the requirements of the situation before accepting. If this is the flight on which you promised yourself you would practice a full ILS right down to the deck, by all means tell ATC that you would prefer the complete approach. Common sense and courtesy suggest that you don't try this at Chicago O'Hare during the morning rush hour; although your request for a full approach will be granted, you will probably hear "Roger, Barnburner 1234 Alpha, cleared direct to the outer marker, climb to and maintain eight thousand, hold east on the localizer course, expect approach clearance tomorrow!"

RADAR APPROACHES

"Barnburner 1234 Alpha, this is Disneyland Approach Control, turn right heading two two zero, vectors for a surveillance approach to runway one eight." Should you hear such a transmission in today's IFR world, chances are the Barnburner is either doing practice approaches or is in trouble; the use of radar for actual approaches has dropped off to just about zero. Radar "did itself in" by virtue of the very feature that promoted it not too many years ago. The fact that an aircraft—*any* aircraft—could be brought safely to earth if the pilot had basic instrument skills and one radio receiver, led many in the flying business to practice self-conducted approaches only for emergencies, such as a radar failure. But it was not in the cards, for air traffic has increased by such leaps and bounds that communications channels would be unbelievably clogged if every IFR flight had to be "talked down." A radar approach requires a lengthy and nearly continuous stream of instructions and corrections from the Controller, limiting him to handling one airplane at a time—air traffic would be backed up all the way to Constantinople if all the flights coming into Kennedy Airport had to be radar-controlled.

So the tables have turned on radar. Once hailed as the best way to get from clouds to ground, it now takes a distant back seat to the cockpit-display type of approach in which one Controller can point several pilots in the right direction and turn them loose, trusting to their navigational skill and keeping communications channels open for directing other flights. But like an understudy waiting in the wings for the leading lady to falter, radar is always standing by for that situation when somebody *needs* a bit of vocal assistance.

When the weather is not too much of a factor and traffic is light, Controllers will be most happy to provide you with a radar approach. They realize that it is a good training exercise; as a matter of fact, it is not unusual to be asked if you will accept a radar approach, since a certain number of squares must be filled each month to keep the Controllers qualified. You have an interest in the skill of the man on the other side of the radar scope (don't you want him to be *good* when it's the only way to get out of the sky?), so go along with his request whenever you can.

There's not much to be gained by practicing radar approaches—you will have proved that you can do very precisely what someone else tells you to, but your instrument training time can be so much better spent on other types of approaches, the ones where all the navigational responsibility is on *your* shoulders. So, know what radar approaches are all about, and now and then go out and run through one, but consider it something you will do only when everything else has turned sour.

PRECISION APPROACH RADAR (PAR)

Because of the communications problem and the availability of other types of approach procedures, *precision* facilities are available at only a handful of joint-use (civilian *and* military) airports, but nearly every Air Force Base and Naval Air Station is equipped with precision approach radar. The military services call it GCA (Ground Controlled Approach), but it's the same thing. When you are in real trouble, unable to make an approach on your own, don't hesitate to holler for the nearest GCA-equipped airbase, and put yourself in their hands. The military controllers are very adept when it comes to gathering wayward airplanes to their center-striped, edge-lighted concrete bosoms—even though it may be zero-zero, give it a try. When the Controller says you're over the runway, reduce your rate of descent to about 300 feet per minute or less, hold your heading, and hope for the best—it's a lot better to blow a tire than to buy the farm. Somewhere in your mental list of good things to remember, tuck away the common military tower frequency: 126.2 is guarded by almost all of Uncle Sam's finest. If you need it, use it, and someone will answer.

Once you have established radio contact with the Controller, he will issue vectors and altitudes which will line you up with the final approach course. At this point, you will be handed off to a Final Controller, who is monitoring your progress in all three dimensions, altitude, azimuth, and distance. As if it weren't enough for the man on the ground to do all the *navigating* for you, he also assumes the *communication* burden when he says "Barnburner 1234 Alpha, this is your Final Controller, you are in radar contact, do not acknowledge further transmissions." What could be easier? All you have to do is to sit there and drive the machine where he tells you.

The Final Controller will provide plenty of advance notice before you reach the glide path. "Barnburner 1234 Alpha, you are seven miles from the runway, on final approach, prepare to begin descent in one mile." If you are not ready to start down, get that way, as he expects you to commence losing altitude the instant he says "begin descent." This is one of the few times in instrument flying when the vertical speed indicator earns its keep; using the Controller's recommended rate of descent as a base figure (he will have provided this after you tell him your airspeed on final approach), make slight power adjustments to get on, or stay on, the glide slope.

The Controller can interpret only what he sees on the scope, and when your blip moves off course, he must assume that wind is the villain, and he makes a correction accordingly. If the deviation from course is the result of your not holding the heading he has assigned, you may wind up with a double correction: one from him for "wind," and one from you as you return to the original heading. You must hold heading religiously on a radar approach—it's all the Controller has to work with.

The small corrections continue, right down to the decision height, which the Controller will mention at some time during the procedure. Depending on the situation, he may tell you when you are over the approach lights, and when you are over the threshold. You must execute a missed approach at the decision height if the runway is not in sight.

Sometime during your instrument training (which is assumed to continue forever) you should be exposed to a precision radar approach. So, fly over to Affable Air Force Base or Nice Naval Air Station, and ask if you can get a couple of precision approaches. Chances are your request will be granted, for they have currency requirements, too; you will probably be limited to low approaches only—no landings allowed—but it will give you an idea of what it's like—if the day comes when you need it, you will not be a total stranger to Precision Approach Radar.

AIRPORT SURVEILLANCE RADAR (ASR)

Whereas PAR and GCA equipment is intended for use as a landing aid, ASR finds its primary function fulfilled as an *approach* control device. Not limited to the final approach area of one runway, ASR beams sweep out a considerable distance and show the Controller air traffic throughout the vicinity of the airport. Coincidentally, it can also be used as a means of vectoring aircraft to the final approach course for all runways at the airport. (Some installations are limited to certain runways because of terrain features, electronic problems, etc.) ASR is a single-scope operation showing only the two dimensions of azimuth and distance; with no glide slope, it drops into the non-precision category, which means that an ASR approach will be flown to a minimum descent altitude (MDA), not a decision height (DH).

Altitude, airspeed, rate of descent, everything except corrections in heading to maintain the final approach course, is up to the pilot. Recognizing the decreased accuracy of ASR, the law says that the Controller must break off the approach when you are 1 mile out, and he'll make it crystal clear: "Barnburner 1234 Alpha, you are one mile from the end of the runway; if you do not have the runway in sight, execute an immediate missed approach."

Flying a surveillance approach is much the same as precision radar, except that *you* will be concerned about altitude, and how fast to descend. On request, the Controller will compute a recommended rate of descent for you, providing a guideline, but it is always best to get down to that minimum altitude just as soon as practical; it gives you more time to look for the runway, and prevents your arriving over the airfield in solid clouds 50 feet above the ceiling, requiring a needless missed approach.

Use the same techniques for flying the airplane on a surveillance approach that you use for precision radar. It's basic instruments all the way, and as such makes a great introduction to approach work for the fledgling flyer. Most terminals with Approach Control will also be set up for surveillance approaches, and will be happy to accommodate your practice whenever traffic allows.

"BELOW MINIMUMS" APPROACHES

Your military and airline brethren are prohibited by regulation from even *starting* an instrument approach when the weather at the airport is reported below their landing minimums. A different approach to the problem shows up in civilian flying rules, where the only limiting factor is visibility; if you fly down to the appropriate altitude (MDA for non-precision, DH on a precision approach) and can see the runway environment, you are within your legal rights to land the airplane. This philosophy reflects sound thinking on the part of the regulation writers, since it allows the pilot to make his own determination of visibility. And who is in a better position to decide? As long as you stay at the published minimum altitude for the approach (this height is the result of exacting computations of the lowest *safe* altitude) and sight the runway at the appropriate time, the ceiling requirement will take care of itself.

Though it's not always the smartest thing to do, you cannot be denied an approach because the weather is bad, but the Controller will deftly remove himself from the hook when the reported visibility is less than that stated on the approach chart for the procedure in use. Suppose that you are cleared for an NDB approach, for which the charted visibility minimum is 1 mile. As you start the procedure turn, Approach Control says: "Barnburner 1234 Alpha, visibility is now one-half mile in fog. This is below published minimums for the NDB approach. Advise your intentions." Just like the old mule-skinner who got his animals' attention by hitting them over the head with a two-by-four, a transmission like this should start some wheels turning between your ears. If you want to go ahead with the approach (and if it appears to you from past experience and knowledge of the weather characteristics of the local area that this, too, will pass), by all means make that your reply: "Roger, thanks for the report, I'd like to go ahead with the approach." And he'll clear you to continue, having satisfied his requirement to let you know.

Inbound now, over the radio beacon and descending toward MDA, Approach Control clears you to contact Tower for landing clearance. Apparently the fog hasn't cleared out or lifted as you thought it might, for Tower comes back with: "Barnburner 1234 Alpha, the visibility is now one-quarter mile, cleared to land Runway Four if you have landing minimums." (The book actually calls for the Controller to say "minima," but there aren't many of them who speak fluent Latin.) Now, that weight you feel on your shoulders is the visibility monkey; once again, the Controller has complied with the law—he has shifted the responsibility squarely onto the pilot.

IT'S ALL UP TO YOU

Here is where the "pilot becomes the visibility observer" law can really work in your favor. You have eased down to the MDA well ahead of the missed approach point, and when the clock tells you that you're there, you look up and see the runway lights shimmering through the fog. Are you legal to land? You certainly are, as long as you can keep the runway lights in sight the rest of the way—you have just established an official visibility observation at the runway, despite the reported one-quarter mile from the Tower. The airport layout often furnishes a clue to the disparity; control towers are seldom near the approach end of the runway, and the Controller's visibility may indeed be only one-quarter mile, which prevents him from being able to judge conditions on the final approach course. You are in a *much* better position to decide "if you have landing minimums."

There is a decided note of permissiveness in this clearance, and as such there is a very big loophole; you can press on in lower-than-minimum conditions, and if you do a good job of navigating, chances are at least fair that you will eventually see the airport, and be able to land. But don't forget that everything is up against the limits, and you've got to do it all right the first time. For one thing, when the visibility is such that you don't see the runway until you're right on top of it, your effective landing distance is drastically reduced. Restricted visibility is usually caused by some type of precipitation, which means that the runway will probably be wet; at worst it may be covered with ice and/or snow. The winds will invariably choose this instant to die, and the whole thing can add up to less runway than you need to touch down and bring the old bucket of bolts to a stop.

So back off and take a good long look at all the factors before you commit yourself in conditions like these. If your first approach finds you too high, too hot, and too hazardous, execute the missed approach procedure, and come back at a slower speed and mentally prepared to pick up the chips. You can't be faulted if you abide by the rules, which give you the benefit of dynamic observation.

SPEED ADJUSTMENTS DURING AN APPROACH

The basic goal of Air Traffic Control in a terminal area is to provide safe separation for aircraft arriving and departing, and as the number of flying machines grows, the control problems increase accordingly. With more operations in the system every day, Controllers find themselves involved in valiant efforts to sort out the speed requirements and performance limitations of a mixed bag of aircraft. At a busy airport, Approach Control is faced with funneling everything from 747's to 150's into the narrow confines of the approach corridor—speed and timing is the name of the game. A veteran railroader visiting an approach control facility noted the multitude of aircraft approaching from all directions at all speeds, flying into the "small end of the funnel" onto a single runway. He could not help comparing this operation with his own experience, in which the main line spread out into many divergent rails in the terminal, allowing trains to come to a stop on any one of a dozen or more tracks. He allowed that trying to put all those airplanes coming from every direction onto one runway was "a hell of a way to run a railroad!"

It isn't likely that we will see multi-runway airports for a long time, if ever, so we're stuck with adjusting speeds and timing to fit air traffic into the approach funnel. Controllers will cut and fit to achieve their objective, and are furnished a set of guidelines with which to do the job. You needn't know what these guidelines are, only that they exist, so that a request for a speed adjustment won't come as a complete surprise. The jets and some of the faster propeller-driven aircraft have little concern with minimum airspeeds, and are more often than not asked to *reduce* speed, but the light airplane fleet is sometimes required to add a few knots in order to fit into the schedule of approaches —that "a few knots" frequently means maintaining near-cruise airspeeds to the final approach fix. Controllers are aware of the limitations of light aircraft, and would not ask a Musketeer pilot to maintain 160 knots, but in most of the light twins and some of the "hot" singles, these speeds are not unreasonable. In any case, you should deal with speed adjustments as *requests*—if Approach Control asks you to fly at 150 knots and there's no way the Barnburner can do it, or if you feel that such rapid passage through the air would jeopardize your performance, reject the request.

14. The NDB (ADF) Approach

AN ADF RECEIVER, adequate training and practice, and a couple of grains of common sense will outfit you splendidly for an NDB (Non-Directional Beacon) approach. (Everybody still knows what you're talking about when you refer to it as an "ADF" approach, but the official title is NDB; and rightly so, for it's the radio receiver in your airplane which is the ADF, or Automatic Direction Finder.) This procedure enables you to fly to a point on a specific course at a prescribed altitude, and from this point continue to a landing if visibility is sufficient. It's not the most accurate method of finding an airport, because it requires considerable skill and technique on the part of the pilot, but it's a lot better than no approach at all. Even with this lack of precision, a typical NDB approach will bring you to within 500 or 600 feet of the airport surface, and the visibility required for landing will be about 1 to 1½ miles.

At the heart of all ADF procedures is "relative bearing"—a term which could no doubt stand a bit of amplification. The azimuth indicator (needle) of the ADF set will always point to a number on the instrument which represents the bearing from aircraft to station, measured relative to the nose of the airplane

("0" on the ADF dial); hence the term "relative bearing." When the relative bearing is "0," the station is straight ahead; should the relative bearing turn out to be 090 degrees, the station is off the right wing tip; at 180 degrees you'd have to turn around in your seat to see the transmitter, and a relative bearing of 270 degrees puts the station off the left wing.

With this constant readout of relative bearing, the navigational task becomes one of determining whether you are on, to the left of, or to the right of a preselected course to or from the station. When you are on course, flying toward the station with no wind to push you off the track, the aircraft heading will be the same as the desired course, and the ADF will read 0 degrees relative bearing. Pass directly over the transmitter, and the needle will immediately swing to the 180 degree, or tail position; if you really want to make it easy for yourself, think of it as a 0 degree relative bearing *outbound.*

A touch of plane geometry will help you understand what happens when you intercept a course with ADF, as well as the mechanics of drift correction. Some geometrician discovered early in man's research into the properties of straight lines that whenever two of them are crossed, the opposite angles are always equal. You can put this knowledge to work on an ADF problem by thinking of the intended course (track) to the station as one straight line, the aircraft's heading the other. As long as the lines are superimposed (on course, no wind), there are no angles and no problem—but if the aircraft heading changes, the ADF needle will move, creating an angle between heading and track.

Conjure up this situation—you are on course, headed to the station, relative bearing 0 degrees. Now turn the airplane 30 degrees to the left; the ADF needle, always pointing to the station, will appear to move to the *right,* exactly 30 degrees—the opposite angles are equal. So, whenever you are *off* course and are flying at an angle to that course so as to intercept it, you'll know you are *on* course when the angles are the same. Using the same principle, you can remain on course with a drift correction that will keep the two angles equal. Using the intended track as the base, you're ON COURSE whenever the heading and relative bearing are displaced the same number of degrees. *Inbound*, heading displacement will be *opposite* that of the ADF pointer—*outbound*, heading and ADF needle will be displaced on the *same side*.

TUNING THE ADF RECEIVER

Radio stations upon which ADF procedures are based are generally called NDBs, for Non-Directional Beacons, which suggests that the signals from these transmitters may be received anywhere around the antenna; the signal is not concentrated, or aimed, in any particular direction. NDBs are found in the lowest frequency band on the low-frequency receiver (usually 190 to 415 KHz); the manufacturer includes two other bands, so you can listen to music, news bulletins, and ball games.

The function switch should be in the REC (receive) position whenever the set is being tuned. It may be marked ANT, for ANTenna, on some radios, but it means the same thing—in either case, the automatic direction-finding function is not operating until you switch to ADF. Tuning in the ADF position means that the needle will try to point to every station it receives as you turn the dial. Just like a bird dog trying to point every quail in a covey—it doesn't give you much useful information, and it's hard on the dog! Give your equipment a break by finding the proper frequency on REC or ANT, then switch to ADF, and let the needle do its thing.

With the exception of the high-powered beacons (which usually carry a transcribed weather broadcast), don't expect a usable signal until you are within 15 or 20 miles of the station. Most NDBs are intended only for approaches and are not powered for long-range reception, so don't complain to ATC about the quality of the transmitter because you can't pick it up 50 miles out.

The Controller will somehow get you within range before he turns you loose to navigate to the beacon.

There is only one way to make certain you have tuned the right station, and that's by listening to the Morse code identifier. A great many ADF stations are crammed into a rather narrow band of frequencies—it's easy to get a needle indication which looks OK, but it's mighty embarrassing to make an approach on the wrong station. It could also cause you to aluminum-plate a hillside, or reduce the height of a radio tower or two.

THE INITIAL APPROACH

Getting to the NDB to commence the approach is a piece of cake with radar vectors, but you'll have to put on your navigator's hat when the Controller clears you "from your present position direct to the beacon." Since the ADF needle always points to the station, you can turn the appropriate number of degrees to put the needle on the nose (or 0 degrees relative bearing), keep it there, and you'll wind up over the station. True, and on a windless day you'll fly directly to the station, just what ATC wants you to do. But throw in a crosswind, and the picture changes. Now instead of making good a direct line, or track, your needle-on-the-nose method will result in a curved path across the ground. This is called "homing," is done best by a specific breed of trained bird, and is not at all what is expected of you; you were cleared *direct*, and ATC would like you to go in a straight line. Leave homing to the pigeons.

In a typical situation, when you receive clearance "direct to the beacon," your heading is 360 degrees and the ADF needle is 40 degrees to the left of the nose. A left turn of 40 degrees will put the needle on 0 and the station directly ahead of you, and that's fine, as long as it lasts. But a right crosswind will eventually drift the airplane off course to the left; you maintain a heading of 320 degrees, and the needle shows the drift by moving slowly to the right. Here is a key point: Whenever the aircraft heading is the same as the desired course, and the ADF needle is off to either side, *it always tells you which way to turn to get back on track.* In this case, it indicates that your intended *track* of 320 degrees is to the *right.*

You must obviously set up a drift correction, but first get back on course (you were cleared *direct*) by turning 30 degrees to the right. When this new heading puts you on the intended course, the ADF needle (always pointing to the station) will point exactly 30 degrees to the *left* of the nose (opposite angles equal). Had you turned right 45 degrees to get on course faster, the ADF will indicate 45 degrees to the left when you are on course. The number of degrees turned is immaterial as long as you remember that a corresponding number of degrees to the *opposite* side on the ADF will tell you when you're on course again.

Now apply some drift correction—start with 10 degrees. As long as your heading is 330 degrees (the intended course of 320 degrees plus 10 degrees drift correction) and the ADF reads 10 degrees left, you're on course, and the drift correction is just right. By the cut-and-try method, you'll soon find a heading that will balance drift correction and wind effect—you are proceeding "direct" to the station, as cleared. (You should apply the principle of course bracketing, Chapter 8.) Drift correction is not so difficult if you will think of your situation as one in which heading and ADF needle displacement must remain balanced. If there's no wind, your heading will be the same as the desired course, and the ADF needle will read 0—no angle between the two straight lines, everything in balance. When a 15-degree drift correction to the *left* is needed to stay on track, it will be reflected in your heading, and to balance that, your ADF should read 15 degrees to the *right*; opposite angles equal, everything in balance. A change in ADF indication (maintaining a constant heading, of course) means that your drift correction is not doing the job; if it creeps back toward the nose, you haven't enough crab, and if it goes the other way, you have overcorrected.

A directional gyro that includes some sort of heading "bug" is really a blessing, because it helps you solve the memory problem. As soon as your track to the station is determined, set the bug on that number, and you can tell at a glance how many degrees you have turned to counter the crosswind. Another glance at the ADF indicator will confirm the balanced situation or show the need for another heading change.

STATION PASSAGE AND TRACKING OUTBOUND

When the ADF needle swings past the wingtip position on either side, you have passed the station. Assuming for now that a full approach procedure is required, you must track outbound on a specified course, turn around, and come back to the airport. There are a number of things to do in addition to flying the airplane, so get yourself organized.

As soon as you recognize station passage, use the Four T's: TIME, TURN, THROTTLE, TALK. Note the TIME (with a stopwatch if you have one), TURN to the outbound heading (you can make drift corrections in just a minute; the outbound *heading* is more important now), THROTTLE back to begin descent to procedure turn altitude (if you're not already there), and finally, after everything is settled down and under control, TALK; tell the man you have passed the beacon outbound. You can make it a very brief report: "Tampa Approach, Barnburner 1234 Alpha, Kapok outbound." He'll reply with instructions appropriate to the situation.

Now, if drift correction is required, put it in; remember that when tracking *outbound*, the ADF needle will point rearward, and the "balance" between heading and ADF indication will be on the *same side*. If the outbound course is not significantly different than your inbound track to the station and if the wind stays the same, your 10-degree drift correction will now show up on the ADF as a needle indication 10 degrees to the *right* of the tail. In other words, when the outbound *heading* is off 10 degrees to the right to correct for wind, and the ADF needle is *also* off 10 degrees to the right, you are on course. If things stay just like that, you have the proper drift correction.

To intercept a track outbound, turn to the new heading, note the position of the ADF needle relative to the *tail*. If the needle is off to the right, that's where your new track lies, and vice versa, so head that direction, with one minor change—when outbound, it's important that you get on course as soon as possible, so turn 45 degrees toward the needle right off the bat. When the ADF shows a 45-degree deflection on the *same* side, you are on track; return to the desired heading, plus drift correction if needed. Try 10 degrees, and as long as the ADF needle stays 10 degrees to the same side, everything's shipshape. If it creeps toward the tail, you've too much wind correction—if it moves away from the tail, too little. Even though your ADF dial is imprinted with "18" at the tail of the aircraft, think of it as just another "zero point," and you'll be able to handle the problem more easily.

PROCEDURE TURN

When it's time (two minutes is a safe, practical figure), begin your procedure turn in the direction published on the chart; the headings outbound and inbound are always printed, so turn directly to the proper heading. If you started the turn on course, the ADF needle will have moved 45 degrees from the tail when you roll out on the published heading (opposite angles equal!) and once again note the time. If you miss the 45-degree indication, start the clock when you level the wings, and you'll not be far off.

Fly outbound for one minute (or forty-five seconds plus or minus wind correction if you prefer that type of procedure turn) and then turn 180 degrees in the opposite direction to intercept the final approach course. If ATC has requested that you report "procedure turn inbound," now is the time to do it. When you are on course again, the ADF needle will be 45 degrees from the nose, and it's back to a simple problem of tracking to the station. You may now descend below procedure turn altitude on your way to the next altitude published for the approach.

POST-PROCEDURE TURN AND THE FINAL APPROACH

You've a couple of minutes to kill inbound to the station, but don't get behind the airplane. There are three things you can do here: First, compensate for wind drift—most final approach courses (from station to airport) are the same as the inbound course you are on at this point, and wind direction *generally* becomes more southerly as you descend, so anticipate it. Second, slow the airplane to approach speed, and third, configure the airplane for the final approach; gear down, flaps as required, so all you'll have to do at station passage is to reduce power to descend comfortably to minimum altitude.

When the needle swings, note the TIME (the Missed Approach Point is always based on timing on an ADF approach, unless the beacon is located on the airport), TURN to the final approach course if necessary, THROTTLE back for descent, and when a comfortable rate of descent is established, TALK—"St. Petersburg Tower, Barnburner 1234 Alpha, Kapok inbound." Nine times out of ten you'll be cleared for landing.

Now you're down to the nitty-gritty of the approach, and your objective is to get to the MDA as soon as practical, so that you can look for the ground. Be sure to arrive at MDA well ahead of the missed approach point—it's embarrassing and terribly inefficient to miss an approach because you didn't get down to the MDA soon enough.

Your rate of descent from final approach fix to MDA is based on the estimate ground speed for this segment, and the surface winds from the Tower are as good an input as any at this point. Your approach chart furnishes the time-distance figures (Jeppesen usually provides the required rate of descent for a no-wind situation), but it's a better practice to get down to the MDA well in advance of the missed approach point. You are guaranteed terrain and obstacle clearance for the entire final approach segment if you remain at the MDA—the sooner you can see the ground, the better off you'll be, so choose a comfortable rate of descent—one that you can handle, and one that will get you to the MDA quickly. When you get there, STAY THERE until you either see the airport or your time has elapsed. Airport in sight? Go ahead and land, in accordance with the Tower's clearance.

But suppose the clock hands race around to the appointed mark, you're at MDA, and still "in the suds." Don't hesitate, *don't* go down further to take a look, *do* execute the missed approach procedure NOW!

THE RADIO MAGNETIC INDICATOR (RMI)

NDB approaches fall into the shooting-fish-in-a-barrel class if you are fortunate enough to have a Radio Magnetic Indicator installed in your airplane. Fundamentally, it is a slaved gyro heading card which moves under the ADF needle. (Some installations include a second needle which points to a VOR.) Now, instead of the non-RMI presentation in which "0," or the nose of the airplane, is always at the top of the dial, the aircraft's magnetic *heading* appears under the top index; therefore the ADF needle *always* points to a number that represents the magnetic course to the station.

In the previous example, when you are cleared direct to the beacon, the ADF needle would still indicate that the station is 40 degrees to the left of the nose, but it would also show that the course to the station is 320 degrees. When you turn to the left, roll out on that heading (320 degrees), and as long as the needle stays on that number (which will also indicate a zero relative bearing), there is no drift, and you are proceeding direct to the NDB. If wind begins to drift you off course, the ADF needle will again tell you which way to turn to get back on track, but with the RMI at work for you, the correction is much easier. Use the same method of turning toward the needle, but rather than having to go through the mental calculation of balancing heading change and relative bearing, hold your into-the-wind correction until the needle once again reads 320 degrees. From here on, do whatever is necessary to keep that needle on 320 degrees, and you can rest assured that you're tracking direct to the station. (You may notice that whenever the ADF needle is on the prescribed course, it will also show a relative bearing that balances the drift correction, but you don't have to figure it out—the RMI does it for you.) Track outbound the same way, keeping the needle over the number that represents course to the station (it will be the reciprocal of your inbound track), and you will be on course. The inbound portion of the procedure turn is made much easier with an RMI; just fly on the inbound heading until the needle points to the inbound course, at which time you turn to that heading, and keep the needle where it belongs.

A less expensive version of the RMI consists of a manually-rotated compass card; with this system, it's up to you to put the aircraft heading under the index (don't forget to change it whenever you turn!). Otherwise, it is used in the same way as its electrically-powered big brother.

15. The VOR Approach

BY THE VERY NATURE of the electronic equipment involved, the VOR approach climbs a rung higher on the accuracy ladder; but it still must be ranked with the non-precision procedures, since it lacks a glide slope.

The number of VOR approaches has grown steadily through the years, as the criteria for an instrument procedure are met at more and more small airports. Since an already-in-place VOR has the potential of serving several airports, you'll find that it is the most-used approach aid. The surrounding terrain has a lot to say about which airports qualify for approaches from a given VOR, as does distance. The latter will furnish some surprises though, because there are many airports located 8, 10, sometimes 12 miles from the omni—Maxton, North Carolina, has a VOR-DME procedure which is practically a cross-country trip in itself; the airfield is 27 miles from the VOR!

TUNING THE RECEIVER

Tuning a VOR is as easy as falling off the bottom wing of a Stearman—it's simply a matter of making the proper numbers appear in the windows. Whether you have to turn a crank or twist knobs, make it an unfailing habit to IDENTIFY the station after tuning—it can ruin your whole day when you fly a beauty of an approach, only to run into a mountain because you didn't have the right station tuned. The FAA people are careful to separate frequencies so that you will pick up only one VOR during an approach, but don't forget Murphy's Law: "If there's a way for something to go wrong, it will." TUNE AND IDENTIFY—a rule that will keep you out of trouble.

So you're not a Samuel F. B. Morse—maybe the only code you can really understand is S-O-S. Fear not, the coded identifiers are transmitted slowly enough for you to follow them, matching what you hear with the dots and dashes on the chart. After a while, close-to-home stations will become familiar patterns of dits and dahs. If you like to become constantly more professional about this flying business, there are a number of quick-learning techniques for remembering Mr. Morse's brainstorm—for example, the VOR at Zanesville, Ohio, is identified with ZZV, and it sings "Old-Man Riv-er, Old-Man-Riv-er, this-is-a-Vee" twenty-four hours every day (- - • • , - - • • , • • • -). Not much of a melody, but great lyrics!

Some stations even identify themselves with a recorded voice, saying, for example, "Indianapolis VOR." And if you want your spirits lifted some dark, stormy night, tune in one of the omnis down south, and let a lovely southern FAA belle whisper the name of the station in your ear as only a Dixie gal can do—the whole world suddenly seems brighter!

THE INITIAL APPROACH

By turning to the inbound heading and holding it, you will soon be able to tell whether or not you are drifting, and which way—the rate at which the CDI moves away from center gives you an idea of how *fast* you are drifting. As soon as the needle moves, go after it—start bracketing the course, as outlined in

Chapter 8. The secret is to recognize drift, turn to a heading to correct for it, and hold the heading until something happens. Your technique from here on out depends on the direction and velocity of the wind; store the correction in a corner of your memory so you can anticipate headings and ground speeds during the approach.

STATION PASSAGE AND TRACKING OUTBOUND

You've done a good job of tracking to the station when the TO-FROM indicator reverses itself in the blink of an eye—the faster it flips, the closer you are to the station. But even if it takes several seconds, you have officially passed the VOR as soon as FROM appears, and it's time to proceed with the next segment of the approach.

The best way to start is with the Four T's: TIME, TURN, THROTTLE, TALK. Start your stopwatch or note the TIME, TURN to the outbound heading, THROTTLE back to slow down and descend to the procedure turn altitude, and finally, when everything's under control, TALK to the man—let ATC know that you are outbound from the omni. Don't be in a rush to make this report; the Controller knows what you are doing, since he cleared you for the approach, so get the airplane going in the right direction before you pick up the mike.

You are obliged to get on the outbound course before starting the procedure turn, so after station passage, put the right numbers on the OBS, and take a look at the CDI—it will tell you which way to turn.

You've been descending all this time, of course (gets a little like rubbing your head and patting your stomach, doesn't it?), and your target is the procedure turn altitude, on course, ready to begin the turn. A VORTAC (VOR station with distance-measuring capability) makes it a simple matter to determine your distance from the station. In the absence of DME, keep track of the time outbound.

PROCEDURE TURN

Procedure turn altitude is a minimum to be observed until you are on course inbound, at which time you can usually descend. (Sometimes terrain requires that you stay up there all the way to the station.) During the turn, change the OBS to the inbound course. As the CDI begins to center, start your turn to the inbound course, applying drift correction as necessary. (Detailed techniques for the various types of procedure turns are found in the first section of Chapter 13, "Instrument Approaches.")

POST-PROCEDURE TURN AND FINAL APPROACH

Unless obstructions make this airspace untenable, the post-procedure–turn course to the station will be lined up with the final approach, that electronic line down which you're going to fly to the minimum altitude. Take advantage of this opportunity to really nail down the drift correction; you can get a general idea which way the air is moving as you fly this segment. You should also be slowing the airplane to approach speed, and accomplishing your "Before Landing Checklist." Having these things done early will let you focus your attention on precise flying during the final approach segment, when the chips are down.

The closer you get to the station, the more the CDI seems to defy your efforts to keep it centered—the needle will move more frequently and rapidly, but think of this as increased accuracy (which it really is), and make the most of it with very small corrections. When the CDI begins to move, start bracketing—a few "cuts and tries" will establish a heading just right for the wind that exists. Here's where the needlechaser will rack his airplane around 30 or 40 degrees, whereupon the CDI comes roaring back across center and off to the right, prompting a 2g turn the other way, which then makes the needle zip to the other side—all this is happening while he is getting closer to the omni, which makes the CDI even *more* sensitive. By now, fixation has set in, and the needlechaser has lost all interest in altitude and airspeed; as if that weren't enough, Approach Control will always choose this moment to ask, "Barnburner 1234 Alpha, what are your intentions after this approach?" The reply to that question is frequently unprintable!

Over the VOR, the TO-FROM reversal will be abrupt, and it's your cue to exercise the Four T's again. You are required to report over the final approach fix inbound, but all you need to say is "Barnburner 1234 Alpha, VOR inbound."

The final approach segment is the climax of your short love affair with this VOR station; everything depends on your making the right moves. Your attention should be devoted to, first, keeping airspeed, altitude, and heading right where you want them; second, descending on course at a rate that will get you to the MDA well before your time runs out; third, keeping track of the time elapsed so you'll know when to pull up should it become necessary; fourth, looking for the airport. Don't expect to see it, and you'll get a nice surprise when it comes into view!

Give yourself a break by getting down to the minimum altitude just as soon as practical, because you'll likely establish ground contact that much sooner. Remember that as ground speed increases, rate of descent must increase if you are to lose the same amount of altitude in a given distance.

A typical VOR approach (excluding those situations where unusual terrain features and/or distance from omni to airport require higher minimums) will bring you to the missed approach point about 300 or 400 feet above the airport elevation, and will require from ¾ to 1½ miles visibility. Keep the CDI centered, descend to MDA, fly out the time, and if the weather man cooperates, you'll find yourself all set up for a normal landing.

THE VOR APPROACH WITH DME

Distance measuring equipment (DME) adds a second dimension to the capabilities of a VOR station. Without DME, the best you can do is to locate yourself somewhere on a radial, dependent on timing to provide information relative to distance. Considering changes in wind velocity and airspeed, and the interpolation required on the time-distance tables, your position on a VOR approach is nothing but a good estimate at best. With DME, the added precision is reflected in more favorable minimums for the approach.

Approaches using DME fall into two operational categories: those in which DME provides step-down fixes and lower minimums than the VOR-only procedure, and those in which DME is an absolute requirement. In the first case (DME optional), a pilot experiencing DME loss could continue the approach, but at the higher VOR-only MDA. The second category requires *both* VOR and DME equipment, and makes no provision for pressing on if the mileage-meter falls out of the instrument panel.

Check the approach chart to determine whether the distance measuring equipment is required, or is considered an adjunct to the procedure. The key is the inclusion of a separate set of minima for DME-equipped aircraft, indicating one MDA when you've got it, another when you don't. In the illustration, Category A and B aircraft are permitted to descend to 2,620 feet MSL until the 3½-mile fix is identified, then are cleared down to an MDA of 1,860 feet. If no DME is available, or is not part of the aircraft equipment, you must maintain 2,620 until reaching the missed approach point—it has in effect bought you 760 feet (and 1 mile of visibility). If you frequently use such an airport, DME might pay for itself in one season by permitting landings from approaches which otherwise would have been missed.

On the other hand, a VOR-DME procedure which does not offer the option will have only one set of minimums listed—that approach *cannot be executed* unless you are equipped with *both* VOR and DME receivers, in working order (assuming that both transmitters are also operative).

Phelps-Collins Airport at Alpena, Michigan, displays still another means of putting DME to work for a more efficient ap-

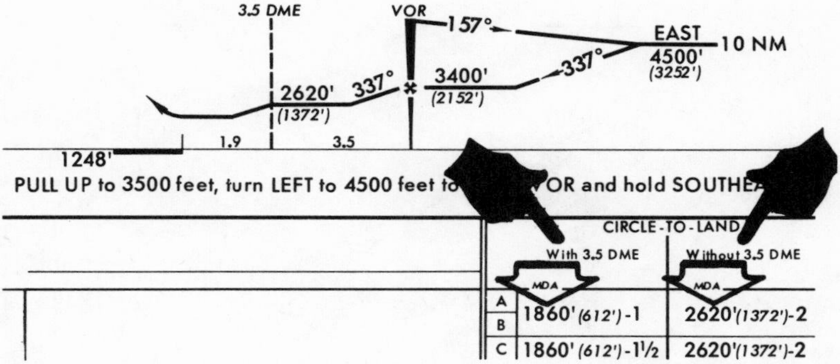

With DME available for more accurate positioning on the final approach, the MDA is considerably lower. © 1969 Jeppesen & Co., Denver, Colo. All rights reserved. Not to be used for navigation.

proach procedure. Instead of maneuvering your way around a procedure turn, you could be cleared to intercept the 10-mile DME arc, to proceed around that circle until reaching the final approach course, and then fly straight in to the airport. Although it requires a bit more technique and some diligent practice before it can be accomplished smoothly, flying an arc approach can save you time and give the Controller additional flexibility in spacing inbound traffic. For example, suppose you are inbound to Phelps-Collins from the west, and are instructed to proceed inbound on the 260 radial until intercepting the 10-mile arc, cleared for the VOR Runway 12 approach. Nothing different about it so far, but when the DME indicator gets close to 10, be ready to make your move. Remember that you are approaching on a 90-degree intercept heading, and things will happen rapidly when the time comes; here's where practice comes booming through in spades, where you should know what mileage lead to use for your airspeed. For groundspeeds of 150 knots or less, a lead of ½ mile should be used—in other words, start turning when the DME reads 10½ miles. As groundspeeds increase, you can compute the proper lead by using this formula: ½% of

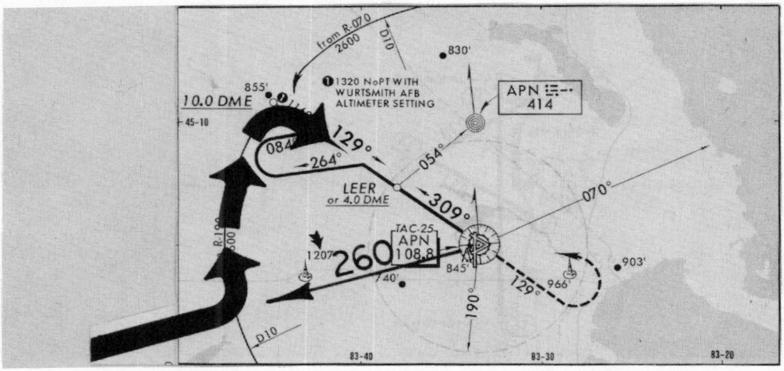

"Intercept and proceed via the 10-mile arc, cleared for the approach." Note the minimum altitude and NoPT on the arc. © 1968 Jeppesen & Co., Denver, Colo. All rights reserved. Not to be used for navigation.

your GS = lead in nautical miles. A standard rate turn is assumed in both situations.

It is obvious that you must turn left 90 degrees, but don't attempt to fly in a continuous circle to keep the DME on 10—that would require your complete attention, to the detriment of all the other things that are going on. Your flight path should be a series of segments which are tangential to the arc, and it is convenient to use 20-degree heading changes as a guideline. When you complete the turn to 350 degrees, the DME should read very close to 10, and it should stay there for a short while, depending on the wind, and your airspeed. If a strong west wind appears to be drifting you toward the station, the DME may move slightly toward 9 miles, but will eventually slide back to 10 as you fly into the arc again. In a no-wind situation, you should turn to the right 20 degrees (new heading of 010 degrees) as soon as the indicator starts to move away from ten miles. Hold this heading until you once again observe the mileage increasing, then turn another 20 degrees to the right. Keep it up, turning farther and farther to the right to keep the DME as close to 10 as possible, until you notice the CDI beginning to center (you set the OBS on the inbound course of 129 degrees as soon as you intercepted the arc). You are on another 90-degree intercept, and should keep turning to the inbound course to center the CDI. From here on, it's just another VOR approach—fly straight down the chute to the missed approach point. A procedure turn is neither desirable nor permitted, since you are already lined up on the final approach course.

The pilot whose instrument panel sports a Radio Magnetic Indicator (RMI) has one more thing in his favor when he is cleared for an arc approach—it takes most of the work out of staying "in orbit." At the completion of the first 90-degree turn, the RMI will point to the right wing-tip position (or the left, depending on the situation), and will immediately begin moving toward the tail, unless you're flying head-on into a hurricane. When the RMI pointer has moved tailward 10 degrees, make your first 20-degree heading change, observing the DME to confirm that you're still close to the 10-mile arc. In a light wind, the 20-degree turn will put the RMI pointer 10 degrees ahead of the wing-tip position, and you can wait until it returns to 10 degrees behind before changing heading again.

16. The ILS Approach

THIS IS THE GRANDDADDY of 'em all when it comes to getting down close to the ground! That point to which any instrument approach procedure leads you is at its "brass-tackiest" using ILS, and with the most sophisticated equipment the point can be literally right on the runway—a zero-zero approach. Special authorization for airport, airplane, and pilot is required for Category II and III (reduced minimums) ILS approaches, but the "normal" procedure, available to all adequately-equipped aircraft and any instrument-rated pilot, allows landings from a Decision Height of 200 feet if visibility is ½ mile or better. CAUTION: This is the typical situation—some approaches have DH's somewhat higher than 200 feet, and visibility minimums greater than ½ mile, so check each approach chart you use and know what you're getting into!

In strict legalese, an ILS approach may be conducted only if all four electronic components of the system are operating and receivable in the aircraft. These four, localizer, glide slope, outer marker, and middle marker (defined in Chapter 2, "The Language of Instrument Flying"), are supplemented by the Approach Lighting System (ALS). The important thing to understand is that you may not descend to "full ILS" minimums if your aircraft is not equipped with all the black boxes, or if all of them aren't black-boxing properly, or if the transmitters on the ground are out of business. The localizer is the backbone of the ILS; when it's inoperative, you might as well request some other procedure—without a localizer to line you up with the runway, the approach is impossible.

Lack of an approach lighting system raises the minimums a bit, losing (or not having) an outer marker receiver bites even deeper, and no glide slope capability really takes a toll on how low you may descend. Without a glide slope, you are automatically pushed into the "non-precision approach" category, which will raise the minimums significantly.

FLYING THE LOCALIZER

It's the same receiver and the same indicator (the CDI) you use for VOR navigation, but some important electronic changes take place when you select a localizer frequency. First, the CDI becomes four times as sensitive, since the localizer course is only about 5 degrees wide—this means that the needle moves much more rapidly and the displacements are much larger. (It's roughly four times as sensitive as it was when tuned to a VOR.) Second, the omni bearing selector (OBS) with which you select VOR courses for navigation is cut out of the system; the CDI is now responsive only to a left-of-course or right-of-course signal, or a blend of the two, which gives you an on-course indication. (Even though the OBS is inoperative, it's a good idea to set it on the localizer course as a reminder of the track you want to maintain on the approach.)

The instrument designers made it easy for you when they set up the left-right needle—if the CDI *points* to the left, you should *fly* to the left to get back on centerline. When it moves off to the right, turn to the right; it's really that simple. The CDI will always show you which way to turn to get back on course as

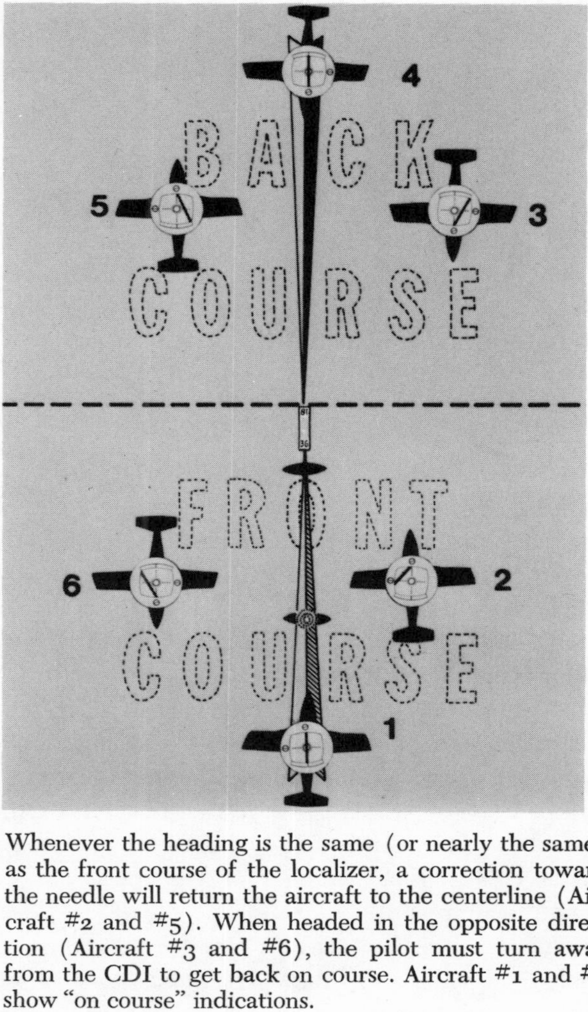

Whenever the heading is the same (or nearly the same) as the front course of the localizer, a correction toward the needle will return the aircraft to the centerline (Aircraft #2 and #5). When headed in the opposite direction (Aircraft #3 and #6), the pilot must turn away from the CDI to get back on course. Aircraft #1 and #4 show "on course" indications.

you are *flying toward the runway on the front course* (during a normal approach), or *away from the runway on the back course* (executing a missed approach). You will always fly *toward* the needle on an ILS approach.

TUNING THE ILS RECEIVERS

Since you are about to make use of a *system* of navaids, there is more than one receiver involved. First, set up the localizer frequency on the VOR receiver, and listen for the identification; it will always be three letters in Morse code, preceded by the letter "I" (• •). So, the localizer at Los Angeles is I-LAX, at Minneapolis it's I-MSP, and so on.

When the localizer frequency is selected (always an odd tenth, such as 109.1, .3, .5, .7, .9, etc.), it will automatically tune the glide slope receiver, a completely sēparate unit. Since there is no way you can identify it aurally, don't worry about it. If you are reasonably well lined up for the approach, the localizer and glide slope needles will come alive when the frequency is selected. Don't panic if the needles refuse to budge when you're approaching from the side; the ILS signals are somewhat directional in nature, and are not very strong except on the approach course, where they are intended to be used.

Tuning the next navaid is not really tuning at all, because the 75 MHz marker beacon receiver is a single-frequency, non-tuneable radio. *Every* outer marker, *every* middle marker, transmits a signal on 75 MHz, the only difference being in the pattern; the OM sends out continuous dashes (- - - -), while the MM transmits alternate dots and dashes (• - • - • -). So make sure that the receiver is turned on, and the volume turned up. (Check the blue [OM] and amber [MM] marker beacon lights if you have them—they are not required, but help you identify these markers as you pass overhead.)

Although not a requirement or an official component of the ILS, you will find compass locators (LOM) installed at many airports. (Some Controllers call them "Outer Compass Locators.") The LOM is really just a low-powered NDB sited at the same place as the OM, providing navigational guidance to the OM (that's why it's called a "locator"). It also serves as an additional indication of *passing* the outer marker, and you may legally substitute your ADF receiver for the marker beacon receiver to comply with the "four components" rule. (A radar position is also acceptable.) The compass locator is tuneable, with a frequency (from 190 to 415 KHz) printed on the chart, and with a Morse code identifier. It is usually the first two letters of the localizer's three-letter identification; hence, the LOM at Los Angeles (LAX) will probably be LA, at Minneapolis (MSP) it will be MS.

INITIAL APPROACH

A terminal with enough traffic to justify an Instrument Landing System will probably be radar-equipped, which means that the initial approach will consist of vectors until you are established on the localizer. Because of this, procedure turns on an ILS approach are as outdated as narrow neckties—but there may come a time when you have to accomplish the approach all by yourself, with no help from radar, so you should know how to do it.

Notice that the ILS Runway 27 Approach Chart for Metro Wayne County Airport in Detroit indicates several points from which flights are normally cleared to the OM to begin the ILS approach. Each of these initial approach routes has its own course to the OM, the distance, and a minimum altitude; from the Salem VOR, it's 126°, 20.7 NM, and the lowest safe altitude is 2,500 feet—from the Carleton VOR, the course is 051°, 15.3 NM, and no less than 2,500 feet.

Some initial approach routes are nearly lined up with the localizer course, and do not require a procedure turn. When this situation exists, the route will be labeled "NoPT," and you are expected to proceed as charted, straight in, with no procedure turn. An example is the route shown from LaSalle Intersection;

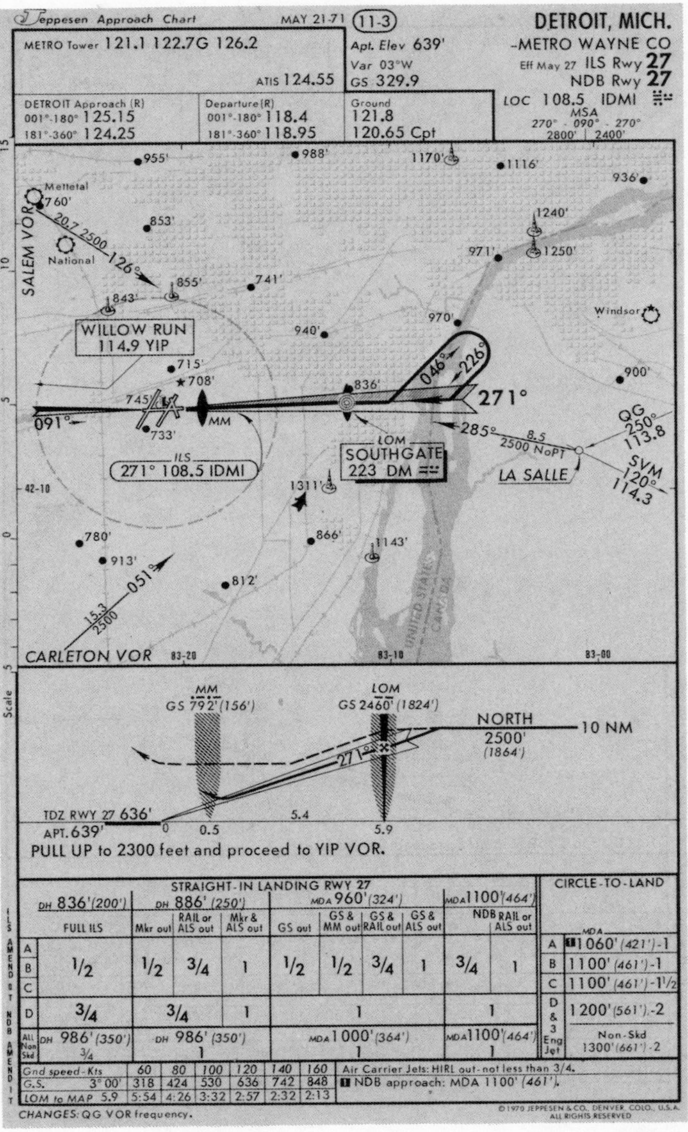

Approach and landing chart for the ILS to runway 27 at Detroit's Metropolitan Airport. © 1970 Jeppesen & Co., Denver, Colo. All rights reserved. Not to be used for navigation.

notice that the minimum altitude (2,500) coincides with procedure turn altitude, and you should be ready to commence descent upon intercepting the glide slope. The Controller should have you down to a compatible altitude by the time you cross LaSalle, but if you need a procedure turn to lose altitude (ear problems, maybe), by all means ask for one, and chances are you'll be cleared. But don't do it without clearance, because Approach Control may have a 747 breathing down your neck! (Another situation which precludes a procedure turn is one in which you have been radar vectored to the final approach course [the localizer] and have been cleared for the approach; in this case, you're all lined up, courtesy of radar, and there's no need to turn around.)

Assume you have been cleared "from over the Salem VOR direct to the Southgate compass locator, descend to 4,000 feet, cleared for the ILS Runway 27 approach." You're on your own now, and after acknowledging the clearance, begin descent to 4,000 feet and track inbound to the OM via the Salem 126 radial. You should be tuning radios, cleaning up the cockpit, listening to other aircraft, and in general getting your ducks in a row for the approach. If you have two VOR receivers, tune #1 to the localizer frequency and check the identification—leave #2 on Salem, so you can continue on the 126 radial. Use the same receiver for approach work every time and you'll spare yourself the embarrassment of flying the wrong needle, to say nothing of the dangers involved!

The localizer needle (CDI) will be a long time moving, since the signal is so narrow, but as you get closer to the outer marker, the CDI will begin to center, cueing you to start turning to the outbound heading of 091 degrees. With practice, you will develop the proper lead to prevent overshooting the localizer course—it's a function of airspeed, rate of turn, and wind component, and all three must be taken into consideration.

STATION PASSAGE AND TRACKING OUTBOUND

A pilot flying a fully-equipped airplane has no excuse for missing station passage at the outer marker. Think of all the indications at work for you; the most obvious will be the strident blare of the marker's continuous dashes (following which you will turn the volume to "LOW," where it should have been anyway!), at the same time the blue light is doing its thing, and the ADF needle will swing from nose to tail—it's time for the Four T's.

Plan your rate of descent to be at the procedure turn altitude by the time you turn inbound, and make your descent at a practical yet comfortable rate. Keep the welfare of your passengers in mind—for most non-pilots, a descent of more than 800–1,000 feet per minute can cause problems.

PROCEDURE TURN

After two minutes outbound, turn to the appropriate heading, and your procedure turn is under way. When it's time (depending on the type of procedure turn you elect), turn right to 226 degrees, which sets you up for intercepting the localizer once again. As your heading approaches 226 degrees, watch the CDI out of the corner of your eye—if it's beginning to center, continue your turn and you'll roll out on course. If at 226 degrees it hasn't moved from the left side of the instrument, roll out on 226 degrees and hold it until the CDI starts moving—the proper lead comes with practice. In the opposite situation, the CDI starts moving toward center during your turn inbound; obviously the result of a northerly wind component, it will require an increase in the rate of turn so that you won't overshoot the localizer and wind up doing a series of S-turns trying to get back on course.

The time from localizer interception to the outer marker is a golden opportunity to find out what heading will keep you on course; you can get a good idea of what's going on windwise right here. As soon as you are on course, begin a descent that will put you at 2,500 feet before intercepting the glide slope.

POST-PROCEDURE TURN AND FINAL APPROACH

Finally inbound to the airport, the CDI is making sense again (turn left when it's off center to the left and vice versa), and it's time to configure your airplane for the final approach; drop the rollers, maybe a touch of flaps, and stabilize pitch attitude to obtain approach airspeed. A convenient, comfortable, and safe number to use is power-off stall speed times 1.3—as your experience, ability, and confidence increase, it is good practice to keep your airspeed somewhat higher until just before intercepting the glide slope. (At large, busy terminals you will often be asked to maintain *cruise* airspeed to the outer marker, but don't do it if the resultant "too many things at once" is more than you can handle—tell Approach Control you can't comply, and let *them* handle the traffic separation problem.) By setting up the airplane in approach configuration, at approach airspeed, you will need only to reduce power a bit to establish a rate of descent that will keep the glide slope needle right where it belongs.

Still inbound to the OM, maintaining 2,500 feet, you will note the glide slope indicator begin to move from its full "UP" position; this is a good indication that you are very close to the marker. If you are carrying some extra airspeed, it's time to bleed it off—the final scene in this drama is about to commence. As soon as the glide slope needle centers, reduce power and begin the descent, even though you have not yet crossed the marker. It's completely legal, and is an important part of the approach procedure. Check the profile view of the approach, and you'll see that if the glide slope is followed, you will cross the OM at an indicated altitude of 2,460 feet, and a glance at the altimeter will provide an accuracy check before continuing the approach; if it's way off (how much is up to you), you may have second thoughts about going ahead with the approach.

On course and on glide slope, the marker indications will be just as numerous as they were outbound, and at station passage, only two T's apply—TIME and TALK—"Metro Tower, Barnburner 1234 Alpha, marker inbound." That's all you need to say, for two reasons: First, it's merely a confirmation, since Approach Control has already called the Tower by phone and informed them that you're on the way; second, you are mighty busy flying the airplane, and you really haven't time to waste carrying on a conversation. Likewise, you shouldn't be concerned if you don't, or can't make this report until some seconds have slipped by—your primary job is controlling the airplane, setting it up as accurately as you can on the localizer and glide slope. Tower will usually come right back with clearance to land; they've been expecting you.

And down you go; down, down, down—from outer marker to runway-in-sight or missed approach can be one of the longest periods of time in a pilot's life! Slight power corrections keep the glide slope needle centered (it's always directional; down means fly down, up means fly up) and small heading changes will correct for drift and keep the CDI centered. Don't try to "fly" these two needles—you'll inevitably chase them back and forth and up and down, and you can't win, because the needles can move faster than you can! The only technique that really works well is to plug in the CDI and glide slope as additional instruments in your cross-check. Make corrections on the *attitude* instruments to put the ILS needles where you want them to be. If the CDI slides off a bit to the right, turn to the right 5 degrees (just press the rudder a bit; don't try to bank the airplane for a 5-degree turn) and watch to see what happens—it's important to pick a corrective heading and *hold it* until you can determine the effect on the CDI. Still sliding right? Turn another 5 degrees and see what that does—when you finally get the needle centered, take out corrections in small increments with rudder only, and before long you'll have a heading that will maintain the localizer course. The same technique is used for vertical corrections, increasing or reducing power *slightly* to change your rate of descent so that you will fly back onto the glide slope.

Down, down, and down some more until, with localizer and glide slope needles centered, you see 836 feet on the altimeter. You are at the Decision Height (DH), and you can do one of two things: Either continue to a landing, or execute a missed approach. The regulation-writers, who usually play "Philadelphia lawyer" with flight rules, came up with one of their best efforts here, as far as being brief and concise and crystal clear. "Decision Height" is very relevant nomenclature, because when you get there on a *precision* approach, you've got to make up your mind—either fish or cut bait! If the runway environment (this includes the Approach Lighting System) is visible, and if you are in a position to make a normal landing (they leave that determination to you), you may proceed to touchdown. That's the "fish" situation—but if those conditions are not met, you'll have to "cut bait"; execute the missed approach procedure.

There will be very few times when you start an ILS approach and don't complete it, for two reasons: First, the weather just doesn't get down to ILS minimums and stay there that often, and second, you will probably not be out flying when the weather is that bad. Especially in a single-engine machine, you are pulling the string out rather far in such conditions—if you should experience that increasingly rare occurrence of power failure, you've nowhere to go but down, and since the glide slope requires a rather flat approach path (it's only a 2.5 to 3 degree slope), you're going to need some power to get to the runway. Loss of that power will certainly result in a sudden and intimate meeting with terra firma at some point other than the touchdown zone on the runway.

If you spot the runway from ½ mile out (which is about where you'll be on most ILS approaches when you reach DH), you'll more than likely be able to go the rest of the way to a landing. The law is equally clear regarding your actions if you lose sight of the airport after you go below Decision Height. You must execute an immediate missed approach—no hesitation, no hunting around for the field, get out of there, NOW! Come back for another try if you like (with ATC's blessing, of course), but don't press your luck if the runway doesn't show up at the Decision Height. (When you are cleared for the ILS approach, then to circle for landing on some other runway, you must observe *circling* minimums, which will limit you to a minimum descent altitude [MDA]. You *may not* go down to the DH, even though the Barnburner is fully equipped and all the transmitters are functioning properly. That Decision Height is a safe level for only *one* runway.)

Measured above the highest elevation in the touchdown zone of the runway (the first 3,000 feet beyond the threshold), Decision Heights are accompanied on the approach charts by another figure, called "height above touchdown" (HAT). Most ILS approaches are set up so that you will be 200 feet above the runway when you reach the decision height, but sometimes it will be considerably higher because of local terrain. For example, at Roanoke, Virginia, the DH is 615 feet above the runway, and visibility for the approach is hiked way up to 2 miles because the clouds around Roanoke are mostly cumulus granitus—full of rocks!

The safest, most professional procedure is to fly the glide slope right down to the roundout (the glide slope signal usually flares about 20 to 30 feet above the concrete—it will guarantee that you will clear all obstacles in the approach path and will encourage you to develop the very good habit of considering the runway and its environment as just another "instrument" in your crosscheck). One of the quickest ways to get into trouble at the end of an approach is to attempt a change from all instrument clues (while you're still in the clouds) to all visual clues as soon as you see the runway. Do it the right way—when it becomes visible, begin to include in your crosscheck what you see through the windshield, making it an increasingly larger percentage of primary information, and the transition will be accomplished smoothly and safely. Even when the visibility is only half a mile, you will find that you can effect this transition quite smoothly in the fifteen seconds or so between "runway in sight" and touchdown.

THE LOCALIZER APPROACH

Many general aviation aircraft are without glide slope receivers, and not a few airports have only a localizer transmitter installed. In addition, glide slope transmitters have been known to develop malfunctions—any of these circumstances dictate a localizer approach, which means that everything is there to help you except the vertical guidance of the glide slope. This automatically becomes a *non-precision approach*, with attendant higher minimums. You will be limited to a Minimum Descent Altitude (MDA), and you must rely on timing for determination of the missed approach point.

A localizer approach is therefore flown very much like a VOR approach (it's up to you to begin descent at the appropriate time, get to the MDA, and determine the missed approach point all by yourself), with the increased accuracy of the localizer to line you up with the runway more precisely. The final approach fix on a localizer approach is frequently a marker or an NDB, but it can also be a VOR intersection, or a bearing to an off-course radio beacon. On occasion, the approach chart carries the notation that two VORs are required—one for the localizer, one to determine the intersection making up the final approach fix. If the FAF depends on an NDB or a bearing to another nearby radio beacon, you'd also better have an ADF receiver on board!

Initial approach, procedure turn, and final approach are flown just like the full ILS, with one exception—plan to arrive at the MDA well before your time runs out, to give yourself more opportunity to look for the runway.

Controllers don't have time to ask if you have all the goodies, and will normally clear you for "the ILS approach." If your airplane does not have a glide slope receiver, it's up to you to realize that you cannot execute a precision approach, and you must look up the "Localizer Only" numbers on the chart. *Do not* attempt an approach down to a DH unless you are receiving a usable glide slope signal; that's really asking for trouble! And don't always assume that a localizer approach is authorized for each ILS procedure. On some approaches, the angle required to clear terrain is so extreme that the full procedure is required—no glide slope, no approach at all.

THE LOCALIZER BACK-COURSE APPROACH

One statement, "a back-course approach is the same as a front-course approach without the glide slope," should suffice to explain this procedure; but because the localizer indicator (CDI) seems to work in reverse, everyone develops a hang-up about back-course approaches.

A back-course procedure always lines you up with a specific runway, and although it is not a "precision" approach, it offers minimums much lower than either VOR or ADF. It's up to you to determine by timing when you have reached the missed approach point, and the final approach fix is frequently an intersection rather than a marker or a compass locator. Other than that, the back-course approach is as easy and as accurate to fly as the front-course.

Initial approach and procedure turn techniques are the same as before, so this discussion begins after you have turned around and are flying toward the runway on the back course, and just before reaching the Final Approach Fix. Since completing the procedure turn or intercepting the localizer, you have been flying away from the needle to effect your course corrections. The technique of making a heading change and *holding* it until you see a change on the CDI is just as relevant as it was on the front course, and as you approach the FAF, get the airplane ready to begin descent. When the marker or intersection is passed, three "T's" apply: TIME, THROTTLE, and TALK—you owe ATC (usually the Tower) a report.

There are no approach procedures which require an unsafe rate of descent, but remember that a tail wind will necessitate going downhill somewhat faster. You might consider slowing your airplane a bit when the wind is really pushing you along, so that things don't happen so rapidly.

The LOC(BC) approach is subject to the same regulations as all the others regarding MDA, landing conditions, and missed approach procedures. If you can get to the runway using ground references and you're reasonably lined up with the runway, go ahead and land. If these conditions don't exist, or if they cannot be maintained after leaving MDA, you must "go around."

Some automatic pilot installations have a "Localizer Reverse" function, which allows George to interpret back-course signals properly during a coupled approach (that's where the autopilot does all the work and you record "IO" time in your logbook—"Interested Observer"). A less sophisticated setup permits you to flip a reversal switch on the VOR indicator so that you can fly toward the CDI on a LOC(BC) approach; if you paid for it, go ahead and use it, but don't forget to switch back to the normal function at the completion of your back-course approach, or you'll wind up in a state of complete confusion the next time you try to fly a front-course procedure. Murphy's Law again: If there's any possibility of doing something wrong, somebody will do it.

Flying a back course properly is more a state of mind than anything else. The procedures, principles, and restrictions are not that much different than any other approach; you've just got to sit there, in firm and complete control of the airplane, and ignore the snickering from the back seats as you mumble to yourself "fly away from the needle, fly away from the needle, fly away from the needle."

17. High-Altitude IFR

THE TURBO-SUPERCHARGER, that marvelous pumper of air which makes reciprocating engines think they're running at sea level all the time, has literally boosted light-plane operation into volumes of airspace previously denied to all but the jets, turboprops, and older business aircraft powered by the big radials. Until the coming of the small, relatively inexpensive "blowers," the practical altitude limit was 10,000 feet, and most light aircraft spent so much time getting up there it was hardly worth the effort except on long trips, or when you had to cross the mountains. The single-engine ceiling of normally-aspirated light twins left more than a little to be desired—in essence, when you finally got to the higher levels, there just wasn't much power left.

But now, you can "slip the surly bonds of earth" behind a supercharged engine or two, and climb into the wonderful high-altitude world of crystal-clear air. Up where altitudes change to flight levels, where the winds often move faster than a J-3 can fly, you look down from your oxygenated perch at all the murk below and wonder why you didn't do this sooner. And there's almost as much power available up here as you had at takeoff, which makes for spectacular single-engine performance in light twins. (If the fan stops on a supercharged single, you've got the same old forced-landing problem, but a heck of a lot more time to solve it!)

A wealth of benefits awaits the pilot who shells out the extra dollars to have "supercharged" lettered on the nacelles:

— flight above most of the weather, especially that troublesome twosome, turbulence and icing.
— much faster climb through the weather to "on top."
— the ability to see most thunderstorms and avoid them.
— higher true airspeeds at altitude.
— much greater latitude in selecting the best altitude for winds or weather.
— you can take advantage of fantastic tail winds.
— when it's clear up there, it's *really* clear; no problem seeing other aircraft.
— able to leap tall buildings at a single bound.
— comparatively little traffic, and everyone else in this airspace (above 18,000 feet) is under positive control.
— the ride will almost always be smoother than lower levels.
— if you have an obnoxious passenger on board, you can slyly unplug his oxygen hose and watch him go to sleep.
— in addition to all this, when was the last time you flew *through* a rainbow?

And so on, with every new turbo pilot adding his own pet joys to the list. But like anything worthwhile, all this has a price (in addition to the cost of the equipment) which must be extracted in the form of additional pilot knowledge, new techniques to be learned, and increased vigilance. You'll have to become familiar with a whole new set of enroute charts, because the low altitude paperwork won't do the job above 18,000 feet—it's like trying to take an all-interstate–highway trip with a county road map. Some new techniques will crop up, like changing course over a VOR so that you don't go outside the airway, or learning how far out to request descent when you are cruising at Flight Level 240, or getting used to handling your high-flying bird in a high-speed descent. When you haul people to altitudes which might affect them adversely, they have a right to expect you to know all about this new environment, to be the guardian of eardrums, sinuses, and breathing apparatus. High altitudes are not necessarily dangerous, but the hazards are insidious and unforgiving.

BABY, IT'S *COLD* OUTSIDE!

There are several things that you should check more thoroughly than usual as you preflight for a high-altitude trip, and one of these is the cabin heater. On a sweltering summer day, you may look forward to the cooler air of the 5,000- to 10,000-foot levels you used before you got the turbos, but when you keep right on climbing into the teens and twenties, you won't want the fresh air vents open! Temperatures remain rather low throughout the year up there, with the OAT gauge seldom climbing above the zero mark (Fahrenheit), even in midsummer. In the wintertime, temperatures of twenty below zero are not uncommon. If the cabin heater fails, or won't start, there's no doubt that you can survive, but preoccupation with keeping yourself warm can trigger a chain reaction of inattention and forgetfulness. Besides, it's just plain uncomfortable to sit in a cold airplane—a simple preflight check of the heater saves you all the trouble. If the BTU-maker in your airplane doesn't fire up right away to full output when you ground check it, take the time to get it fixed, or plan the flight for a lower altitude—especially if you have passengers on board for their first flight. No one will walk away from an airplane with as much distaste for the whole business as the one who walks away on benumbed feet, trying to restore circulation to his frost-bitten fingers, and mumbling anti-aviation epithets through blue lips.

There's nothing like a cup of steaming hot coffee to complete the settling-down process at altitude, after the autopilot has taken over the chores and you can relax for a few minutes. But if you wait until this point to open the jug, be prepared for a real surprise—nearly all thermos bottles are purposely designed with a very effective seal around the cap, and as a result you will suddenly expose boiling coffee at sea level pressure to the sharply reduced pressure of high altitude. It's a lot like pulling the plug on Old Faithful, with the painful difference of having the geyser right in your lap! No one can do a good job of flying an airplane with superhot boiling coffee all over, and there's always the chance that you may get it in your eyes—'nuff said. Remember to loosen the cap a bit on the way up so that the pressure can equalize. This is a good practice even when climbing to only 10,000 feet. (If the contents of a sealed container are under pressure to start with, the opening will be even more dramatic. Consider one pilot who popped the cork on a bottle of champagne at FL 230; his airplane *still* smells like the mashing room at Manischewitz!)

WHAT YOU DON'T KNOW *CAN* HURT YOU!

You should have a carbon monoxide (CO) indicator pasted firmly and conspicuously on the instrument panel. Some pilots, especially former coal-miners, insist on carrying a live canary, but it's a good deal easier to glance at the indicator, which turns dark in the presence of CO. Up till now, this may have been of concern only in the wintertime, when heater malfunctions or leaks could fill the cabin with undetectable and very poisonous CO fumes, but you'll be using the heater on nearly all high altitude flights. Have something on board to let you know when a problem exists.

OIL IS IMPORTANT

Another preflight area which is not adequately served by the "kick tire, light fire" school is the oil supply. The engines are not only going to be putting out more than normal power in the turbo-boosted climb to those ever-lovin' high altitudes, they will be doing it for a longer period of time and at a relatively low airspeed. Because of this, the powerplants need all the oil specified in the aircraft manual to help dissipate the thermal energy that is the inevitable result of higher power settings. When you push the nose over at altitude, the increase in airspeed and the well-below-zero air whistling by the cylinders will improve the cooling situation, but during the climb, the oil coolers help get rid of a lot of BTU's. Give your engines a break by making sure that the oil level is right where it belongs before you turn a blade. On some installations, the oil supply for the turbo is a separate system, and must be checked—it too is responsible for heat transfer in addition to its lubrication chores.

TAKE ALONG SOMETHING TO BREATHE

Check the oxygen gauge for full pressure as you continue the specialized walkaround for a high-altitude flight. You should keep this system filled for a number of reasons, not the least of which is always having oxygen when you need it. How frustrating to have the capability and the smarts to climb above an area of icing or turbulence, only to be forced back down where you don't want to be because you didn't fill the oxygen bottle before takeoff! And when you *do* refill it, be very sure that nothing except AVIATOR'S BREATHING OXYGEN goes into the system. Anything else, even medical oxygen, contains a small amount of water vapor, which has a nasty habit of freezing in the lines, shutting off the flow completely. You may save a couple of dollars a tank buying lower grade oxygen, and lose the whole shootin' match when the system freezes shut.

One parting shot about preflighting the O_2 system: Plug in the passengers' masks and put them where they can be seen so that no one gets a big surprise when you break out the nose hoses on the way up. Some folks just don't take kindly to sticking their faces into a big plastic nose with a balloon on the end, and it's much better to find out who these people are when you're on the ground and able to reason with them. (Trying to settle down a near-panicked passenger in the back seat when your hands are full flying the airplane can be a horrendous experience.) With masks plugged in, open the valve and assure yourself that all the indicators show oxygen flow; you'll want each passenger to check his supply later on at altitude, but now is the time to make absolutely certain everything is right.

DON'T FORGET THE CAPTAIN

The extra time spent preflighting the airplane is a complete waste if you neglect the most important system of all—YOU. The nagging cold, the slight headache, can assume monumental proportions when carried to high altitudes—not only are your aches, pains, and bad mood magnified by the environment (in an unpressurized airplane, your body is subject to probably less than half the atmospheric pressure under which it normally functions), but you will find your basic piloting and navigational skills taxed by the increased speed with which things happen. Here's the situation that really develops the "snowball" effect—less than ideal physical and/or psychological condition, coupled with high altitude effects, leads to mistakes and uncertainties, which lead to apprehension and tension, which lead to increased oxygen consumption, and on and on until the worst may happen. If you don't feel up to it, don't make the flight at all.

MAKE THOSE TURBOS WORK FOR YOU

Planning for a high-altitude IFR flight involves more than just picking out a convenient route, eyeballing the distance, and guestimating how long it will take. On relatively short flights, you'll discover an optimum altitude for almost any day (excepting really strong winds, icing, or turbulence), and it will probably be higher than you've been flying! With turbos providing the capability for rapid climbs, you will make money in direct proportion to your altitude, and passengers will be more comfortable in the bargain. It's amazing how people will remember the ten or fifteen minutes in smooth, clear air even though you climbed through lumpy sky for ten minutes to get them there. Common sense dictates that you shouldn't go to 15,000 feet for a fifteen-minute trip, but when you fly high, you'll be more comfortable, safer (because you will be up there where you can *see*), and remarkably close to the elapsed time of the same trip flown at lower altitudes, down in the murk where everybody else is groping along.

On the longer, more critical trips, you want those expensive air pumps to work most effectively for you, so set your sights high. Considerable advantage can be gained even without penetrating the High Altitude Airway system (above 18,000 feet), especially when you are headed west. The upper air over the United States moves mostly from west to east, and sometimes at three-digit speeds—so a general rule would be to fly lower westbound, and as high as practical eastbound. It's picking out that westbound altitude that becomes tricky, since even though you may be flying upstream, the increase in true airspeed at altitude could more than make up for the head wind.

You can't go too far wrong using the 2 percent-per-1,000 feet rule of thumb to help make the altitude decision. If your airplane indicates 150 knots at 10,000 feet, you can figure on a *true* airspeed of close to 180 knots—this will hold up as long as the turbos can maintain constant power. The difference becomes quite dramatic at high altitude, where true airspeed may often be half again what the indicator shows!

Of course the price to be paid is the time you spend climbing to altitude at a high power setting and a low airspeed. How far you intend to go becomes important, too—the extra knots generated by the turbos may not be justified by the many-gallons-per-hour pouring through the fuel injectors. Sometimes it becomes a matter of deciding whether to go fast for a short distance, or to give up some speed in exchange for making the trip non-stop. Remember also that turbine-boosted engines don't always have to be run wide open.

Comfort and weather conditions bear heavily on your decision, so there's really only one way to arrive at *the* altitude for an extended trip—get out your computer and weigh performance figures for several altitudes against all the other factors.

HIGH ALTITUDE CHARTS

It's not as thrilling as breaking through the sound barrier, but when the snout of the *Turbo*Barnburner pokes through 18,000 feet, you've flown into a new world of regulations. Some major restrictions affect your operations up here, and they should be recognized in the planning phase. For example, you *must* use the separately-published High Altitude Enroute Charts (either U.S. or Jeppesen).

A number of differences are apparent when comparing the High Altitude charts with their below–18,000-foot counterparts; the most striking change is that a whole bunch of charts is missing—but you get your money's worth, even though there are only two pieces of paper in the mail at revision time. Because of the tremendous increase in true airspeed at high altitude, fewer checkpoints are needed, and consequently the coverage of the charts is greatly increased. Just think how far you can fly without having to refold a chart! You may also notice right away that the Jet Routes (even the name "airway" changes up here) have legs much longer than low-altitude airways.

Selection of a route in the high-altitude structure is easy—pick out the Jet Route that runs closest to a straight line between here and there, and depend on radar to get you started and stopped. Almost every high-altitude flight gets under way with vectors to a nearby VOR, or until intercepting the desired route. The same situation prevails at the other end, where you will be worked into the approach environment with the all-seeing eyes of radar. Be especially cognizant of Standard Instrument Departures

(SIDs), Preferred Routes (which are published separately for high-altitude operations), and Standard Terminal Arrival Routes (STARs) when filing—you're working with the big-leaguers, and should expect to receive the same kind of ATC handling, so be prepared. When you get right down to it (beg your pardon, right UP to it), route planning for a high altitude flight is much easier, with fewer checkpoints and more direct legs.

POSITIVE CONTROL AIRSPACE

All the airspace above 18,000 feet MSL over the entire United States is rather special in nature—it's called "Positive Control Airspace," and a better name couldn't have been chosen. ATC has an electronic tag on every flight that operates up there, which tends to keep high-speed airplanes from running into each other, and that's *got* to be good for everybody! In order to exercise this positive control, some very specific restrictions and requirements have been legislated for all who seek the advantages of flight above 18,000 feet.

In the first place, there is *absolutely no VFR allowed*—every flight within PCA must be on an instrument flight plan, with an assigned altitude. The IFR-only requirement also limits the type of pilot and airplane permitted to use the upper air, since you and your flying machine must be IFR rated and equipped. And not just normal IFR equipment either, since PCA standards must be observed: You must have a transponder; when above FL 240, you need DME; and at all times within PCA you must be able to communicate with ATC on frequencies they assign. For all practical purposes, this means 360-channel capability, because you will frequently be requested to "contact the Center now on one two four point niner five," or some other 50 KHz-spaced number.

If you insist on flying VFR at high altitude, you can do it legally, but you'll have to go out over the ocean and climb to FL600, which is the upper limit of Positive Controlled Airspace.

SUPPLEMENTAL OXYGEN

An average person will begin to feel the effects of altitude at about 10,000 feet, which no doubt accounted for the long-standing recommendation for oxygen above that level. Today, you as the pilot (and your co-pilot and flight engineer if the aircraft manual requires them) may not operate an unpressurized airplane between 12,500 and 14,000 feet for more than thirty minutes without supplemental oxygen. Above 14,000 feet you must use oxygen *all* the time. The rule was not devised to *encourage* non-oxygen flights at those levels, but to *permit* them for short periods to get you over weather and high terrain. (The law requires you to provide supplemental O_2 for all occupants when flying above 15,000 feet.)

With turbos, you are on your way to heights at which some help in supplying the breath of life is necessary to function properly, and since you probably don't have an "average" person on board, why not plug into the oxygen system at, or soon after, 10,000? It gives you plenty of time to recheck the system before any physiological damage can be done, and helps acclimate you and your passengers to the environment in which you'll be operating for the next hour or so.

Make sure that everyone on board understands that he must remain on oxygen until you give the word to unmask on descent. Now open the valve and have everybody check and let you know that they are "on" as evidenced by the individual flow indicators. Most people just don't realize how quickly they can join the "blue fingernail set" without oxygen at high altitudes, so make it a practice to check your entire complement at least every fifteen minutes—they'll appreciate your concern. The effects vary with individuals, but here's what can happen at turbo altitudes without oxygen:

8,000 to 10,000 feet for over four hours—fatigue, sluggishness.

10,000 to 15,000 feet, two hours or less—fatigue, drowsiness, headache, poor judgment.

15,000 to 18,000 feet, one-half hour or less—false sense of well being, overconfidence, faulty reasoning, narrowing of field of attention, unsteady muscle control, blurring of vision, poor memory. *You may pass out.*

Over 18,000 feet—above symptoms come faster, loss of muscle control, loss of judgment, loss of memory, loss of ability to think things out, no sense of time, repeated purposeless movements, fits of laughing, crying, or other emotional outbursts.

Small children represent a special liability at high altitudes in an unpressurized airplane, and very wee ones probably shouldn't be exposed at all to oxygen-requiring flight levels. Allowing passengers to sleep while at altitude can hardly be avoided, but make frequent checks of their condition.

It is absolutely mandatory that the smoking lamp be out while oxygen is in use.

At the first suspicion of *any* kind of oxygen trouble, descend NOW, and do it FAST, so you can trouble-shoot at an altitude where the dangers are minimized. The pilot's well-being is more important than anyone else's, because if YOU get into difficulty, don't look for much help from a plane-load of hypoxic passengers.

FLIGHT LEVELS

Everyone in the upper reaches (above 18,000 MSL) must fly at an assigned *pressure altitude*. This means that you will set 29.92 in the window on your altimeter, and leave it there until you're once again under 18,000 feet. You are now *flying* at a certain number of feet above the 29.92 pressure *level* (which on a standard day will be at sea level), and so the vice-president in charge of names put the two together and came up with "Flight Level"—the designation for assigned altitudes above 18,000 feet.

There are going to be times when the 29.92 level is so low (as around the center of a deep depression or "low" in the atmosphere) that 18,000 or 19,000 or maybe even 20,000 feet above it would sag down into the Low Altitude Route structure, and would be unusable. When this happens, you will not be assigned a Flight Level unless it is safely above the Low Altitude aviators.

Altimeter Setting	Lowest Usable Flight Level
29.92 or higher	180
29.91 to 29.42	185
29.41 to 28.92	190
28.91 to 28.42	195
28.41 to 27.92	200

Part of your clearance when descending from high altitude will be the altimeter setting in the terminal area, and as soon as you go through 18,000, place that setting in the adjustment window, and rejoin your low-altitude brothers.

HIGH ALTITUDE WEATHER

When you're flying high, weather avoidance doesn't amount to much, except when going through fronts or the hearts of low pressure systems. There is the occasional problem of getting through some nasty conditions on the way up, but once you're there, most of the weather that causes trouble for pilots is below you. Having the capability to operate at the higher levels goes a long way toward all-weather flying, but some days there will be heavy icing and severe turbulence at all levels, with solid lines of thunderstorms lying across every route between here and there —these are the days when it's *much* better to "have loved not at all," than "to have loved and lost!"

Icing is not often a problem at altitude except over high mountainous terrain, because clouds that form on high are usually the cirrus type, composed of ice crystals which for the most part just bounce off the airplane. But the turbocharged engine does have one drawback in this situation—the ice crystals will sometimes collect in the air intakes, partially closing off the supply, and you may experience a significant drop in manifold pressure. You'll be able to limp along at a reduced speed, but your thinking must change as you plan ahead—start checking the weather at terminals this side of where-you-originally-planned-to-go-Municipal. An alternate air source which can be selected if the intakes ice up completely will help, but you'll pay a price in reduced power. The only way to get rid of the ice is a descent to warmer altitudes, if there are any.

Turbulence associated with thunderstorms is one thing, clear air turbulence (CAT) is something else—the very visible presence of a cumulo-nimbus operating at full throttle should serve to warn you away, but CAT can claw at you invisibly, when you least expect it, and it will be the surprise of your life! Thunderstorms are rather well forecast, and there's no excuse for blundering into one. Clear air turbulence is not so easily pinned down, although the weathermen are getting better at it every day—when CAT is suspected along your route at the altitudes you wish to fly, take a long second look. When you spot thunderbumpers ahead (and from your high-altitude vantage point you can see most of them), ask for a route deviation around them—ATC is almost always willing to go along with you. When it appears that there's no way around, and the tops are out of sight, it's time to do something else—implement "Plan B." (*Always* have a "Plan B.")

The sustained high-power and rapid-climb capability provided by your turbos will stand you in good stead in an icing situation, *if you act promptly.* Two sets of circumstances usually prevail: You may be faced with getting through an icing layer while climbing to clear air or too-cold-to-freeze conditions, or you may find yourself picking up the white stuff unexpectedly in a cruise situation. In either case, the ice-producing layer is often no more than a couple of thousand feet thick (check the forecasts—sometimes there are *many* thousands of feet of icing conditions!), so your best bet is to change altitude, and do it NOW! When climbing through a relatively shallow layer, watch for the first evidence of icing—when you see it, slow down your rate of climb, let the airspeed build up, then haul back and get through it in a hurry. When encountering icing in a cruise situation, use that turbo power to get to a higher altitude as rapidly as you can. (Check *Weather Flying*, Chapter 13, for more detail.) It's unrealistic to dictate a climb in *every* icing situation, but if you go up, at least you'll have some more altitude to work with if things get worse. There are two things that are utterly useless to a pilot: altitude above and runway behind.

FAST DESCENTS

A very large payoff of high-altitude flight comes during the descent, when you take advantage of going downhill. You stored up a lot of potential energy in the airplane by climbing, so when ATC clears you to descend, let 'er run—leave the go handles at cruise power and watch the airspeed build. Almost all turbo installations have a manifold pressure limit which is automatically controlled, so don't worry about overboost; the engines think they're still at sea level, and they love to run under those conditions. Descending at cruise power will more than likely push the airspeed indicator up into the yellow caution arc, which is quite all right unless you encounter something greater than light turbulence—if it feels uncomfortable, slow down to a safe speed. (Easy on the throttles!—prolonged descents at low power settings are bad news for engines. Keep them warm with a reasonable amount of power.)

Now you must do some calculating; groundspeed will increase in a high-speed descent, and you must adjust your rate of descent to arrive in the terminal area at an altitude compatible with the approach in use. It's easiest to settle on a rate of descent of 1,000 feet per minute, and let the airspeed stabilize—DME with a groundspeed readout is a big help, but in any event, estimate how fast you are moving over the ground versus your 1,000 feet-per-minute rate, and you'll have a good idea of how things are going to work out. Cruising at FL 200 and anticipating a rate of 1,000 feet per minute, you should request descent perhaps 75 miles from destination (based on a groundspeed of

3.5 miles per minute, and going to a sea-level airport). If you are at a higher altitude, or picking up a real buster of a tail wind, you may want to start down even sooner—ATC is well acquainted with these problems, and will usually grant your request.

EAR PROBLEMS

One thousand feet per minute on the way down is an easily-computable number, but sometimes it just won't get you down fast enough. Here's where you must take your passengers' welfare into consideration, because if you plunge downhill much more rapidly than that, you can bet that somebody on the airplane will leave his ears at altitude, and that hurts a lot! Fortunately, the rate of pressure increase in a descent is very gradual down to about 15,000 feet, but below this altitude, ear blocks and malfunctioning sinuses can really become a problem. If you have a limited distance in which to descend, or if tail winds are strong, do the going-downhill-fast act while you're still above 15,000 feet, and you'll be doing yourself and the people with you a big favor. When you find it necessary to limit your rate of descent, let ATC in on the secret. ANYTIME you or a passenger begins to suffer and the various ear-clearing tricks don't work, level off (advising the Controller you have an ear problem on board will get you any altitude you want) and let the pressures equalize. If one of your passengers is *really* suffering, climb a few hundred feet, which will usually relieve the pain—then start down slowly, making sure he hollers, swallers, yawns, laughs, or whatever else is required to keep inner and outer ear pressures close together.

Most non-flyers, unaware of the dangers involved, will hide their discomfort behind a shield of pride, and before long the problem may solve itself, with a great deal of pain, and certainly a very black public relations eye for you and aviation in general.

Sinuses can be even worse, and you as the house doctor on the airplane should be very familiar with the Valsalva and other methods of relief, as well as knowing when *not* to use them. (Consult a qualified Aviation Medical Examiner.) Better yet, don't take yourself or anyone else to high altitudes when suffering from colds, hay fever, or other respiratory maladies.

HIGH-SPEED APPROACHES

If all has gone well in the descent, there's no need to slow down for the first stages of an instrument approach; in busy terminal areas, where you're being mixed with other high-speed traffic, Approach Control will usually *request* that you keep up your speed as long as possible, sometimes right up to the Final Approach Fix. No problem at all, if you're on top of the situation, meaning that you have to shift into "approach gear" very early. All the suggestions and good operating practices in Chapter 12, "Getting Ready for an Instrument Approach," apply, *in spades*. You'll undoubtedly be radar-vectored onto the final approach course, and things happen in very rapid succession—remember that you have been *requested* to maintain a high airspeed, and if you are uncomfortable, uneasy, and just don't think you can handle it, turn it down. You may be vectored through a less-direct approach, but if it's better for you, don't hesitate to leave the high-speed approaches to them that wants 'em.

18. Proficiency Exercises

SOMEDAY, an edict is going to come down from on high, requiring pilots to demonstrate their proficiency in accordance with the ratings they hold. Air carriers and the military have had such programs for years to check the skill levels developed in intensive training and practiced in day-to-day flying. About the only time a general aviation pilot finds out that he is not quite as sharp as he ought to be is when he gets himself into a bind. In most cases, nobody else knows about it, but on occasion the headlines proclaim his lack of proficiency. When you get right down to cases, is your neck less valuable in your own airplane than when you are a passenger on an airliner? You place complete faith in the man with four stripes on his sleeve because you know he must maintain a high level of competence; there's no reason why you should not demand the same of yourself when *your* hands are on the controls.

Flying, particularly instrument flying, is an art—a sophisticated skill—and unless you fly IFR regularly and frequently, you *know* that you must practice that skill to be as good as you want to be. An occasional IFR cross-country won't do the job, because a typical "real-world" flight consists of following radar vectors and airways until you get into the terminal area, then some more radar vectors to the final approach course, and relatively simple navigation to the runway. When the chips are down and you are required to fly the approach all by yourself, with procedure turns, climbs and descents to predetermined altitudes and headings, missed approaches, and no-radar navigation, your rusty techniques don't do you much good. There's only one way to be sure, to be safe, to be sharp, and that's a regular program of practice—one that will lead to precise control of the airplane almost as an afterthought, with most of your attention and thought processes devoted to staying ahead of the situation. If you're a beginner, the exercises in this chapter will help get you that way, and if you're an experienced IFR pilot, they will help keep you that way. Whether you need to use all or a selected portion of these maneuvers will depend on your particular needs, your skill level, and how often you fly on the gauges. Are you the type who likes to accept a challenge? Run through the entire series next time you're under the hood—you'll soon know whether or not you need the practice.

EXERCISE #1—STRAIGHT AND LEVEL FLIGHT

It's more difficult to keep all the needles, pointers, and numbers standing still than it is to make them move in the proper direction at the proper rate. Flying straight and level, with no changes in heading or altitude or airspeed, is a great deal harder than turning, climbing, or descending, but it's not impossible, so set yourself up in level flight and adjust the little airplane on the attitude indicator so that it rests exactly on the horizon—that's your best reference for what's happening, or what's about to happen. As long as you keep the pitch attitude where it belongs, and the wings level (the ball in the turn-and-bank is assumed to be centered all the time), you will maintain straight and level flight. The altimeter will indicate immediately any climb or descent, and the directional gyro will keep you honest in the heading department. The very instant you detect any change on either of these instruments, apply corrective pressure to stop the movement, then additional pressure to return things to their proper places. The procedure is very simple, and should become an unconscious three-step method to be used in all your instrument flying. First, cross-check the instruments (all of them, as rapidly as possible but with emphasis on the attitude indicator); then, interpret the indications so that you can decide what to do about it; third, apply control pressures to control the situation.

Straight and level flight is difficult because your task is to keep things from happening, and satisfying because it will develop a mental discipline that will carry through to other maneuvers—if you can do a good job of straight and level flight, you're well on the way to precision instrument flying. Stay at it until you can keep the needles steady, narrowing your tolerances as you progress.

EXERCISE #2—STANDARD RATE TURNS

Starting from straight and level flight on a cardinal heading, practice turning at the standard rate of 3 degrees per second. The secret of smooth, accurate turns is PRESSURE; all that you should have on your mind is applying enough aileron pressure to make the miniature airplane begin to bank. A smooth, slow increase in bank attitude is what you're looking for—as long as you maintain the pressure, the airplane will continue to bank, so keep pressing until the turn needle indicates a standard rate turn. (You should know the angle of bank required for a standard rate turn at two airspeeds—cruise and approach. There's an easy rule of thumb which you can apply: Divide the *true* airspeed in knots by ten and add five. This number is the bank angle for a 3-degree/second turn. For example, cruising at 130 knots true airspeed, bank 18 degrees for a standard rate turn.) At this point, relax the bank pressure, notice the amount of bank on the attitude indicator, and make small corrections as necessary to keep it right there. As instrument indications begin to change, cross-checking becomes vitally important—you know that banking the airplane changes the distribution of lift produced by the wings, so as soon as the altimeter moves even the tiniest bit, apply a tad of back pressure to stop it.

The heading indicator should be consulted during the turn, but only with a glance, since your objective is to maintain the bank angle that will produce a standard rate turn. Don't forget about the heading completely, because you want to roll out on a certain number. You may want to experiment with this a bit, but for starters, begin the roll-out when the heading indicator passes through a number that is one-half of the number of degrees of bank from the desired heading. If your standard rate turn requires 20 degrees of bank, start your roll-out pressure when you are 10 degrees from the heading you want. Use the same, slow, deliberate process that got you into the turn, remembering to remove any back pressure you needed to hold altitude—as the wings return to level, the lift you redistributed in the turn will show up as a tendency to climb. A rapid, complete cross-check will help you stop the altimeter before it moves very far. As soon as the turn needle lines up with its center index, you've stopped turning, and you should go right back to the old straight-and-level bit. If you've done it properly, you will run out of bank at the same time the heading indicator comes to rest on the sought-for number. Remember that you are maintaining constant pressure to reduce the bank attitude, which means a constantly reducing rate of turn. After a few practice runs, you should know just how much lead to use to make everything come out even. Most pilots have a strong tendency to roll out of a turn considerably faster than they roll in, so you may have to force yourself to slow down. Slow, smooth application of pressure to effect the desired change in attitude is the secret. You'll soon be making turns that will not even be noticed by your passengers when there are no outside references—this is the target you should set for yourself.

EXERCISE #3—STEEP TURNS

A safe limit in actual IFR conditions is 30 degrees of bank, but there's nothing like the ability to handle your airplane in a steep turn to build your confidence. Start your practice with enough bank to push the turn needle a little past the standard rate mark, and as your skill builds, keep it going until you can fly around confidently and smoothly in a 45-degree bank, rolling out right on the headings you desire.

There are a couple of things to watch for. Roll into the turn at a slow, deliberate rate, and as the bank angle progresses, pay more attention to the altimeter—you are changing the lift situation rapidly as the wings get farther and farther from the horizontal. A steep turn requires a great deal of back pressure, and it's not a bad idea to roll in some trim to help you maintain altitude. Your lead on the rollout headings will have to increase, too, to compensate for the faster rate of turn. When rollout time comes, use the same slow, deliberate pressure that got you into the turn. Don't forget all that back pressure and elevator trim, either.

EXERCISE #4—CONSTANT AIRSPEED CLIMBS AND DESCENTS

Before you can start this one, you'll have to go back to the drawing board to discover the attitude that will produce the best rate-of-climb speed. When you have it nailed down, make a mental note of the picture you see on the attitude indicator—within the limits of available power, you can rest assured that when you apply climb power and rotate the little airplane to that predetermined position, the same airspeed will result. Next, set up an attitude and power setting for practice descents—since this is just an exercise, not an approach situation, leave gear and flaps up, reduce power to just above idle, and play with the pitch attitude until you are descending at 500 to 1,000 feet per minute at the same airspeed used for climbing. Once you've established this, remember the attitude and power setting.

Now you're ready to go to work. From straight and level flight at normal cruise, simultaneously increase the attitude to the predetermined position and smoothly add power to the climb setting. Don't worry about airspeed, it will take care of itself; but you *will* have to increase the speed of your cross-check to keep the heading indicator from wandering off to the left. Feed in whatever rudder pressure is required to maintain your original heading. Sail right on up for 1,000 feet; don't change a thing until you are within 20 feet of the desired altitude, when you should SMOOTHLY press the wheel forward until the little airplane rests on the horizon bar, and hold it there, rudder pressure controlling the heading. As the airspeed builds up to cruise once again, reduce power to normal and that's all there is to it! The higher the climb performance of your bird, the more you will have to lead the level-off, so start with 20 feet and work down from there. As soon as the altimeter hands stop where you want them, they become your primary source of pitch information.

The downhill technique is only slightly different, but of course everything works in reverse. From normal cruise, reduce power to the descent setting you worked out earlier, and hold the little airplane on the horizon bar until the airspeed approaches the proper number for descent. You'll notice a need for left rudder pressure to keep the heading constant, and as your cross-check shows the gyro numbers creeping off the mark, press with the appropriate foot. When the airplane is slowed to the speed you want, SMOOTHLY press the nose down to the attitude you set up in your test, and you're on your way. Descend 1,000 feet, but before you get to the bottom, consider the effect of both gravity and inertia resisting your attempts to level off—increase your lead to 50 feet, at which time you should begin a slow addition of power and a SMOOTH increase in pitch attitude to bring the little airplane to rest on the horizon. As in the climb, you'll have to experiment a bit to find the proper lead for your airplane, the airspeed you're working with, and your personal technique. Coordination and SMOOTH pressure are the keys.

EXERCISE #5—CONSTANT RATE DESCENTS

Descending at a constant, controlled rate is useful when trying to stay on a glide slope, or when you must reach an MDA within a certain distance from the Final Approach Fix. The objective is to set up the descent airspeed, then control the *rate* of altitude change with power. A reasonable figure for most light aircraft is 500 feet per minute, but the power loading of your airplane may indicate a rate higher or lower. Make the power changes small, keep the little airplane steady in the descent attitude, and remember how much manifold pressure or how many RPMs are required. Go down a thousand feet, and accomplish a normal level-off.

You may have noticed that 1 inch of manifold pressure or a 100-RPM change produced roughly a 100-feet-per-minute rate change in both situations. If it's more or less for your airplane, remember the figure—it will smooth out your glide slope corrections later. This is also a good time to calibrate the vertical-speed indicator, by checking the altimeter readings at the beginning and end of a fixed time period. VSIs are notoriously inaccurate, and the amount of error seems to change daily, but at least you'll have a rough idea of how much yours is out of calibration, if at all.

EXERCISE #6—THE VERTICAL S

This is a coordination-builder, and requires constantly changing thought patterns; you've got to start planning ahead. Like flying into a funnel without touching the sides, the Vertical S gets more demanding as you proceed. It starts with a 500-foot altitude change, next time it's only 400 feet, then down to 300, and finally 200. You'll hardly have time to make the attitude and

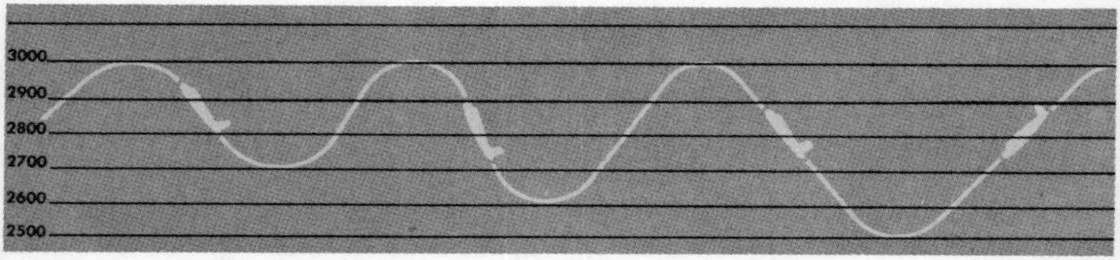

The Vertical S.

power changes for a 100-foot dip, so be satisfied when you can go through four successive ups and downs.

Start from normal cruise and descend 500 feet at constant airspeed. When level-off time rolls around, DON'T! Keep the nose coming right on up to the climb attitude while you're adding climb power. The objective is to touch the bottom altitude and enter a climb without any change in airspeed. Talk about coordination!—this will really try your patience until you discover the right combination of altitude lead, rate of pitch and power change, and a soft touch on the rudders. During the transition from descent to climb, everything imaginable is undergoing change.

Climb back to your original altitude, *start* the level-off at the normal lead point, but *don't level off*—instead, press right over into a constant airspeed descent. You're trying to just barely brush the top altitude before starting down again. From here on, it's simply a repetition of what has gone before, but each time you bottom out, chop off 100 feet.

EXERCISE #7—THE VERTICAL S-1

If you happen to be a roller-coaster nut, and dream of the big day when you get to ride the world's wildest, one that not only goes up and down, but changes its direction of turn every time, dream no more! Your wishes have come true in the Vertical S-1, and the only disappointment will be that you won't get to see what's going on; you'll be inside, under the hood, making it happen. This is the last "challenge" maneuver in the series, and when you master it, pat yourself on the back—you are doing a good job of flying your airplane on the gauges.

Start from normal cruise, but don't begin any maneuvering until you reduce airspeed to the climb/descent speed used in Exercise #4. When this is achieved, take a deep breath, and enter a descending standard rate turn. So far, much like Exercise #6, but the similarity ends when you have descended 500 feet—at this point, repeat the Vertical S "soft bounce" and enter a constant airspeed climb, *and at the same time, reverse the direction of your turn.* In other words, if you started the S-1 with a descending right turn, you should go down 500 feet, turning all the time at standard rate, then climb 500 feet while turning to the left. When you reach the top, enter another descent and reverse the direction of turn again. Continue through the same series of altitude changes as in the Vertical S, changing the turn each time you transition from climb to descent, or descent to climb. Don't be concerned about how many degrees you turn during the exercise; the objective is to accomplish smooth, positive, and coordinated changes in aircraft attitude at the proper times. You'll have your hands full, and after a couple of times through the Vertical S-1, you may have another name for it, one that is not necessarily acceptable in mixed company.

EXERCISE #8—SIMULATED HOLDING PATTERN

Now you can begin applying your instrument artistry to more practical matters, such as a standard holding pattern. Get squared away on a heading in straight and level flight, and at a cardinal point on the clock, simulate station passage. Using the Four T's (Time, Turn, Throttle, Talk), enter the holding pattern by noting the *Time,* roll into a standard rate *Turn* to the right, *Throttle* back to holding power, and pretend you are *Talking* to ATC, making the required report entering a holding pattern. This procedure will form a habit that will stand you in good stead later on.

The first turn when entering the racetrack is more than just a standard rate turn, because you are also changing airspeed and are required to hold altitude precisely. You will notice that all three controls call for changes in pressure—you need a higher angle of attack because of the lift change in the turn as well as the decrease in power and airspeed; unless you decrease the bank angle, your rate of turn will pick up as airspeed goes down, and rudder pressure will be needed as you change power and bank. Roll out at the 180-degree point, and fly level for exactly one minute. Now another 180 degrees to the right, fly for one minute, and you're finished. You could go on flying in the racetrack pattern all day long, but it wouldn't prove much—you should be aiming for smooth entry technique. Try a couple of left-hand patterns for kicks.

EXERCISE #9—THE 45-DEGREE PROCEDURE TURN

When a procedure turn is required, this one comes as close to "standard" as anything else. From straight and level flight at your approach airspeed (clean airplane), roll into a standard rate 45-degree turn to the right and fly for one minute. When that time has elapsed, turn left 180 degrees—the second turn will *always* be made in the opposite direction, taking you away from the station, and helping to guarantee that wind will not blow you back toward the airport shortening the time available to line up on the final approach course.

At the completion of the 180-degree turn, maintain heading

for thirty seconds, then turn left 45 degrees to put you back on course, but going in the opposite direction. That's the entire purpose of the procedure turn—to get you turned around on a specific course. Head wind or tail wind will of course change the time on that thirty-second leg when you are actually flying to an approach course, but at least this exercise will instill the principle.

For variety, try a couple of procedure turns to the other side of the course, always making the second turn in the opposite direction.

EXERCISE #10—THE 90-270 PROCEDURE TURN

When time is of the essence, this little gem will get you turned around *tout de suite*, and it's a good exercise in coordination. To get the most out of it, plan to make your turns greater than standard rate—use 30 degrees of bank throughout. At approach speed in straight and level flight, roll into a turn to the right, and begin the roll-out pressure as if you were going to stop the turn at the 90-degree point.

But instead of levelling the wings, keep right on going, into a 30-degree bank in the opposite direction. Continue the turn through 270 degrees, and bring the airplane back to straight and level on the reciprocal of the original heading. So that you won't develop a right-hand pattern "groove," do a few of these to the left as well. Once again, the second turn is *always* made in the opposite direction from the first.

EXERCISE #11—MODIFIED PATTERN B

Ask any pilot who has been through a military flying school, and he'll tell you that the Pattern B was a sort of "final exam" of instrument technique before graduating to approaches. In addition to including all of the maneuvers you have been through in the previous exercises, this one requires a good bit of planning ahead, the essence of good IFR operations.

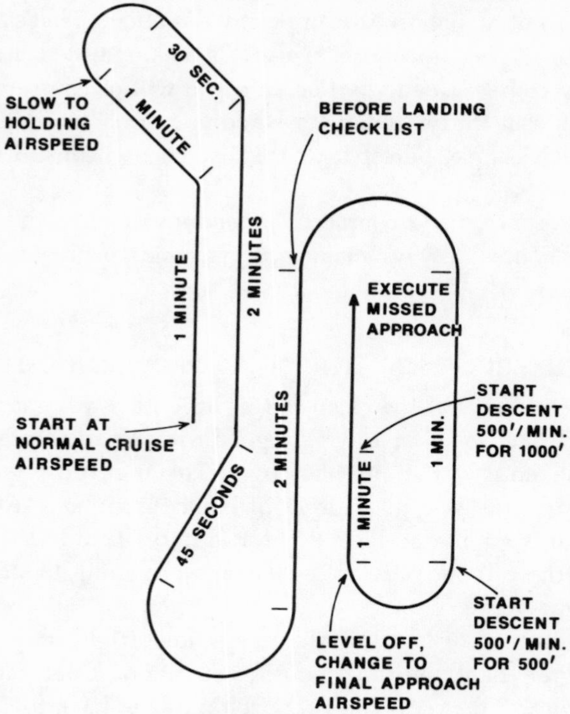

Modified Pattern B.

Because of its complexity, sketch out the pattern and its instructions on a card which you can clip to the control wheel, or your knee board, or wherever you plan to put approach charts when you get to the real thing.

There is one ground rule for Pattern B that makes it a little different from the other exercises. All timing is done with reference to cardinal times on the clock, regardless of the bank attitude of the airplane. If you find yourself getting increasingly more behind, check your rate of turn, and the rate at which you are rolling into and out of turns—the whole pattern is based on precise 3-degree-per-second turns; no more, no less. Start the pattern on a north heading—this exercise is *not* a test of your ability to add and subtract!

At the end of the final leg, you are pretending that you have just arrived at the missed approach point, and unless the hood falls off, you'll still be on instruments, so execute a missed approach. The objective is to accomplish the transition from descent to climb as smoothly and rapidly as possible, with a minimum loss of altitude. Climb out for 500 feet, and take off the hood—you've been hard at it for almost fifteen minutes of concentrated IFR practice, and you deserve a break.

EXERCISE #12—UNUSUAL ATTITUDES AND STALLS

There is a purpose to be served by "unusual attitudes" practice, but it is *not* the satisfaction of your instructor's sadistic psyche. Ever since instrument flight instruction was invented, there have been CIFIs with a strong Beelzebubbian desire to devise complicated, stomach-turning, vertigo-producing attitudes which rank as truly unusual—but not necessarily useful in helping the student become a safer instrument pilot. It is doubtful that in the course of an actual IFR flight you will allow your attention to wander completely away from the array of gauges on which your very life depends; so why should you practice recoveries from attitudes that are suddenly thrust upon you after a period of sightlessness during which the guy in the right seat has been flying the airplane? Since complete inattention is impossible to simulate as long as you can see, it is expedient for you to close your eyes while the unusual attitude is set up, but YOU should fly the airplane into the abnormal situation. You will have sensation of movement, but no idea of how much, and after a couple of turns you likely will not be able to tell which way. Under the direction of the instructor or the safety pilot, enter and roll out of turns in each direction—you may think you're doing just great, but sooner or later your inner ear and deep muscle senses will begin to fool you, and when your companion recognizes an attitude other than one required for normal instrument maneuvering, it's time for him to say, "recover."

You may have gotten yourself into a nose-low, 60-degree bank; or a wings-level, nose-high attitude. The airplane may be headed for the ground and about to go through the redline, or it could be valiantly struggling upward, ready to stall. The important part of the exercise is that YOU have flown yourself into the situation, and now it's up to you to get yourself out of it. These two attitudes, nose-low with airspeed building and nose-high with airspeed decreasing, are the themes upon which the recovery procedures are based. Allow the former to continue building and the airplane is likely to come apart if it doesn't collide with the ground first—ignore the latter and the airplane will stall, a less-than-desirable situation any time other than when you're 2 inches above the runway.

This is *not* the place for "do anything, even if it's wrong"—pulling back on the wheel when you recognize the high-airspeed-if-you-don't-pull-out-of-this-dive-we'll-hit-the-ground situation, may be followed by a sharp report as the wing tips meet directly above the cabin. With this in mind, force yourself to make a thorough but rapid check of the instrument indications before you take action. There are only two basic problems, and you can experience only one at a time, so things aren't really so bad after all. And even more to your advantage, the same control is the one to reach for first in either situation—if the airspeed is high and moving higher, reduce power—immediately, rapidly, and significantly. Looking at the instruments and recognizing a near-stall, your hand should instinctively go to the throttle and keep right on moving, adding power to get you out of trouble.

If the wings are not level when "recover!" sounds (and they probably won't be), apply aileron pressure to get things back where they belong. The only problem yet to solve is that of pitch, which in either case should be returned to the level flight attitude; but the sequence is important, especially in a nose-low, high-airspeed situation. Unload the wings by taking out the bank before easing the nose up to the horizon—it doesn't matter quite so much in the nose-high problem, since the addition of power will probably keep you from stalling.

The ideal recovery from any unusual attitude consists of a split-second interpretation of what's going on, followed by a completely coordinated, rapid return to level flight with little loss of altitude, direction, or aplomb. It seldom works out that way, especially the problem of which controls take precedence in a particular situation. For the sake of structural integrity, organizing your thoughts, and providing guidelines, here's the order in which you should get things done when you recognize an unusual attitude (some bank will usually be present):

First Case—Nose low, airspeed increasing, steep bank.
1. Reduce power.
2. Level the wings.
3. Pitch attitude back to level (smooth and easy does it).

Second Case—Nose high, airspeed decreasing, steep bank.
1. Add power (full power, if necessary).
2. Pitch attitude back to level (smooth and easy again, but it's not as critical here as in the high-speed case).
3. Level the wings.

While you're at it, run through a few stalls while under the hood. Stalls? Under the hood? Why not?—you know that you have plenty of control over the airplane's attitude in a stall when you can see outside, and there's no difference with the blinders on. Set the power, gradually bring the nose up, keep the wings level with aileron, nail the heading indicator on the proper number with rudder pressure, and when your sturdy bird shudders and quits flying, make a normal recovery—it's just another unusual attitude. Try stalls in various aircraft configurations and power settings, and with different amounts of bank. You'll exude confidence when you can handle all these situations, and isn't it nice to know that should that one-in-a-million chance catch up with you, a stall in actual IFR conditions, you are prepared to solve the problem?

PARTIAL PANEL IFR

The reliability of today's flight instruments is almost legendary, but don't ever forget that Murphy's Law was expressly invoked for aviators—"If anything can go wrong, it will." Every now and then, make yourself cover up the heading indicator and the attitude indicator, and fly "partial panel." It's not really attitude instrument flying, because all you have to work with are the *reactions* of the gauges that are left—there's no direct way to put the airplane in a specific attitude. If you think you have a fine touch on the controls when *all* the instruments are working, you may want to sandpaper your fingertips for partial panel; it requires the ultimate in smooth pressure and oneness with the airplane.

Any of the exercises in this chapter will provide ample opportunity for development of your partial panel skill—pay particular attention to those involving timed turns, and you won't have to worry about all those magnetic compass errors which have been known to drive pilots up the cockpit wall. If you roll in and roll out at the same rate, always applying pressure at the exact elapsed time, a standard rate turn for thirty seconds will result in a heading change of ninety degrees; keep it up for one minute and you've turned 180 degrees, and two minutes will give you a full circle. The magnetic compass should be used only to check the heading once you're in straight and level flight, because that's the only time it's going to tell you the truth. Now you know why most aircraft instrument systems are set up with the turn needle powered from a different source than the other two gyro gauges—lose that turn indicator and it's all over. The original catchword of instrument flying—needle, ball, and airspeed—had a lot going for it; without those basic indications, flight in the clouds is impossible.

Another tip that will serve you well when on partial panel concerns the altimeter. Especially when recovering from an unusual attitude without the gyro horizon, you can rely on the altimeter to let you know when the airplane is in level flight. It has nothing to do with bank, but *when the climb or descent has stopped, the altimeter will stop moving*—and at this point, you should be grateful for all the information you can get! When you notice the altimeter has come to rest (you'll have to watch closely), ease off whatever pitch pressure you happen to be holding at the time, and make the altimeter stay put. This will give you a short respite during which you can get the rest of the airplane going the right way.

Don't be satisfied until your control of the airplane is *good*, and don't let up—keep proficient with frequent and regular practice. It's the only way to fly.

INDEX